ORDNANCE SURVEY MEMOIRS OF IRELAND

Volume Twenty-eight

PARISHES OF COUNTY LONDONDERRY IX
1832-8

Published 1995.
The Institute of Irish Studies,
The Queen's University of Belfast,
Belfast.
In association with
The Royal Irish Academy,
Dawson Street,
Dublin.

Reprinted 2013 by Ulster Historical Foundation

Grateful acknowledgement is made to the Economic and Social Research Council and the Department of Education for Northern Ireland for their financial assistance at different stages of this publication programme.

Copyright 1995.

All rights reserved. No part of this publication may be reproduced, stored in a retrieval system or transmitted, in any form or by any means, electronic, mechanical, photocopying, recording or otherwise, without the prior permission of the publisher.

British Library Cataloguing-in-Publication Data.
A catalogue record for this book is available from the British Library.

ISBN: 978-0-85389-516-9

Printed in Ireland by SPRINT-print Ltd.

Ordnance Survey Memoirs of Ireland

VOLUME TWENTY-EIGHT

Parishes of County Londonderry IX
1832–8

West Londonderry

Edited by Angélique Day and Patrick McWilliams

The Institute of Irish Studies
in association with
The Royal Irish Academy

EDITORIAL BOARD

Angélique Day (General Editor)
Patrick S. McWilliams (Executive Editor)
Lisa English (Assistant Editor)
Dr B.M. Walker (Publishing Director)
Professor R.H. Buchanan

CONTENTS

	Page
Introduction	ix
Brief history of the Irish Ordnance Survey and Memoirs	ix
Definition of terms used	x
Note on Memoirs of County Londonderry	x

County Londonderry

Cumber parish (Upper and Lower)	1

List of selected maps and drawings

County Londonderry, with parish boundaries	vi
County Londonderry, 1837, by Samuel Lewis	viii
Claudy, OS map, 1830s	2
Foot-bridges across Glenrandal and Faughan rivers	10
Mether from Dungiven parish	29
Catholic chapel in Mullaboy townland	33
Plan and views of Brackfield Castle	36
Giant's grave in Tamnyreagh townland	38
Grocers' coat of arms from Ervey schoolhouse	78
Bell Stones in Tamnyreagh townland	82

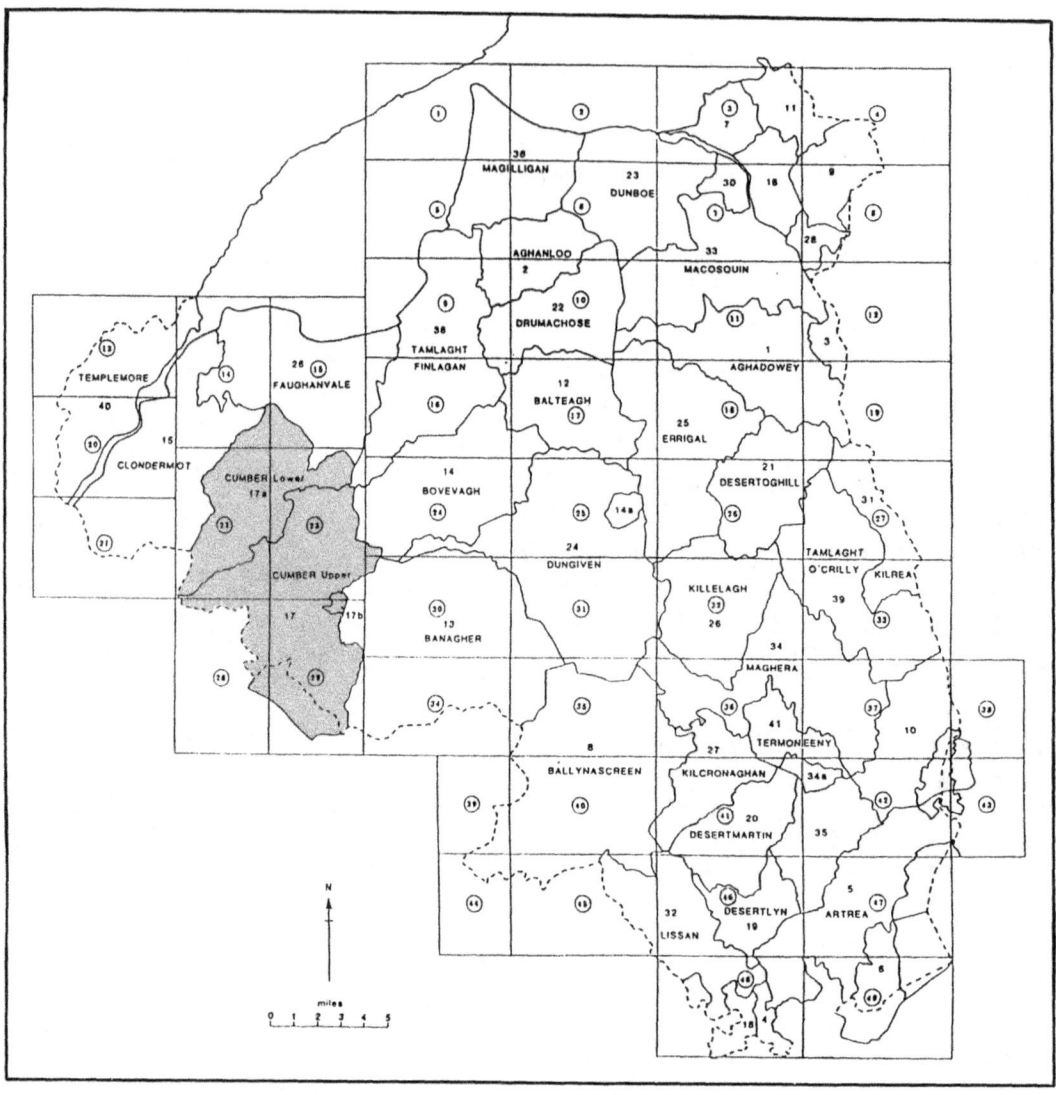

ACKNOWLEDGEMENTS

During the course of the transcription and publication project many have advised and encouraged us in this gigantic task. Thanks must first be given to the Royal Irish Academy, particularly former librarian Mrs Brigid Dolan and her staff, for making the original manuscripts available to us. We are also indebted to Siobhán O'Rafferty for her continuing help in deciphering indistinct passages of manuscript and wish to make particular acknowledgement to her for valuable help with the preparation of this volume.

We should like to acknowledge the following individuals for their special contributions. Dr Brian Trainor led the way with his edition of the Antrim Memoir and provided vital help on the steering committee. Dr Ann Hamlin also provided valuable support, especially during the most trying stages of the project. Professor R.H. Buchanan's unfailing encouragement has been instrumental in the development of the project to the present. Without Dr Kieran Devine the initial stages of the transcription and the computerising work would never have been completed successfully: the project owes a great deal to his constant help and advice. Dr Kay Muhr's continuing contribution to the work of the transcription project is deeply appreciated, as is that of former editor Nóirín Dobson. Mr W.C. Kerr's interest and expertise have been invaluable. Professor Anne Crookshank and Dr Edward McParland were most generous with practical help and advice concerning the drawings amongst the Memoir manuscripts. We would like to thank the Director of the Ordnance Survey, Dublin and the keepers of the fire-proof store, among them Leonard Hines. Finally, all students of the nineteenth-century Ordnance Survey of Ireland owe a great deal to the pioneering work of Professor J.H. Andrews, and his kind help in the first days of the project is gratefully recorded.

The essential task of inputting the texts from audio tapes was done by Miss Eileen Kingan, Mrs Christine Robertson, Miss Eilis Smyth, Miss Lynn Murray and, most importantly, Miss Maureen Carr.

We are grateful to the Linen Hall Library for lending us their copies of the first edition 6" Ordnance Survey Maps: also to Ms Maura Pringle of QUB Cartography Department for the index maps showing the parish boundaries. For providing financial assistance at crucial times for the maintenance of the project, we would like to take this opportunity of thanking the trustees of the Esme Mitchell trust and The Public Record Office of Northern Ireland.

Left:

Map of parishes of County Londonderry. The area described in this volume, the parishes of West Londonderry, has been shaded to highlight its location. The square grids represent the 1830s 6" Ordnance Survey maps. The encircled numbers relate to the map numbers as presented in the bound volumes of maps for the county. The parishes have been numbered in all cases and named in full where possible, except those in the following list: Agivey 3, Arboe 4, Ballinderry 6, Ballyaghran 7, Ballyrashane 9, Ballyscullion 10, Ballywillin 11, Bovevagh 14a, Coleraine 16, Derryloran (no Memoir) 18, Kildollagh 28, Killowen 30, Maghera 34a, Magherafelt 35.

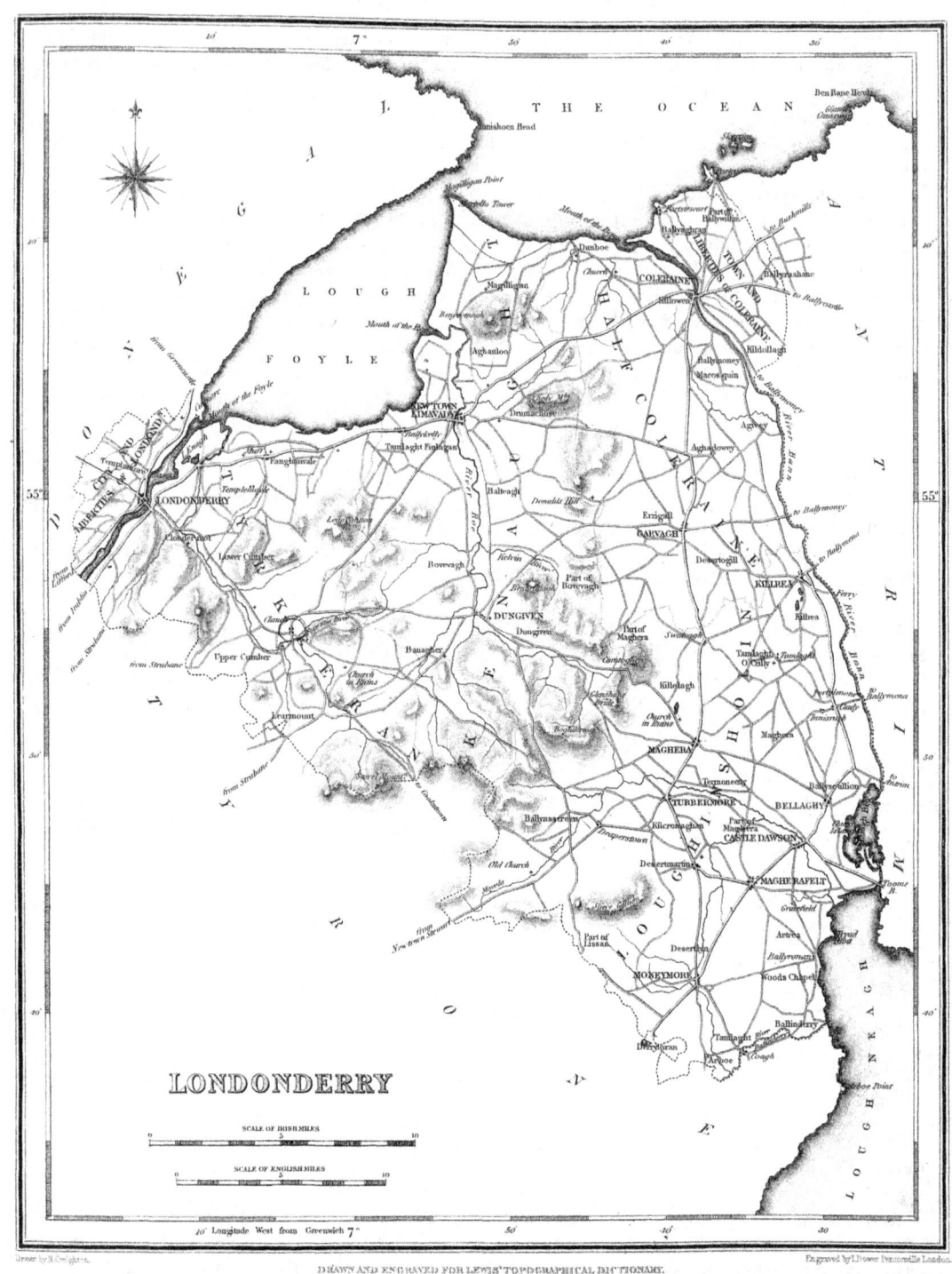

Map of County Londonderry, from Samuel Lewis' *Atlas of the counties of Ireland* (London, 1837)

INTRODUCTION AND GUIDE TO THE PUBLICATION OF THE ORDNANCE SURVEY MEMOIRS

The following text of the Ordnance Survey Memoirs was first transcribed by a team working in the Institute of Irish Studies at The Queen's University of Belfast, on a computerised index of the material. For this publication programme the text has been further edited: spellings have been modernised in most cases, although where the original spelling was thought to be of any interest it has been retained and is indicated by angle brackets in the text. Variant spellings for townland and lesser place-names have been preserved, although parish and major place-names have been standardised and the original spelling given in angle brackets. Names of prominent people, for instance landlords, have been standardised where possible, but original spellings of names in lists of informants, emigration tables and on tombstones have been retained. We have not altered the Memoir writers' anglicisation of names and words in Irish.

Punctuation has been modernised and is the responsibility of the editors. Editorial additions are indicated by square brackets: a question mark before and after a word indicates a queried reading and tentatively inserted information respectively. Original drawings are referred to in the text, and some have been reproduced. Manuscript page references have been omitted from this series. Because of the huge variation in size of Memoirs for different counties, the following editorial policy has been adopted: where there are numerous duplicating and overlapping accounts, the most complete and finished account, normally the Memoir proper, has been presented, with additional unique information from other accounts like the Fair Sheets entered into a separate section, clearly titled and identified; where the Memoir material is less, nothing has been omitted. To achieve standard volume size, parishes have been associated on the basis of propinquity.

There are considerable differences in the volume of information recorded for different areas: counties Antrim and Londonderry are exceptionally well covered, while the other counties do not have quite the same detail. This series is the first systematic publication of the parish Memoirs, although individual parishes have been published by pioneering local history societies. The entire transcriptions of the Memoirs made in the course of the indexing project can be consulted in the Public Record Office of Northern Ireland and the library at the Queen's University of Belfast. The manuscripts of the Ordnance Survey Memoirs are in the Royal Irish Academy, Dublin.

Brief history of the Irish Ordnance Survey in the nineteenth century and the writing of the Ordnance Survey Memoirs

In 1824 a House of Commons committee recommended a townland survey of Ireland with maps at the scale of 6", to facilitate a uniform valuation for local taxation. The Duke of Wellington, then prime minister, authorised this, the first Ordnance Survey of Ireland. The survey was directed by Colonel Thomas Colby, who had under his command officers of the Royal Engineers and three companies of sappers and miners. In addition to this, civil assistants were recruited to help with sketching, drawing and engraving of maps, and eventually, in the 1830s, the writing of the Memoirs.

The Memoirs were written descriptions intended to accompany the maps, containing information which could not be fitted on to them. Colonel Colby always considered additional information to be necessary to clarify place-names and other distinctive features of each parish; this was to be written up in reports by the officers. Much information about parishes resulted from research into place-names and was used in the writing of the Memoirs. The term "Memoir" comes from the abbreviation of the word "Aide-Memoire". It was also used in the 18th century to describe topographical descriptions accompanying maps.

In 1833 Colby's assistant, Lieutenant Thomas Larcom, developed the scope of the officers' reports by stipulating the headings or "Heads of Inquiry" under which information was to be reported, and including topics of social as well as economic interest. By this time civil assistants were writing some of the Memoirs under the supervision of the officers, as well as collecting information in the Fair Sheets.

The first "Memoirs" are officers' reports covering Antrim in 1830, and work continued on the Antrim parishes right through the decade, with special activity in 1838 and 1839. Counties Down and Tyrone were written up from 1833 to 1837, with both officers and civil assistants working on Memoirs. In Londonderry and Fermanagh research and writing started in 1834. Armagh was worked on in 1835, 1837 and 1838. Much labour was expended in the Londonderry parishes. The plans to publish the Memoirs commenced with the parish of Templemore, containing the city and liberties of Derry, which came out in 1837 after a great deal of expense and effort.

Between 1839 and 1840 the Memoir scheme collapsed. Sir Robert Peel's government could not countenance the expenditure of money and time on such an exercise; despite a parliamentary commission favouring the continuation of the writing of the Memoirs, the scheme was halted before the southern half of the country was covered. The manuscripts remained unpublished and most were removed to the Royal Irish Academy, Dublin from the Ordnance Survey, Phoenix Park. Other records of the Ordnance Survey, including some material from the Memoir scheme, have recently been transferred to the National Archives, Bishop Street, Dublin.

The Memoirs are a uniquely detailed source for the history of the northern half of Ireland immediately before the Great Famine. They document the landscape and situation, buildings and antiquities, land-holdings and population, employment and livelihood of the parishes. They act as a nineteenth-century Domesday book and are essential to the understanding of the cultural heritage of our communities. It is planned to produce a volume of evaluative essays to put the material in its full context, with information on other sources and on the writers of the Memoirs.

Definition of descriptive terms

Memoir (sometimes Statistical Memoir): an account of a parish written according to the prescribed form outlined in the instructions known as "Heads of Inquiry", and normally divided into three sections: Natural Features and History; Modern and Ancient Topography; Social and Productive Economy.

Fair Sheets: "information gathered for the Memoirs", an original title describing paragraphs of information following no particular order, often with marginal headings, signed and dated by the civil assistant responsible.

Statistical Remarks/Accounts: both titles are employed by the Engineer officers in their descriptions of the parish with marginal headings, often similar in layout to the Memoir.

Office Copies: these are copies of early drafts, generally officers' accounts and must have been made for office purposes.

Ordnance Survey Memoirs for County Londonderry

This volume, the ninth for the county and twenty-eighth in the series, contains the

Memoir papers for the parish of Cumber, situated in western Londonderry bordering on Tyrone, beside the Faughan river and beneath the western flank of the Sperrins. This parish was so large that it was divided into Upper and Lower districts.

This area was principally agricultural, with the villages of Claudy and Park as the main settlements, and was strongly influenced by the London Livery Companies (the Fishmongers, Goldsmiths and Skinners).

The complicated archive of material surviving for this parish indicates both the strengths and weaknesses of the team method of collecting and compiling information preparatory to the writing up of the Memoirs. There is no single Memoir account, but rather subject sections for the Memoir; and there are numerous draft accounts and working papers. These have been linked together, following the Heads of Inquiry, to form whole Memoir accounts.

Particular emphasis was given to Productive Economy, in the form of statistical tables completed under the indefatigable Captain J.E. Portlock. This statistical material of April and July 1838 is dated later than other accounts. There is some earlier information from the 1820s relating to schools and dispensary but the bulk of material dates from the mid to late 1830s, culminating in the extraordinarily detailed Productive Economy tables which are similar to those found in Memoirs of Banagher, Clondermot, Errigal, Faughanvale and Magherafelt.

Several drafts in George Petrie's hand show that he was involved in trying to gather together the different sections of Memoir to produce a coherent overall account. The Irish scholar John O'Donovan also provided information on place-names and we know these two members of the Topographical department were sometimes called in to provide final drafts of Memoir accounts, as, for example, in Dungiven parish.

Through the different Memoir sections, descriptive and statistical, a fascinating picture of this traditional district is built up, with unusual detail of ordinary inhabitants and cottiers' income; and mention is made of workers' migrating from this parish to Dublin, Cork and Galway. It reveals the survival of rundale farming, and herding practices which must have harked back to the old pastoral economy of early Ireland, as well as showing how petty jobbing or trading in cattle and other commodities grew up to supply the income lost by a serious decline in the domestic linen industry.

Although there were important bleach greens in the parish, farming was the main occupation; and there is some detail in the Fair Sheets by John Bleakly about model farmers which complements the statistical tables. Portlock also provides an interesting analysis of the statistics he provides for each townland's landholding, farming and labour.

Thomas Fagan's Fair Sheets as usual are rich in tales and descriptions of the antiquities of the area. Traditional beliefs too were still fairly widespread, and marriage celebrations are recounted as well as May Eve rituals and beliefs in cures and witchcraft.

Drawings in the Memoirs are listed below and are cross-referenced in the text. All unique drawings have been included and are listed below; some are illustrated. There are some comments on the drawings in Box 36 III 26. The manuscript material is to be found principally in Boxes 35 and 36 of the Royal Irish Academy's collection of Ordnance Survey Memoirs. The following sections which contain working papers and duplicate drafts have been omitted: Box 35 III 4-8. Box 36 I 1-3, 7-10, 12, 17-18, 25, 28-29, 32, 34, 42.

Section references in this volume are given below in their printed order:

Box 36 I 23; 6; 15; 36 and 31; 22; 36, 30 and 35; 26; 35 III 1; 36 I 36; 21; 39; 38; 33; 5; 41; 40; 24; 19; 27; 11, 6 and 2; 16; 37; 35 III 2; 36 I 26; 14; 13; 20; 43; 35 III 9; 3; 36 I 4.

Drawings

(Box 35 section 1, Box 36 sections 9, 13, 15, 22, 26, 30):

The Bell Stones, annotated plan with dimensions and scale.

Monument in Ervey, view of a stone circle [by J. Stokes].

Ornamental iron braces of Learmount church.

Iron foot-bridge across the Glenrandal with 2 persons on bank [illustrated].

Claudy chapel, annotated ground plan (by G. Downes) [illustrated].

Turf spade or flagger.

Cromlech in Barr Cregg.

Ancient fence in Altahoney, with dimensions.

Stone pillar in Killycor.

2 drawings of urns: one in Killycor and type found in bog.

Decorated vessel of burnt earth found in Carnanbane, with dimensions.

Ground plan of Kilcluggah church with dimensions and annotation.

Cross at the yew trees, with dimensions [most of the above by J. Stokes].

Fort in Dungorkin, ground plan and section with annotations [by J.B. Williams].

View of the home of Shane Crossach the robber in Carnanreagh.

Mether of yew from Bond's glen, 2 views with dimensions [illustrated].

Mutilated cross, 2 diagrams [by R.K. Dawson].

Cromlech of Slaughtmanus, tracing from G.V. Sampson.

Diagram of method of raising stones of cromlech (Bell Stones) in Tamnyreagh.

Bell Stones; and detail of interstices of stones and of ribbing on stone.

Ancient fence or mearing between Ballygroll and Highmoor.

Views of Brackfield castle from west and east [illustrated].

Annotated plan of Brackfield Castle with dimensions [illustrated].

Traced plan of the Bell Stones in Tamnyreagh, with dimensions and scale.

The Bell Stones from the south east with dimensions [illustrated].

The Bell Stones showing holes, with annotations.

Parish of Cumber xiii

Another view of Bell Stones on Robert Steele's farm with dimensions.

The Bell Stones from the west with dimensions [illustrated].

Plan of the Bell Stones to show position of the ringing stone.

Plan of monument in Tamnyreagh with dimensions.

Same monument with dimensions; view of junction of stones.

Giant's grave in Tamnyreagh.

Giant's grave in Tamnyreagh from the west.

Giant's grave in Tamnyreagh from the north, with dimensions [illustrated].

2 views of ancient fence in Robert Thompson's farm, with dimensions.

Fence in Highmoor with dimensions.

Plan of fences in Slaughtmanus with dimensions.

Plan of upper house with scale and dimensions.

View from point in upper house in Slaughtmanus.

Lower house in Slaughtmanus with dimensions.

Plan of the lower house in Slaughtmanus, with dimensions and scale.

Plan of upper house in Slaughtmanus, with dimensions and scale.

Distant view of Slaughtmanus from the east, with section of the door.

Another view of Slaughtmanus.

Plan of remains of a monument in Mullaboy, with dimensions.

Ground plan of standing stones on Sliebh Gore, with annotations and dimensions.

Plan of Cranagh Fort with scale [most of the above by J. Stokes].

Grocers' Company coat of arms over schoolhouse in Ervey [illustrated].

Hugh Lyle's suspension bridge across the Faughan, with scale [illustrated].

Parish of Cumber (Upper and Lower), County Londonderry

Statistical Report for Upper Cumber by Lieutenant Edward Vicars, November 1832

NATURAL STATE

Situation and Boundary

The parish of Upper Cumber is situated in the western part of the county of Londonderry, in the half-barony of Tirkeeran <Tyrkerin> and diocese of Derry. The main road from Londonderry to Dungiven enters the parish at about 6 miles from the former place.

Upper Cumber is bounded on the north by the parish of Faughanvale, on the south by the parish of Donaghedy <Donagheady> in the county of Tyrone, on the west by Lower Cumber and on the east by Banagher and Bovevagh. The townland of Stranaganwilly belonging to the parish of Upper Cumber is in the county of Tyrone and barony of Strabane. It is a wild uncultivated tract.

The boundary of the parish is well defined: where it passes on the range of hills which separate it from Donaghedy the mearing <meering> is lockspitted.

Extent and Divisions

The greatest length of the parish is 10 miles 2 furlongs 14 perches in a line from Mullockclogher (or Straw Mountain) towards Lockermore Pole (close to the road leading from Claudy <Clady> to Newtownlimavady) or in a direction from Straw Mountain of 10 degrees 20 minutes to the east of north. The greatest breadth (taken at right angles to the above line) is 6 miles 5 furlongs 20 perches, from the junction of the 3 parishes of Upper and Lower Cumber and Donaghedy, about 1,100 feet north of the top of Slieve Brice mountain, meeting the [?] river below the village in Ballyrory, close to the mearing between it and Gortscreaghan <Gortscregan>.

The parish contains 26,663 acres and is subdivided into 40 townlands.

Upper and Lower Cumber were formerly united and formed only one parish. The division was made about 36 years since, when the Earl of Bristol was bishop of the diocese, and the lower parish given to the son of the incumbent.

MODERN TOPOGRAPHY

Towns and Villages

There is not any market town in the parish of Upper Cumber, and the only place deserving the rank of a village is Claudy. It is situated on the main road from Londonderry to Dungiven, about 7 miles from the former place. It is a police station and contains the petty sessions house, which has lately been built.

There is not any trade carried on in Claudy. It is chiefly composed of public houses which derive their prosperity from the number of fairs held in the village.

MODERN TOPOGRAPHY AND SOCIAL ECONOMY

State of the Church

The parish church is in the townland of Cumber and is in very good repair. There is also another church (or chapel of ease), called Learmount church, in the townland of Tireighter, for the accommodation of the parishioners in that neighbourhood, both in Upper Cumber and Banagher.

In addition to the clergyman who officiates here (who is supported conjointly by the rectors of Upper and Lower Cumber and Banagher), there is a curate kept. The tithes of the parish are under the Composition Act for 21 years from 1828, at 760 pounds per annum. The glebe lands attached to the living are valued at 417 pounds per annum, including the house which is in good repair.

The glebe house is in the townland of Upper Alla, about 1 mile from the church.

The advowson is in possession of the Bishop of Derry. There are not any parochial funds whatever, and the only support the aged and infirm have to look for is the collection made during divine service and the charity of the parishioners.

Meeting Houses and Chapels

There is a Roman Catholic chapel in the townland of Gortscregan and one close to the village in the townland of Claudy.

The meeting house, which has been lately built, is in the townland of Craig.

Dispensary

The Fishmongers' Company have established a dispensary in the townland of Mulderrig, and allow a salary of 100 pounds per annum to the medical man who constantly resides. The situation is ballotted for in London by the members of the company and testimonials as to character, experience and ability strictly looked into. The candidates must belong to the medical department of either the army or navy.

There is a good new house and abundance of medicines supplied [to] the medical attendant.

Abstract of the dispensary in the parish of Upper Cumber. Average number of patients per annum 1,400: from rheumatic complaints 36, dyspeptic or indigestion 62, catarrh 80, the rest consisting chiefly of bowel complaints and diseases of children.

Schools

There are 9 schools in the parish of Upper Cumber. The annexed table will show the numbers of scholars of each, how the teachers are supported. [Table contains the following headings: name of townland, religion and sex of pupils, remarks as to how supported].

Alla, 88 Protestants, 42 Catholics, 94 males, 36 females, total 130; the parish school of Upper Cumber, in the foundation of the late Erasmus Smith Esquire. The total annual support of this establishment is estimated to be worth about 60 pounds, derived from various sources.

Ballyarton, 68 Protestants, 38 Catholics, 63 males, 43 females, total 106; supported by the London Hibernian Society, from which it receives the annual stipend of 12 pounds. A small contribution of 1s per quarter is paid by such of the pupils as are able to pay; this amounts to about 8 pounds.

Ballycallaghan, 53 Protestants, 30 Catholics, 50 males, 33 females, total 83; formerly received a grant from the Kildare Street Society, none held out as likely this year. Receives no other support but what is paid by the scholars, which averages about 7 pounds per annum.

Craig, 60 Protestants, 60 Catholics, 70 males, 50 females, total 120; supported by the London Hibernian Society, annual stipend 10 pounds, and a small contribution of 1s per quarter from the parents of such as are able to pay, amounting to about 4 pounds.

Gortilea, 45 Protestants, 54 Catholics, 65 males, 34 females, total 99; supported by the Fishmoners' Company, annual stipend averages 45 pounds per annum.

Kilcaltin, 34 Protestants, 17 Catholics, 23 males, 28 females, total 51; receives no support whatever

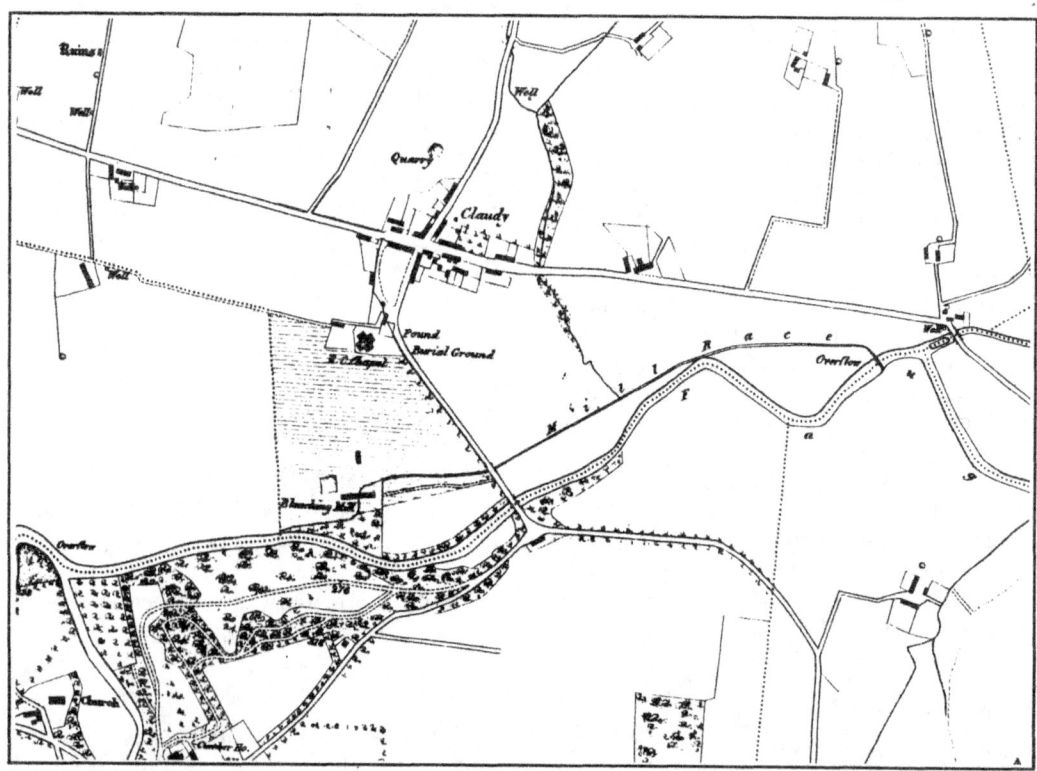

Map of Claudy from the first 6" O.S. maps, 1830s

but from the parents of the children, who pay about 1s 6d per quarter, and this amounts to about 14 pounds 16s per annum.

Killycor, 40 Protestants, 45 Catholics, 47 males, 38 females, total 85; supported by the Fishmongers' Company, annual stipend averages nearly 40 pounds per annum.

Park (Tireighter), 8 Protestants, 78 Catholics, 72 males, 14 females, total 86; receives no support but what is paid by the scholars, which averages about 4 pounds per quarter.

Stranaganwilly, 6 Protestants, 50 Catholics, 35 males, 21 females, total 56; receives 4 pounds annually from James Sinclair Esquire and a small contribution of 1s per quarter from such of the pupils as are able to pay.

Total number of scholars: 402 Protestants, 414 Catholics, 519 males, 297 females, total 816.

PRODUCTIVE ECONOMY

Manufactories

There were formerly 4 extensive bleach greens in this parish: at present there is not one at work. The linen trade in its different branches is nearly lost. All the small rents were paid by the earnings of the spinning wheel, but at present all that can be earned by one woman is from 1d ha'penny to 2d per diem.

Weaving is greatly on the decline and with hard work barely pays the labour.

There is a paper manufactory in the townland of Lettermuck, at which about 1,000 reams of coarse paper is annually made and sold for grocers etc., at from 3s to 4s per ream. From 3 to 4 hands are employed, at from 6s to 8s each per week.

Agriculture

Most of the land in this parish is occupied by farmers of a low rank, holding from 5 to 15 Cunningham acres, at from 5s to 20s per acre for arable and from 1s 6d to 7s 6d for mountain land and green pasture. The quality of the land is much inferior to that of Lower Cumber. In very good years it will yield equal crops of oats, barley, flax etc., but in wet and cold seasons the crops suffer much [crossed out: are destroyed and famine ensues; while in the low and warm soils they have tolerable crops in the worst of seasons. For this reason the county rates are lower in the mountainous district than in the lowland, possessing a more genial climate].

There was formerly a large proportion of each farm under flax, and by this the tenants looked to pay their rent; but at present a quantity sufficient only to give occupation to the family is raised.

There is not any wheat grown in the parish, and very little barley. An acre of oats will produce on the average about 7 barrels.

Value of an acre of oats on the ground from 3 to 6 pounds; value of an acre of barley on the ground from 5 to 8 pounds; value of an acre of flax on the ground from 10 to 12 pounds; value of an acre of potatoes on the ground from 10 to 12 pounds.

The quantity of potatoes raised depends entirely on the number of the family to be supported; it generally averages about 1 acre to 10 acres arable, though holders of only 4 or 5 acres may have as much.

The largest farmers in Upper Cumber generally sow about an acre of flax and the smallest from a rood to a rood and a half.

Wages

The wages given in the parish average from 10d to 11d in summer and from 8d to 9d in winter without victuals, except in harvest time when they are not in regular employment.

Manures

The manure chiefly used is a compost of lime (which is to be obtained in all parts of the parish), rotten bog (unfit for fuel) and animal manure, for in the reclaimed land, nor in any part of the parish, is there a good subsoil of clay or loam to be met with. When the deep bog is removed a wretched unproductive till of hungry gravel usually appears that only after potatoes can return a tolerable crop of oats; while high in the hills flax will not grow.

Markets

Londonderry is the nearest and surest market town for this district. In consequence of the great exportation of grain to Liverpool, the farmer meets with a ready sale for his oats.

NATURAL FEATURES

Mountains

The altitude of many of the mountains in this parish is very considerable. The highest are: Straw Mountain, 2,083 feet (this is close to the south mearing of the parish), Aughdoorish, 1,864, Aughtawaddy, 1,611, Crookdooish, 1,062, Menie mountain, 1,198, Main mountain, 918. They are composed principally of mica slate and limestone. The low ground is of a cold gravelly nature and [a] great portion covered with thick bog, and both barren and [blank].

Rivers

The Faughan, which rises in the parish of Banagher, in the neighbourhood of Sawel mountain, divides that parish from Upper Cumber for a considerable distance after it passes Park bridge, and then flows through the parish in a north west direction, meeting the parish of Lower Cumber. It is joined near Claudy by the Fore <Four> Glen river, running west from the parish of Bovevagh in the low grounds between Ballymaclanigan and Mulderrig.

At the townland of Cumber the Glenrandal meets the Faughan from the south, taking its rise in the neighbourhood of Straw Mountain. It is an insignificant stream except in wet weather, when swelled by the torrents from the surrounding mountains.

The course of each of these streams is most marked and picturesque, running for the most part in valleys between high hills which present a beautiful and magnificent outline. Great quantities of salmon ascend these rivers, and are destroyed almost with impunity at a season they are quite unfit for food.

PRODUCTIVE ECONOMY AND MODERN TOPOGRAPHY

Quarries

There are not any quarries of consequence in the parish. Abundance of limestone is to be got in all parts of the parish. Quarries of mica slate are worked for the purposes of building and the repair of the roads.

Roads and Bridges

The main road from Londonderry to Dungiven is kept in very good order. It is repaired with gravel, mica slate and stones brought from the river and broken for the purpose.

The crossroads of the parish are remarkably good, from the quantity of gravel of a very good quality which is to be had in abundance in the vicinity of the Faughan river and indeed in all the low grounds of the parish.

There are 3 stone bridges across the Faughan in Upper Cumber, one at Ballyarton, one at Cumber and one at Park; also one across the Glenrandal <Glenrandle> at Cumber, close to the church.

The other bridges in the parish are over the [?] numerous small glens formed by the streams from the mountain, and it is no uncommon circumstance in wet weather to find some of them have been swept away by the mountain torrents and the communication quite impeded.

Fairs

There are 8 fairs held annually at Claudy and the same number at Park. Custom is demanded at each fair at Claudy, though only 4 annually are held by patent. The tolls belong to J. Brown Esquire, those at Park to Barre Beresford Esquire.

Mills

There are several corn and flax mills in this parish, but none of any consequence. They are all worked by water.

Gentlemen's Seats

Cumber House, the residence of J. Brown Esquire, is close to the church.

Learmount, the seat of Barre Beresford Esquire, is in the townland of Lear.

The Glebe House in Alla and Alexander Ogilby's house in Kilcaltin are the only principal residences of gentlemen in the parish.

Mines

There is not any iron ore to be met with in the parish. Some large pieces of lead from 16 to 18 lbs weight have been found lower in the Glenrandal river, but no vein discovered. Rock crystal is found, some of a fine brown colour; quartz very abundant and in large masses.

Chalybeate springs are to be met with in different parts of the parish; a very fine one in Killycor, which was enclosed and covered in, was much resorted to some years ago.

ANCIENT TOPOGRAPHY

Antiquities

In the townland of Dungorcan there is a circular [?] plot 45 feet in diameter surrounded by a ditch 85 feet wide and having a causeway leading into it, most likely a secure place to enter into in times of trouble.

There are forts (supposed to be Danish) in different parts of the parish. A very remarkable one close to the paper mill, and a very short way from this a cairn or heap of stones is to be seen, supposed to be the burial place of some chieftain. An urn was lately found adjoining one of these mounds, surrounded by large flagstones.

Parish of Cumber

Urns of baked clay of rude workmanship, to hold about 3 pints, have been met with.

On Bollabracken a single stone of quartz is to be seen, supposed to have formed part of a druid's altar, but I could not discover or trace the tradition.

NATURAL FEATURES

Woods

There is a good deal of old timber at Learmount and also fir plantations, as well as at Cumber House, but the general appearance of the country is very bleak, as if to show more plainly the bold and beautiful outline of the surrounding hills.

SOCIAL ECONOMY

Population

[Insert note: The principal proprietors R. Ogilby Esquire, Fishmongers' Company, "Barre" Beresford Esquire, John Brown Esquire, Revd R. Alexander].

By a census taken in 1821, the number of houses in the parish amounted to 1,182 and that of the inhabitants to 6,568. By the census taken in 1831 the number of houses amounted to 1,375 and the inhabitants to 7,751 (males 3,790, females 3,961), showing an increase in the 10 years of 193 houses and only 183 inhabitants. Of the above number (7,751), about 3,095 are Protestants and 4,656 Roman Catholics. [Signed] Edward Vicars, Lieutenant Royal Engineers.

Forwarded to Lieutenant-Colonel Colby, 28th November 1832, [signed] M. Waters, Captain Royal Engineers.

Draft Memoir, with Notes by George Downes

NATURAL STATE

Locality

This parish is situated on the south western part of the barony of Tirkeeran, excepting 1 townland, Stranagalwilly, which is in the barony of Strabane and the county of Tyrone. It is bounded on the north by Lower Cumber, on the east by Bovevagh and Banagher, on the west by Lower Cumber and county of Tyrone, and on the south by the same county. Its extreme length is about 10 miles and its extreme breadth about 6 and a half. It contains, exclusively of Stranagalwilly, 23,325 acres 1 rood 15 perches, of which [blank] are cultivated, and is subdivided into 40 townlands; valuation to the county cess [blank].

NATURAL FEATURES

Hills

The surface is almost entirely mountainous. The parish is described in the Down Survey as being for the "most part mountainous pasture with some arable meadow." The following are the greatest elevations above the sea: Straw Mountain, 2,083 feet, Aughdorrish, 1,864 feet, Lear hill, 1,612 feet, Aughtawaddy, 1,611 feet, Menie hill, 1,198 feet, Crookdouish, 1,062 feet, Ballymaclanighan Top [blank], Claudy <Clady> Top [blank], Main mountain, 918 feet, Slaboy, 854 feet, Letterlogher Top, 763 feet.

Straw Mountain is situated in the county of Tyrone and its highest point is about one-quarter of a mile southwards of the parish. This is the most elevated part of the Stranagalwilly range, which extends about 3 miles from north west to south east parallel to the River Glenrandal, from which it rises with a gentle slope falling more abruptly to the south west without the parish. The north eastern side, however, is varied by glens and ravines, the beds of rivulets tributary to the Glenrandal; and secondary ridges are thus formed at right angles to the first, the tops of which vary in height from 1,100 feet to 900.

On the north east of the Glenrandal rises the precipitous face of a range exactly similar and parallel to the former. Of this, the most important points are Lear hill to the south and Menie hill. From these the ground slopes more gradually to the north east, this face being intersected by a deep valley called Glen Graniagh, which separates Lear hill from Menie hill.

Crookdouish [insert alternative: Crookdooish], a mountain in the north west of the range last mentioned, partakes of the general character of the country, rising gradually from the north and falling almost precipitously towards the south; it is, however, separated from the mountains above mentioned by the deep valley of the Glenrandal. On the northern side, after a gentle descent of 1 and a half miles, it expands into a broad flat top, the boundary of which, 4 miles to the north west, is the deep valley of Bond's glen; on the north and north east it falls gradually towards the Faughan.

To the east of Crookdouish, and separated from it by the Glenrandal, rises Slaboy, which resembles Crookdouish but it is inferior to it in boldness as well as height. It is connected with the Lear hill and Menie hill to the south, and like them falls gradually towards the north east to the Faughan, the valley of which, running from south east to north west, separates the mountains above mentioned from those in the north of the parish. These, which are divided into 2 distinct ranges by the Fore Glen river, run parallel to the bed of that river, and to each other, from east to west.

The most important points in the northern range are Claudy Top and Ballymaclanigan Top; in the southern, Letterlogher Top. These hills also fall precipitously towards the south, but have on the north a very gentle slope.

Lakes

About 1 and a half miles to the south east of Claudy, and on the road to Learmount, are 2 insignificant lakes. They are situated on a flat tract of bog about 400 feet above the sea and take their names from the townlands in which they lie, the larger being called Tullintrain lough, the other Binna lough. The former is about 7 or 8 feet deep, the latter only 3 or 4; its bottom is much overgrown with weeds and long grass.

Rivers

There are 3 rivers and 1 stream of greater or less importance: the Faughan, the Glenrandal river, the Fore <Four> Glen river and the Burntollet stream.

[In another hand] For the general description of the Faughan, see the parish of Clondermot. The Faughan divides this parish from that of Banagher for a distance of 3 and a half miles. It then flows through this parish in a north westerly direction, until it enters Lower Cumber at the junction of Ballyartan and Gortnaran with that parish. Its breadth varies from 15 to 20 yards and, being a rapid river, it is very shallow, except where artificial overflows have been made. Of these, there are but few along its course through the parish, but many more could be constructed with advantage. The first is at Park in Tireighter, the next in Killicor, 1 in Claudy, 1 in Craig and 1 in Lettermuck. The fall is more than 250 feet in a course of 8 miles.

The banks of this river are varied, but their general character is precipitous. In 3 places they are peculiarly beautiful, although of a different appearance, that is at Learmount, where the river enters the parish, at Cumber close to Claudy, and at Kilcaltan, where it enters Lower Cumber. At Learmount the scenery is bolder, and the wildness of nature shows itself through the cultivation of man. At Cumber art has conquered, and the richness of the trees and the meadows is in better accordance with the more placid course of the river. At Kilcaltan again the banks resume their boldness and are enriched by natural wood. In connection with a very picturesque old bridge thrown over the river they form most beautiful scenery.

[First author] The Glenrandal river rises at the southern extremity of the parish near Straw Mountain. Its course is short. After running nearly 4 miles in a north westerly direction through a very deep valley, it proceeds due north for 4 miles and then enters the Faughan in Cumber demesne. This river is very rapid, especially in the first half of its course, during which it falls about 200 feet in a mile; during the remainder it falls about 40 feet in a mile. It is subject to great and sudden floods which subside with equal rapidity, seldom, however, without having caused much injury. The soil deposited by the floods consists of sand and fine gravel, which are both bad for the land and destructive to the crops.

Except during the few dry months of summer, the supply of water is constant and capable of being turned to more advantage than at present. The bed of the river is chiefly of coarse gravel. Near its rise the glen through which it runs is very wild and bold, being overhung on all sides by high mountains. On approaching the Faughan it is enriched by planting and the view is confined to the mere banks of that river.

The Fore Glen river and the Burntollet stream are mere rivulets, except in wet weather when they are swollen into rapid torrents. They both [insert correction: the former] rises in Bovevagh and enter the Faughan after a course of 7 and a half miles westward. [Insert marginal query: Do they rise in Bovevagh?]. [Insert note: The latter rises in Tamlaght Finlagan and enters the Faughan after a course of 11 and one-third miles].

The parish is well supplied with water from smaller rivulets, and the springs are good and numerous.

Bogs

The mountainous part of the parish is covered with bog, which increases in height from about 300 feet above the sea to 2,000. Timber occurs imbedded throughout, even on the top of mountains, but least abundantly in the elevated districts. It is generally fir, but oak is often met with, especially on the edges of the bog near the clay. The oak is generally large, the fir of various sizes, the stumps of the smaller trees being broken at less height from the roots than those of the larger. These stumps are invariably upright and generally vary from 3 feet to 1 foot in height. Stumps or

Parish of Cumber

blocks are occasionally found lying on one another in the deep bogs. Trees also are sometimes found lying in a similar position, and generally in a direction from west to east.

The bog varies in depth from 9 or 10 feet to 1 or 2; the average depth may be about 5. Throughout the mountainous districts the substratum is of a cold blue clay, ill suited to repay the labour of reclaiming it. At the foot of the hills the soil is better, being often alluvial. [Insert marginal query: Productive Economy?].

Woods

Along the Faughan, and there only, does natural wood remain. In Binn, on the southern precipitous bank of the Faughan, there is a narrow skirting of natural oak, one-third of a mile in length. The trees are neither strong nor healthy, and few exceed 30 feet in height. Natural oak is also found at Beaufort, in Cregg, on the northern precipitous bank of the Faughan, but not much stronger or larger than that of Binn. At Kilcaltan it again makes its appearance, and there also is of stunted growth. In the intermediate spaces, on precipitous banks inaccessible to cultivation, are found some solitary stunted trees, which lead to the supposition that the patches now in existence were once connected so as to form part of a larger woody district.

At Learmount, Cumber House and Alla Glebe much wood has been planted within the last 30 years, chiefly various kinds of fir. It is healthy and well distributed along the Faughan and Glenrandal. On the side of the Crookdouish next to Altaghoney there was once a forest of yews, some of which continued growing until a few years since. On the sides of some ravines also, in the neighbourhood of Stranagalwilly, traces still exist of a more extensive forest.

MODERN TOPOGRAPHY

Towns

There is no town in the parish, and the only villages of any importance are Claudy and Park. Claudy (otherwise Clady, Cumber-Claudy and Cumber-Clady) is situated in Claudy, about 9 miles [insert marginal query] from Derry, at the point where the road by Dungiven between that city and Belfast is crossed by that between Newtownlimavady and Strabane. It consists of 25 indifferent houses, of which some are so low as to have their signboards fixed on the roof. It contains a Catholic chapel, a petty sessions house combined with a police barracks, and a penny post office.

Roman Catholic Chapel

The Catholic chapel is cruciform and measures 69 feet by 33. The window frames are in the pointed Gothic style, but built up at top so as to admit light through the rectangular part alone. The eastern arm of the transept is walled off and used as a sacristy. In the western arm there is a small gallery which contains the only seats in the building. This edifice, which is but indifferently built, cost 300 pounds, raised by subscription, and was opened in 1820. It can accommodate 600 persons.

Sessions House and Police Barracks

The combined petty sessions house and police barracks, a plain building of 1-storey, was built in 1829 by John Browne Esquire of Cumber House. The road sessions were held here on one occasion, but the house proved too small.

PRODUCTIVE ECONOMY

Post Office

A penny post office was established in June 1832, and the mail bag is carried daily to and from Derry by the Dungiven mail car. This car passes through Claudy at half after 8 in the morning on its way to Derry and at 4 in the afternoon on its way to Dungiven. In summer it passes at 3 on its way to Dungiven.

Table of Occupations

The following table exhibits the occupations of the inhabitants: publicans 8, carpenters 2, farmers 2, grocers 2, blacksmiths 1, butchers 1, weavers 1.

Fairs

There are 8 annual fairs: 1st, 4 stationary, held on the 17th February, 17th May, 17th August and 17th November; 2nd, 4 movable, held on Old Year's Day, the Tuesday after Old Patrick's Day, Tuesday after Old Midsummer Day and the Tuesday after Old Michaelmas Day. To these fairs the spirit dealers owe their principal support.

MODERN TOPOGRAPHY

Hamlet of Park

Park, which is in [insert queried addition: Tireighter], is a group of 6 well-built slated houses in the south eastern part of the parish. Its situation is very retired. It contains a good schoolhouse, a flax mill, a corn mill, a public house termed an inn and a good blacksmith's forge. Besides the inn there are 2 other spirit shops.

Mills

The flax and corn mills, which form part of the one establishment, are situated on the western bank of the Faughan, from which they derive but a scant supply of water, even in winter, so that the proprietor can work only one mill at a time. The corn mill is double geared, that is, it has more than one pair of stones. Its water wheel, which is a breast wheel, is 14 feet in diameter by 3 and a half in breadth. In this, as in most of the flax mills through the parish, there are 4 scutches or rapid wheels for beating and softening the flax.

Public Buildings

In addition to the public buildings already enumerated, there are the following dispersed through the parish: the Protestant church, a chapel of ease, a Presbyterian meeting house, a Catholic chapel and a dispensary.

Church

The Protestant church, which is in Cumber, is supposed to have been built above 90 years. Its site was well chosen, being close to the meeting of the Faughan and the Glenrandal, in a beautiful retired spot. Its form is antiquated, being long and rectangular, with the side walls thicker at the bottom than at the top. In 1806 it was new roofed and in 1824 almost rebuilt. The walls, being very strong, were left standing but raised about 4 feet, and a new roof, windows, pews, etc. were constructed. The expense was 363 pounds, which sum was raised by a subscription in 1824 from the rector and the landed proprietors, that the occupying tenants might be spared the burden of a parochial assessment. This place of worship can accommodate 200 persons.

Chapel of Ease

The chapel of ease in Tireighter, called also Learmount church, was built not only for the accommodation of the upper part of this parish, but likewise of [insert addition: Lower Cumber and] Banagher. Its situation, on the bank of the Faughan near Learmount, is beautiful, and also commanding without being exposed. It is a small, rectangular Gothic building, tasteful and very well finished. The roof is supported by ornamental iron braces, springing from the side walls. It was built in 1831 and cost 747 pounds 5s, which sum was raised by a grant of 400 pounds from the Board of First Fruits, aided by contributions from the Bishop of Derry, the Irish Society, the Skinners' Company and several of the gentry. It can accommodate 140 persons.

Presbyterian Meeting House

The Presbyterian meeting house, which is in Cregg, is near Claudy and within 200 yards of the Derry and Belfast coach road. It was built in 1830 at an expense of 600 pounds, which sum was raised by subscription. It is a plain rectangular building. When pews and galleries are constructed the entire building will accommodate about 500 people. Mr Browne of Cumber House gives the land belonging to it rent free. Before this meeting house was built the congregation used to resort to that of Lower Cumber.

Catholic Chapel

The Catholic chapel, which is in Gortscreighan, was erected in 1822 at an expense of about 200 pounds. This sum was raised by a subscription, to which some of the Protestant gentry contributed. It is neither well finished nor apparently substantial. No part of the space being occupied with pews, it can accommodate nearly 500 persons.

Dispensary

The dispensary, which is intended for the Fishmongers' tenantry alone, is in Mulderg. It was established in 1822, but no house was built for the purpose until 1829. A good one was erected, which included apartments for the physician. The expense was 1,200 pounds, which sum was granted by the Fishmongers' Company, who are also its only support. [Insert note: Descriptions of the schoolhouses are given in Upper Cumber school statistics (initialled) B].

Gentlemen's Seats

Cumber House, the residence of John Browne Esquire, is situated in Cumber and near Claudy. The Faughan and the Glenrandal meet in the demesne. The present house was built by James Ross Esquire in 1810 and cost about 700 pounds, planting included, and other improvements round the house. It is handsome and commodious, and has a western aspect. The plantations, which are of about 28 years' growth, are extensive and judiciously laid out, but want thinning.

Learmount, the residence of Henry Barre Beresford Esquire [crossed out with marginal note: dead], is situated in Lear, at the point where the Faughan separates the parish from Banagher.

The house consists of a small, low rectangular front, with a square building in the rear flanked by 4 small round towers.

The front was built about a century ago by Captain Montgomery, who improved the land and planted a number of trees, which are now large and flourishing. The building in the rear was erected 30 years ago by John Claudius Beresford Esquire, who then planted extensively along the Faughan and in the smaller glens, which have been thus greatly beautified. The house is in bad order, but the proprietor intends to enlarge the front. The shrubbery and pleasure grounds are spacious and tasteful, but in bad order [insert marginal note: query order?].

The Glebe House, the residence of the Revd Francis Brownlow, is in Lower Alla, on the western bank of the Glenrandal and 2 miles south of Claudy. It was built [insert addition: in 1772 at the cost of 1,070 pounds 12s 4d British] during the incumbency of Dean Edward Ledwich, who planted some trees, to which more were added by the Revd Francis Gauldsburry about 25 years ago. [Insert marginal note: "25 years ago," i.e. in 1834 or 1835, say "about 30"]. Of those planted by the dean, only the second growth remains. [Insert addition: In 1818 the house was repaired at the cost of about 1,103 pounds 6s 11d]. There are several beautiful views through the demesne, particularly up the valley of the Glenrandal.

Kilcaltan, the residence of Alexander Ogilby Esquire, is situated in the townland of the same name and on the northern bank of the Faughan, and about 400 yards from the high road leading between Derry and Dungiven. It is at the western extremity of the parish and 8 miles from Derry. The demesne is extensive and the site of the house is very happily choosen, as it commands strikingly picturesque views of the mountains and of the richly wooded valley of the Faughan.

Beaufort, so called from a fort or rath near the house, is on the opposite side of the Faughan from Cumber demesne. It was built in 1764 by William Ross Esquire, but few trees were planted by this gentleman; there is, however, in the grounds a very beautiful bank of natural oak overhanging the Faughan.

Beaufort is the property of John Browne Esquire. The last occupant, John McCleery Esquire, left it in 1830 and it is at present inhabited only by a family of cottiers.

Communications

The main road between Derry and Belfast by Dungiven lies through the parish for more than 4 miles. Its average breadth is 21 feet. It is a county road and repaired by contracts at county expense. The materials employed are broken slate and rolled pebbles, brought from the rivers with gravel. Its direction might be changed with much advantage, so as to avoid steep hills. Thus in Kilcaltan, about 1 and a half miles to the west of Claudy, instead of ascending to a height of about 510 feet it might be made to run nearer the Faughan and ascend only 350; and in Killycor it might have a similiar ascent, instead of attaining an elevation of about 460 feet, by being here also led nearer to the river.

The main road between Newtownlimavady and Strabane also lies for 8 miles through the parish and meets the Dungiven road at Claudy. Its breadth varies from 18 to 21 feet and it is kept in good repair, chiefly with gravel from the rivers.

The by-roads, which are not unnecessarily numerous, were mostly made by the county and are in good order.

Bridges

There are 4 stone bridges across the Faughan. One is at Park in [blank]. It consists of a single arch, well built, and 21 feet broad.

Another is in [blank] Cumber. [Insert marginal note: Fill blanks from Ordnance map]. It consists of 5 arches and is 21 feet broad. It is old but strong, and in good repair.

Another is in Cregg, nearly three-quarters of a mile lower on the river. This is the oldest bridge in the parish and, although it has an antiquated appearance, it is strong and in good repair. It rests on 3 arches and its breadth is only 11 feet, with a triangular recess on each side extending over one of the abutments. Its foundation is on the natural outcropping rock of schist.

The last bridge, which is between Ballyartan and Gortnaran, is known as Tonnduff bridge. It rests upon 3 high well-built arches and forms a picturesque and beautiful feature of the scenery. This is also an old bridge.

There are several stone bridges over the Glenrandal. They are all in good repair, but the only one worthy of special notice is in Cumber. It rests on a single and exceedingly graceful arch, the span of which is 50 feet. It was built about 25 years ago and is in good repair.

Near the northern extremities of Lower Alla and Tullintrain the Revd Francis Brownlow has thrown an iron foot-bridge over the Glenrandal. This has been done chiefly for the accommodation of his tenants on the eastern side of the Glenrandal and of the children that attend Alla

Foot-bridges across the Glenrandal and Faughan

Parish of Cumber

school, who formerly had to wade through the river in wet weather. The construction of the bridge is very simple, the footway, by means of brackets fastened to its sides, resting on 2 round bars of iron, convex towards the river and securely clamped and fastened with lead-in stones at each extremity. Its length is 35 feet and its breadth 2 feet 8 inches. The following is a side elevation: [insert addition: drawing of a footbridge, made by Revd Charles Brownlow, across the Glenrandal, with 2 figures for proportion]. The expense, including bridge and pier, will amount to nearly 20 pounds.

There are 2 wooden bridges over the Fore Glen river, one in Kinculbrack and the other between Ballyholly and Coolnacolpagh. They were built in 1828 by the Fishmongers, the former on a county road, the latter on a company one. The timber employed was fir from Walworth wood. They are now quite out of repair and impassable, except for pedestrians: vehicles must pass through the bed of the stream at the sides of the bridges.

A stone bridge also of 2 arches, which is old but strong, spans this stream at its intersection with the Dungiven road. Its breadth is 21 feet and it is in good repair.

Some of the smaller bridges used to be sometimes swept away in wet weather, but this is now of rare occurrence from the great care and attention bestowed in rebuilding them.

General Appearance and Scenery

On glancing over this parish, the eye has no conspicuous works of art to rest on; but nature, by it beauty and grandeur, fully compensates this deficiency. The prospect up the valley of the Glenrandal is one of the most interesting. In the foreground appear the timber plantations which form the opening of a vista that pierces far into a range of elevations extending on each side and uniting in Straw Mountain, the elevated barrier of the scene.

About Learmount there is the same grandeur, with a greater extent of prospect. Here the river, winding through the extensive plantations which clothes its frequently precipitous banks, offers a variety of beautiful scenes, among which the chapel of ease, owing to its well chosen site, is pleasingly conspicuous; but the eye, unwilling to rest even here, wanders with delight, almost with awe, through the extensive tracts of the Banagher mountains, among which towers that of Sawel. The northern part of the parish presents no interesting objects.

SOCIAL ECONOMY

Progress of Improvement

At the Plantation of Ulster those parts of the parish not appropriated to the Church became the property of the Goldsmiths', Skinners' and Fishmongers' Companies; a portion, however, was as usual reserved for freeholders, of whom Galleyglass, the son of Rory O'Kane, was of native descent. A considerable number of English and Scotch accordingly settled in it, whose posterity still remains: but, as the Irish population were left undisturbed, their descendants constitute the majority of the inhabitants.

The decay of the cottage linen weaving has brought with it an increased attention to agriculture, which has proved very beneficial.

The establishment of the Reformer Coach, which runs between Derry and Belfast, as also that of the mail car between Derry and Dungiven, have operated as improvements. Before 1827 such public conveyances were unknown, and it was only in 1833 that a post began to pass through the parish. [Insert marginal query: Is there any change in these conveyances?].

The liberal exertions of the Fishmongers' Company, in improving the communications and enlarging the holdings on their estate, have been highly advantageous. They attend particularly to the farmhouses of their tenantry, advancing on loan a sum sufficient for erecting a good house, to be repaid by instalments without interest. They also encourage the reclamation of land, grant young trees etc. Most of the landed proprietors, indeed, are dividing into farms the unenclosed mountain on their estates. The injurious practice, however, of letting ground by rundale still exists to some extent. [Insert query by T.A. Larcom: Dear Portlock, what is "rundale?" Give a few words description of it here, once for all; everybody knows its nature generally, but not well in Ireland].

Inhabitants

The Scotch settlers inhabit all the lowest and most fertile districts. The Irish are numerous on the south of the Faughan, especially about Stranagalwilly, which is encompassed by lofty mountains. The name O'Gormely is very frequent at Stranagalwilly; the McLoughlins are the prevailing family in that part of the district called the Ballymullins [insert note: which is between the hills of Menie and Kilgort (compare with Banagher)].

Local Government

The only magistrate resident in the parish is John Browne Esquire of Cumber House. Monthly petty sessions are held at Claudy, at which the neighbouring magistrates occasionally assist.

Police

In Lear there is stationed a party of revenue police, consisting of a lieutenant, a sergeant, a constable and 12 privates. In Claudy there is stationed a party of constabulary police, consisting of a constable and 3 sub-constables. [Insert marginal query: Are those numbers still right?].

Physical and Intellectual Instruction

There is no establishment for physical instruction in the parish.

In some parts of the parish the wants of the lower orders, in respect to that kind of intellectual instruction which is suited for their children, are well provided for. The number of the schools is 9, of which all are public. In the part of Bond's glen within the parish a day school is greatly wanted, there being none along a line of 4 miles from Ballyartan to the parochial boundary.

The Fishmongers' Company have evinced a laudable anxiety for the promotion of education throughout their part of the parish, on which they have built [blank] schoolhouses, one in the year [blank], another in [blank].

Rules of Fishmongers' Schools

The following are the rules for the government of the schools on the Fishmongers' estate, adopted in 1828 and revised in 1832. [Additions refer to 1828 version].

Nature and design of the institution:

1. The important objects proposed to be effected by the establishment of the schools are: to instruct children of both sexes resident on the estate, chiefly those of the poorer classes, the boys in the useful arts of reading, writing and arithmetic, comprising the rules of addition, subtraction, multiplication, division, reduction, rule of 3, practice and book-keeping by single entry; the girls in reading, writing, and the first 4 rules of arithmetic, needlework and knitting. Also to impress on their tender minds the first principles of pure religion, and moral sentiment and practice as contained in the Bible.

2. All catechisms and books of religious controversy shall be excluded from the schools, and no interference with the peculiar religious tenets of the children shall be permitted.

Of the method of instruction:

3. The system or mode of instruction shall be the Lancasterian, and all books and school requisites be supplied at the expense of the company; and the 2 boards of management (hereafter named) shall appoint such books to be used in the schools as they shall deem best suited to effect the ends of their establishment.

4. One chapter of Holy Scripture [insert addition: and no more] shall be read every day by each class competent thereto, selected from such part of the Bible as shall be directed by the board, and one chapter taken from the New Testament shall be read aloud by the master or the head monitor each day in every school.

Of the government of the institution:

[Insert note: The following paragraph contains the substance of the rules from 5 to 12, both inclusive, which are nearly identical with the dispensary rules similiarly numbered as given further on]. The schools shall be under the superintendence of the 2 boards of management which superintend the dispensaries. [Insert addition: Each board shall meet in the beginning of each quarter (or oftener if it shall be deemed necessary), to examine and inquire into the progress of the scholars, to ascertain the amount due to the master or mistress of each school for the last quarter, to give orders to the agent in writing, signed by the chairman, for that or any other payment to be made, or any necessary article to be procured and for general business; and to depute 6 of their members, 2 for each month of the current quarter, for the more immediate superintendence of the schools in the division].

A particular report of each school within their respective divisions is furnished annually by each board to the company through their agent. This report must be first approved of by the board and signed by the chairman.

Of the masters and mistresses:

The masters and mistresses shall be elected by ballot by the boards within their respective divisions, provided always that no person shall be appointed master of any school until he shall have been examined in the presence of a general meeting of the board, summoned for the purpose, and judged to possess a competent knowledge of the Lancasterian system and to be qualified to teach reading, writing, arithmetic and book-keeping; and that no person be appointed mistress until she shall have been examined in the presence of a general meeting of the board, summoned for that

purpose, and judged to possess a competent knowledge of the Lancasterian system and to be qualified to teach reading, writing, arithmetic, needlework and knitting.

13. In the selection of masters and mistresses, the board shall make no distinction on account of religious profession, having respect only to moral character and qualification for teaching.

14. Each master and mistress will keep a correct and regular account of the daily attendance of each of the scholars, in books to be provided for the purpose, which books are to be open to public inspection and to be laid before the quarterly meeting of each board.

15. Each master and mistress shall transmit a return quarterly of the name and place of abode of each scholar, whether residing on the estate or not, and of the amount they receive from the parents of each scholar, exclusive of the allowance granted to them by the company.

16. The payment of the master and mistress shall be founded on the progress of the children: but they shall not be entitled to claim, either from the company or the parents, any renumeration for the tuition of those children whose progress has been adjudged by the board to be unsatisfactory, unless it shall appear that a deficiency arises from the non-attendance of the children, in which case the parents shall be required to make good the quarter's stipend.

17. The rates of quarterly stipends to the masters for each boy learning spelling, reading, writing or arithmetic [insert addition: cypher] shall be 3s per quarter, and to the mistress for each girl learning spelling, reading, writing or arithmetic, needlework or knitting, 3s per quarter, one-half to be paid by the company and one-half by the parents, if they are able; and in the case of those scholars who are admitted as children of poor parents, the whole amount shall be paid by the company.

18. No payment will be allowed by the company for those children who shall have attained the instruction specified in the first rules; and therefore they direct that if any scholars continue longer at the schools the parents shall be required to pay the full amounts of stipend to the masters or mistresses.

Of the scholars:

19. No child shall be received into any of the schools, unless he produces to the master or mistress a certificate signed by 2 members of the board of the division, according to the form annexed to these rules, and which certificate shall be laid before the next meeting of the board. And it shall be in the discretion of each board, by a vote of a majority of its members, to expel a scholar from any school within their respective divisions, for non-payment of the quarterly stipend due by the parents, or for any other cause which they shall judge to be sufficient.

Certificate of Admission to Fishmongers' School

Form of the certificate of admission: we do hereby certify that [blank] is the child of [blank] and now resident in the [blank], townland of [blank] in the manor of Walworth, and we recommend him (or her) to be admitted and educated at the school at [blank]. [Signed] A B C D, members of the board. [Insert footnote: If the parents are poor, add the following words "at the expense of the company"].

Sunday School

[Insert addition: A Sunday school shall be held in each schoolhouse, and one teacher shall be appointed to each school, with a salary of 1 pound per quarter, who shall keep regular returns of the attendance of the scholars and be subject to the directions of the board].

Education: Moral Instruction

The moral instruction of the parish is superintended by the Protestant rector and his curate, with the curate of Learmount church, a part of whose cure is in this parish, the Presbyterian minister, the Covenanting minister of Clondermot, the Methodist preachers by whom the parish is occasionally visited, and the Catholic priest and his curate.

Sunday Schools

[Table contains the following headings: religious persuasions, population, extent of accommodation provided in places of worship, average attendance as stated by the commissioners of public instruction, place of public worship, periods at which divine service is performed, state of congregation, number of clergymen].

Protestant: population 836, average attendance 80, in the parish church; divine service performed twice on Sundays in summer and once in winter, and on the usual holidays; congregation increasing; clergymen: the rector and a curate, they are resident.

Protestant: population [?] 339, average attendance 50, in Learmount church; divine service performed once every Sunday and on the usual holidays; congregation increasing; clergymen: 1, the perpetual curate, he is resident.

Presbyterian: population 2,186, average attendance 225, in the Presbyterian meeting house; divine service performed twice on Sundays in summer and once in winter, and on 3 fast days previous to the sacrament; congregation increasing, 1 clergyman.

Other Dissenters: population 8, [other entries:] see Clondermot.

Roman Catholics: population 2,677, average attendance 600, in the Roman Catholic chapel; divine service performed once on Sundays and on the usual holidays of the Roman Catholic Church; congregation increasing; clergymen: 3, who also officiate in Bovevagh and Banagher.

Roman Catholics: population 1,985, average attendance 650, in the Roman Catholic chapel at Learmount; divine service performed once on Sundays and on the usual holidays of the Roman Catholic Church; congregation increasing; clergymen: 3, who also officiate in Bovevagh and Banagher.

Summary of Education

It appears from the parliamentary returns that in 1821 there was a free school in the parish attended by 30 boys, which is the only school mentioned, and that the number of children at school in 1824 was 354 and in 1834, 678. At present there are [blank] teachers educating [blank] scholars, of whom [blank] are between the ages of 5 and 15, being [blank] of the population between these ages; and by reference to the tables of population, it will be seen that the number of children receiving education has increased in a ratio considerably greater than the rate of increase of the entire community.

Establishments for Mental and Bodily Disease

This parish is within the district of the Londonderry lunatic asylum. There is no general dispensary in the parish, but a part of it is included in the district of that of Dungiven. The Fishmongers have a dispensary on their estate in Mulderg, which is confined to their own tenantry and includes part of Faughanvale in its district. It is open daily from 9 to 11, Sunday excepted, and the physician is obliged after it closes to visit such patients as had been unable to attend. The annual number of patients is at an average 1,200, and the establishment has greatly benefitted the neighbourhood. The physician, who is constantly resident, is allowed 100 pounds a year.

This situation, which is open to the medical department of the army and navy alone, is ballotted for in London, and the fullest testimonials are required as to character, experience and ability. Medicines are supplied in abundance.

Rules of Fishmongers' Dispensary

Rules for government of the dispensaries instituted and supported by the Fishmongers' Company of London, on their estate in the county of Londonderry, adopted in 1828 and revised in 1832. [Additions refer to 1828 version].

1. The dispensary shall be under the superintendence of 2 separate boards of management, one for the northern division of the estate, situated in the parishes of Tamlaght Finlagan and Faughanvale, the other for the southern, situated in the parishes of Banagher and Upper Cumber, including Loughermore.

2. The agent of the company for the time being shall be a member of both boards.

3. The clergymen of all religious persuasions connected with the estate may be members of the boards, within their respective divisions.

4. In addition to these, there shall be 6 members in each board resident tenants in their respective divisions; and any vacancy by death, resignation, change of residence, or otherwise shall be filled up from time to time by ballot by the remaining members of the board [insert addition: such election being always in the month of May].

5. 5 members of the board shall be a quorum.

6. Each board shall meet in the beginning of every quarter, or oftener if it shall be deemed necessary, to examine certificates of recommendation, to give orders to the agent in writing, signed by the chairman [insert addition: and secretary], for further supplies of medicines, payment of medical officers' salaries, and for general business.

7. A special meeting shall be summoned by the company's agent, whenever he shall think it expedient, or whenever he shall be required to do so by 3 members, in writing.

8. Each board shall annually, in the month of May, elect by ballot a chairman and secretary, and it shall be the duty of the secretaries to attend all meetings of their respective boards and make regular minutes of their proceedings in books kept for the purpose, and to furnish annually to the company, through their agent, a full report of their proceedings, of the patients admitted and dismissed, medicines received and dispensed, which report must be first approved by the board and

signed by the chairman [insert addition: and secretary].

9. 2 surgeons, duly qualified as full surgeons in the army, shall be appointed with a salary of 100 pounds per annum each, one for the northern division of the estate, to be resident at the dispensary of Ballykelly, the other for the southern division, to be resident at the dispensary in Mulderg; and they shall attend their respective dispensaries from 9 until 11 o'clock in the forenoon, and afterwards vist such patients as shall be unable to attend.

10. In case any complaint shall be made to the board against the medical officer for remissness or inattention to his duty, which shall by them be thought worthy of, after consideration, the secretary of the board shall reduce the same to writing and shall send a copy to the person so charged, and shall give notice of such complaint to all the members of the board, who at their next meeting shall carefully examine the charge; and should there appear to them just cause, shall forthwith dismiss such medical officer, provided 7 members of the said board shall concur in such dismissal; and in such event the secretary shall furnish the company's agent with a full statement of the case and the grounds upon which they proceeded, that the same may be forthwith transmitted to the company.

11. When case of difficulty may arise, wherein a consultation may be deemed necessary by either surgeon, it shall be in his power to require the attendance of the other surgeon.

12. Each surgeon shall keep regular books showing particularly the number of patients, diseases and medicines dispensed, in the manner to be determined by the boards, and also the time at which the patients are admitted and when discharged.

13. [Insert addition: That the surgeons shall, in the first instance, be appointed by the Fishmongers' Company, and afterwards], as vacancies may occur, shall be elected by ballot of the boards of their respective divisions, notice of the day and hour of such election being given to all the members of such board by the secretary 1 month previously.

14. No person shall be admitted to receive medical aid at the company's expense, who shall not produce to the dispensary officer a certificate in the form hereinafter specified, and signed by a member of the board, and who shall not then actually possess some fixed place of abode upon the company's estate, or be a servant to a tenant resident therein.

15. The medicines shall be of the best quality and procured by the company's agent, according to the orders of the boards [insert addition: either from Dublin or Belfast].

The above regulations for the government of the dispensaries on the Fishmongers' estate, having been determined on by way of experiment, it is proposed that they be reconsidered at the end of 3 years.

Dispensary Certificate

Form of certificate, Fishmongers' dispensary:
I do certify that [blank], resident in the townland of [blank], is a proper person to receive medical assistance, he being unable to pay for the same. Signed A.B., member of the board, to [blank], the medical officer of the [blank] division. NB The above regulations, for the government of the schools and dispensaries of the Fishmongers' estate, shall be reconsidered, whenever the court shall deem it expedient.

Notes on Dispensary

The number of cases of disease prescribed for, from 1st March 1831 to 14th May 1834, was 4,542. From May 1833 to May 1834 the number admitted was 1,391. Of these, 982 were cured, 196 relieved, 2 incurable, 6 died, 76 remained on the books and 129 were found to be free from disease. The parish is in great want of a general dispensary, the nearest being those of Dungiven and Lower Cumber, at a distance of 15 miles from some parts of it.

Idiots

There are 4 idiots in Claudy.

Mulderg Dispensary

Return from the dispensary of Mulderg, extending over the parish of Upper Cumber and part of Faughanvale.

Average on the years 1829, 1830, 1831, 1832 and 1833.

Expenditure: salary of surgeon or physician 100 pounds; salary of apothecary none, salary of midwife none; rent of dispensary none; rent of surgeon's house: cost the Fishmongers' Company 800 pounds, no rent [insert query: 1,200 pounds in another document; which is right?]; amount of medicine 60 pounds; repairs none, house lately built; other expenses none; total 160 pounds; relief afforded: 1,000 recommended, 1,000 dispensations of medicine, 230 gratuitous visits; dispensary opened 6 days each week, 2 hours attendance each day; number of women delivered by midwife: no return; number of vaccinations none; number of governors 16.

Benevolence: Establishments for the Indigent

[Table contains the following headings: name, object, management, number relieved, funds, annual expense of management, relief afforded, when founded].

9 schools partly supported by benevolence; object: the removal of ignorance; management: sundry; 652 receiving instruction; relief afforded: instruction; schools: Lower Alla, Ballyartan, Claudy, Cregg, Gortilea, Kilcaltan, Killycor, Stranagalwilly, Tireighter.

Places of worship; object: the relief of poverty; management: the churchwardens and others; number relieved variable.

Residence of the gentry; object: the relief of poverty; management: the gentry; number relieved variable.

Fishmongers; the office is in another parish; object: the relief of poverty; management: the Fishmongers' agent; number relieved variable.

Establishments for Mental and Bodily Diseases

[Table contains the following headings: name, management, number relieved, funds, annual expense of management, annual expenses of patients, when founded].

Dispensary: management 2 boards appointed by the Fishmongers' Company; number relieved: 1,200 annually on an average, 1,391 from the [blank] of May 1833 to the [blank] of May 1834; how many the [blank] of May 1835; house rent: interest on 800 pounds (or 1,200), the expense of building; salaries 100 pounds. [Insert note: A printed dispensary table gives 800 pounds for the surgeon's house, but is not here identical with the dispensary in which the surgeon has apartments].

Dispensary of Dungiven, which includes a part of this parish in its district: see parish of Dungiven.

Justice and Trade

The array of preventive justice has been detailed under the heading Local Government, and there is but little room for the exercise of retributive. The crimes seldom exceed petty assaults. Illicit distillation is facilitated by the mountainous nature of the parish, but it was formerly more prevalent. In some districts adjacent to the county of Tyrone it has greatly increased the poverty, and in Bond's glen it received no check until 1827.

The scanty trade of the parish is confined to Claudy.

Population in 1821

[Table] Parish of Upper Cumber: 1,159 inhabited houses, 14 uninhabited; 1,201 families, 3,163 males, 3,301 females, total 6,464; 1,290 persons chiefly employed in agriculture, 1,736 chiefly employed in trades, manufactures and handicraft, 391 chiefly occupied in other occupations and not in preceding categories, total number occupied 3,417.

Population in 1831

[Table] Parish of Upper Cumber: 1,273 inhabited houses, 6 uninhabited; 1,304 families, 3,504 males, 3,660 females, total 7,164, 1,719 males above 20 years of age; 967 persons chiefly employed in agriculture, 190 persons chiefly employed in trades, manufactures and handicraft, 147 persons employed in other occupations and not in preceding classes.

Village of Park: 21 inhabited houses, 1 uninhabited house; 21 families, 66 males, 66 females, total 132, 30 males over 20 years of age; 18 persons chiefly employed in agriculture, 2 persons chiefly employed in trades, manufactures and handicraft, 1 person employed in another occupation and not in preceding classes.

Village of Claudy: 31 inhabited houses, 3 uninhabited, 1 building; 33 familes, 85 males, 95 females, total 180, 44 males over 20 years of age; 17 persons chiefly employed in agriculture, 11 chiefly employed in trades, manufactures and handicraft, 5 employed in other occupations and not in preceding classes.

Totals: 1,325 inhabited houses, 10 uninhabited, 1 building; 1,358 families, 3,655 males, 3,721 females, total 7,476, 1,793 males over 20 years of age; 1,002 persons chiefly employed in agriculture, 203 chiefly employed in trades, manufactures and handicraft, 153 in other occupations and not in preceding classes.

Table of Religion in 1834

As determined in the First Report of the Commissioners of Public Instruction.

Parish of Upper Cumber; 1831, according to the enumerator's return: 804 Established Church, 2,573 Roman Catholics, 2,045 Presbyterians, 8 other Protestant Dissenters, total in the parish 5,430; 1834, as determined by the commissioners: 836 Established Church, 2,677 Roman Catholics, 2,127 Presbyterians, 8 other Protestant Dissenters, total in the parish 5,648.

Learmount, perpetual cure; 1831, according to the enumerator's return: 70 Established Church, 1,905 Roman Catholics, 57 Presbyterians, total in the parish 2,032; as determined by the commissioners, 1834: 39 Established Church, 1,985 Roman Catholics, 59 Presbyterians, total in the parish 2,083.

Total. 1831, according to the enumerator's return: 874 Established Church, 4,478 Roman Catholics, 2,102 Presbyterians, 8 other Protestant Dissenters, total in the parish 7,462; 1834, as determined by the commissioners: 875 Established Church, 4,662 Roman Catholics, 2,186 Presbyterians, 8 other Protestant Dissenters, total in the parish 7,731.

Habits of the People

There is a shade of difference in the habits of almost every glen. The cottages are mostly of stone, and those of the Scotch population exhibit superior neatness, at least externally. The dwellings of the Irish population are rarely watertight, properly glazed, or properly ventilated [insert marginal query: cottiers?]. Frequently, even where the family amount to 9, the only bedstead consists of bog timber supported by large stones, with a bundle of straw or rushes for a pallet, a canvas sheet and a blanket made with three-quarter inches of tow yarn to the quarter inch of woollen yarn. The cottier's coat serves for a coverlet, and the family lies promiscuously at each end of their rude lair.

The ordinary diet of the labouring class is chiefly potatoes and buttermilk, with eggs or salt herrings at dinner and supper. Some cottiers endeavour to have porridge for breakfast in summer; many, however, have to subsist on potatoes throughout the year, with sour milk in summer and gruel, onions, salt, salt herrings or eggs in winter. The middling farmers indeed can sometimes afford a little beef or bacon. The fuel is [blank].

Language and Longevity

The Irish language is on the decline.

No remarkable instances of longevity are on record. [Insert marginal note: Compare with Faughanvale].

Marriage Customs

Early and improvident marriages are frequent. The preliminaries are sometimes conducted in the following reprehensible manner, which is called a "runaway." The girl's sweetheart prevails upon her to remove to a neighbour's house, where, previously to their marriage, they are entertained by the owner. To every visitor likewise, a glass of whiskey is offered. After marriage, every wellwisher comes provided with a bottle to treat the bridegroom to "some whiskey," and another entertainment takes place. On the first Sunday after the wedding the bridal party appears at their place of worship, and the day is hence called "Shewing Sunday."

Desertion of Children

Since 1822 but 9 children have been left deserted, 3 of which are at present supported by the parish. In March 1833 one was found dead and disfigured in Ballyholly: an inquest was held, but nothing transpired.

Respect for Heirlooms

The Irish population have a respect for old family furniture: many such articles, especially spinning-wheels, are known to have been preserved for nearly a century. [Insert marginal note: A universal feeling].

Drink and Poteen

There are 21 licensed spirit shops. The law not recognising the existence of poteen <potieen>, the method of recovering debts due for it is peculiar. The creditor steals his debtor's cow, or some of his chattels, taking care to inform him that his property shall be forthcoming on his depositing the amount of the demand with some person specified. The debtor, however, sometimes retaliates by lodging information against his creditor for cow-stealing.

Cattle Herding

In Bond's glen the cows are led out about sunrise and brought home about 11 in the forenoon. When breakfast and the various business of the morning is over, the men go forth to their rural occupations, the women repair to their household business, the cows are sent back to the hills, and all is silent in the dwelling until about 3, when dinner is announced by a white cloth streaming from a pole planted on some eminence. At the signal all hasten home, except the herd boy, to whom dinner is sent. At 8 in the evening the cows are again brought home and milked, after which they are housed for the night.

Emigration and Migration

No change in the average rent of landed property has resulted from transatlantic emigration. The emigrants consist of the youth of both sexes, farmers and cottiers indiscriminately. This drain has increased the wages of labour. It has also, to a certain extent, relieved the parish by removing numbers who were on the verge of pauperism. This advantage has, however, been partially neutralised by the improvidence with which many spend their all in purchasing the deserted farms, with no other prospect than that of subsisting for years on the crop.

In 1833 the transatlantic emigration amounted to 120 individuals of both sexes, varying in age from 2 to 40.

The families of those who migrate to England and Scotland in the harvest season usually beg through other parishes. About one-seventh of the reapers remain in Ireland and range over the counties of Antrim, Louth, Meath and Dublin. These poor men invariably return to their families with their earnings, which usually average 3 pounds.

In 1833 the emigration amounted to 80 individuals, including some young women.

Remarkable Persons and Events

There is no remarkable person on record connected with the parish, either by birth or residence. The only remarkable events are the following which, although of a private nature, may be worth recording, as illustrative of the habits of the district.

In 1833 a gauger, named Lampen, disappeared from Lettermuck, and no trace of him has since been discovered. He was last seen near the paper mill in this townland, against which he was about to strike a heavy fine. The proprietors were arrested on suspicion, but no proof could be obtained against them, and all search for his body was unavailing.

Near the source of the Glenrandal, and in a spot of singular seclusion, there is a small cairn situated at the foot of a cliff. This commemorates the death of a female maniac, which occurred about 20 years ago. Being observed wandering through Stranagalwilly on a severe winter's day, and entering the valley of the Glenrandal, she was asked whither she was going. She replied that "she was walking up to heaven," after which she continued her way to the end of the valley, a distance of nearly 2 miles, where, overpowered by the snow and sleet, she expired. Her body was found next morning, and the peasantry, as they pass, cast a stone upon the spot, in compliance with ancient usage. [Insert marginal query: Ancient Topography, although a modern cairn].

Draft Memoir mainly by J. Stokes, 1834

SOCIAL ECONOMY

Obstructions to Improvement

Many of the farms are still disposed in rundales, particularly on the lands held by R. Ogilby Esquire. The tenantry appear fully to understand the evils of the system. It appears to be the prevailing opinion among the parishioners that small farms are also disadvantageous, and since the passing of the Reform Bill the proprietors have been disposed to enlarge them. The rents are not so high as would appear from the prevalence of discontent, the greatest obstruction to improvement.

Local Government

The resident magistrate is J. Browne Esquire of Cumber House. A monthly petty sessions is held at Claudy, but the number of magistrates in attendance is irregular. The crimes are trivial, seldom exceeding petty assaults.

MODERN TOPOGRAPHY

General Appearance and Scenery

The general appearance of the parish is bare and bleak. More than one-third of it is boggy, but the only extensive field of bog is that of Alla. The scenery of the Ballymullins, especially of the hills which are on each side of the Glenrandal, is wild; around Cumber House and at Learmount it assumes a softer character.

The remarkable points of view are from the bridge in Kilcaltan and from the back of the old house at Beaufort. The scenery of the Burntollet river is very attractive.

SOCIAL ECONOMY

Poor

There are no parochial funds for the support of the poor, but their chief dependency is on sabbath collections and individual charity. They generally resort to other parishes and beg until the potatoes are sufficiently matured. In winter they stay at home. From there being at present but 1 family of superior rank presently resident in the parish, it is not very much infested.

Parish of Cumber

The cottiers are as usual more or less in a state of incipient pauperism. Their average condition is one in which they can pretty well contrive to exist, but all those who are below it lock their houses at certain seasons and beg abroad, the profession of a beggar being by them considered excellent. The cottier obtains ground from the farmer gratuitously, and makes every exertion to raise manure and procure seed for a small kind of potatoes, which with turf, approach to covering for himself and family, and satisfy his wants. Those who are above the average condition are frequently allowed by the farmer to graze a cow.

They are also in many cases supplied with wool, flax and oatmeal, at stated prices, according to market currency. An experiment has been made, whether paupers were willing to work. It completely failed: for although they hypocritically express their gratitude to their employer for the offer, as soon as he had departed after inspecting them for a short time, they all fled.

The number of paupers is apparently not on the increase. The causes of the existence of that class, and the various circumstances by which it is affected, seem to be the same as in the parish of Clondermot. There is no poor shop nor any similiar institution, but many paupers are pensioned by the Fishmongers' Company and the upper classes. Among the paupers there are many infirm and maimed persons.

Clergymen

The present rector is the Revd Mr Brownlow; his curate is the Revd E. Burrowes. The parish priest is the Revd Henry; his curates the Revd Gunnalouge and the Revd McPheely. The Presbyterian minister is the Revd Mr Brown.

Extent of Congregations

The Revd Mr Brown's congregation scarcely exceeds 20 families. The remainder of the Presbyterian parishioners attend meeting in Brackfield or Banagher, or go to church. The Cregg congregation was formed by a secession from that of Brackfield.

The perpetual curacy of Learmount extends over the outskirts of Banagher, Upper Cumber and Lower Cumber. The curate, the Revd Mr Hunter, resides in Straid, a townland of Banagher (see parish of Banagher). [Insert addition: He is paid about 90 pounds a year by the above parishes]. The Fishmongers' Company gives 10 pounds to the Presbyterian ministers and the priest of the parish.

[Insert addition: The prevalent persuasions are the Protestant, Presbyterian and Roman Catholic, to which should be added a few Methodists or mountain men. The proportion of Catholics to the Protestants is about 3 to 2; tithe 740 pounds].

Chimneys

The chimneys are in many instances only half-chimneys, as the smoke must approach the roof before it meets with any conduit whatever.

Longevity

No parochial register whatever is kept, from which the average longevity might be estimated: however, it is not very remarkable.

Sleeping Habits

The family sleep promiscuously, some at the head and some at the foot, the younger members being often but partially covered.

Family Work Habits

The above description properly applies to cottiers who are not in constant employment, and whose children have not yet gone to service through the want of years or opportunity; but if both parents choose to get an employment suited to both, such as harvest work or turf-cutting, the elder children make themselves useful in minding the younger and preparing the meals of the labourers.

Clothing

The better order of cottiers manufacture their own clothing, which consists of frieze and drugget.

Wedding Customs: Showing Sunday

The first Sunday after the wedding day is called "Showing Sunday," from the bride, bridegroom and all their wedding friends showing themselves among their congregation. This custom, which prevails among the parishioners of every class, could be advantageously dispensed with.

Tradition regarding Lough Lohan

It is generally believed through the neighbourhood of Lough Lohan that the fort which stands upon the island in that lough is a place of meeting, feasting, dancing and rejoicing with the "invisible gentry," or fairies, as lighted fires, candles and music of all kinds have been heard and seen at various times by many of the parishioners.

It is also believed that in the bottom of the lough there exists car-loads of firearms, thrown in at the time of the "wars of Ireland." These wars appear to be usually divided into 3 parts: the first is the "Strongbowian wars," or what should be properly called the wars of Ireland; the second is the "wars of Cromwell," or "Phelimy Roe;" the third is the rebellion of 1798. The second division comprises all the wars from 1641 to the siege of Derry.

Fear of Disturbing Sites

The parishioners have the greatest possible fear that "misfortune worse than that of war" will befall anyone who either designedly or inadvertently disturbs any old bush, fort, grave or standing stone, and say that they have often suffered by the experience.

Gift of Curing

Michael Donohoe of Gortilea got, as he states, in early life the gift of curing men or cattle by a charm. He may "have been overlooked by some unlucky person, or in other words by some malicious curious person, who feels an inward envy at the prosperity of their neighbours:" accordingly, the wisdom of the parishioners induces them to look up to him as a very potent doctor.

Elf-stones

Whenever an elf-stone is found, it is left undisturbed, as they believe that it was cast to that place by the "invisible gentry" or fairies, to revenge any injury done to their rightful property, such as cutting or breaking wilfully any part of a bush, levelling, or in any other way demolishing any part of any fort, moat <mote> or wall, speaking disrespectfully of themselves, or any of the aforesaid things.

When one such offence has been committed, the stone is believed to be discharged and the cattle immediately fall ill. If any cattle fall ill on the lands where this small stone was first seen, and replaced, it is immediately looked for; and if again found, is put into a vessel of sufficient size to contain as much water as the beast may have 3 drinks from, after which it is carefully deposited in the original place. If the animal does not on this recover, the wizards are immediately besought to apply the usual remedy.

Ill-starred Persons

The belief is general that many persons of both sexes are born under an unlucky planet, and that if any such persons happen to look, intentionally or otherwise, at the family, cattle or other effects of persons not thus unluckily born, the glance will immediately produce some malignant influences. The remedy usual when any animate object has been overlooked is this: the applicant is ordered to get at one part of the clothes of the unlucky person and burn them under the nostrils of the injured individual; this done, the injury passes away.

Such ill-starred persons generally avoid as much as possible to express, either by word or look, any approbation of the property of another, unless the subject has been introduced in their presence. In that case, if they remained silent, any disaster occurring to the person who had introduced the subject would be attributed to them.

Miraculous Rivulet

In the townland of Lear there is a small rivulet, whither for centuries past people have flocked from all parts of the adjoining country to perform stations and be cured of *every* disorder. The solemn day is May Eve, at which time it is not unusual to see from 400 to 800 individuals assembled. The spot is called Thurusallin, and the hawthorne bush which marks it is as usual profusely ornamented with rags.

Toole's Well

Toole's Well in the townland of Ballycallaghan is said to have the power of curing dumbness.

Migration to Harvest

On the 4th August 1834 25 men passed through Claudy on their way to take shipping at Belfast, with a view to harvest labour, 7 from Upper Cumber, 9 from Lower Cumber, the remainder from the county of Tyrone. They were all without coats and shoes, except 5 who wore slippers. The remainder had small bundles of clothes under their arms, going, and walked at the speedy rate of 4 miles an hour.

PRODUCTIVE ECONOMY

Linen and Weaving

There were formerly 4 extensive bleach greens in this parish, but at present there is not one at work; and the linen trade, in its different branches, is nearly lost. All the small rents were then paid by the earnings of the spinning wheel, but now all that can be made by one woman is from 1d ha'penny to 2d a day. Weaving is greatly on the

Parish of Cumber

decline, and with hard work barely repays the labour.

Growth of Petty Trades

The parish is at present almost wholly rural. Before the extinction of the bleach greens it was a manufacturing one, and there were very few of the parishioners who were not benefitted, either directly or indirectly, by the employment of the 320 individuals engaged in them, all of whom appear to have been residents of the neighbourhood. The linen trade was succeeded by a multiplicity of petty crafts such as broom-making, egg-selling, peddling, and it is probable that cattle-jobbing too has latterly increased.

Many endeavour to support themselves by dealing in soap, tobacco, salt herrings, candles, cured fish, which they obtain in such small quantities as their means permit, and carry them in baskets through the country, barter them with the farmers for potatoes, meal and eggs. Many also endeavour to support themselves by providing heath in the mountainous parts of the parish, making hand and stable brooms, which they sell in Derry, Coleraine, Newtownlimavady and other market towns. Others purchase eggs, fowl, Irish butter, yarn, lint, tow, potatoes, grain of all kinds, and retail them in the same places.

Those of the working class who are not constantly employed have but little to do from the 15th November to the beginning of April, but in many cases those who have any little capital of their own, or can borrow a sum of money from a neighbouring gentleman or farmer, employ the idle part of the year in dealing of some description, such as buying of black cattle, sheep, pigs, corn and various other commodities, in some fair or market, and conveying them to those parts of the country where they can be sold at advanced price. There are supposed to be 411 labourers of all descriptions; of these, 206 are in constant employment.

Steeping of Flax

The steeping of flax appears to be conducted in this parish in a rather careless and slovenly manner. In 1831 a considerable quantity was steeped at the bottom of the Glenrandal, which was dammed up for the purpose in many places. This forgetfulness of floods initiated much carelessness. Mr Smith of Ballyartan gives out yarn to weavers and receives from them in turn 6,001 webs annually, which he scalds and sends to Belfast.

Tanning: the tanning is doing well.

Paper Manufactory

[In a different hand: At the paper manufactory about 1,000 reams of coarse paper are annually made, which are sold to grocers at from 3s to 4s a ream; from 3 to 4 hands are employed at from 6s to 8s each, weekly].

Fairs and Markets

In the 8 fairs held annually at the village of Claudy, none of which comes under the denomination of "whiskey fairs," cattle of every description and all other commodities for country accommodation are exhibited for sale. These fairs are well attended both by buyers and sellers. "Fair custom" or "stipulated tax," on every saleable article brought to market, is levied at Claudy. All persons passing the custom gate are required by the collector to pay the sum annexed to whatever article he has. If he has not been able to sell the article, an oath is immediately administered, upon his taking [of] which the custom is remitted.

The schedule is as follows: for every cow 2d, for every horse 4d, for every sheep or lamb 1d, for a pig of any size 1d, for a goat of any size 1d, for a hawker's stand or flat 4d, for a hawker's stand covered 5d, for a basket or sack 3d, for any stand of farming tools 3d, for any stand of kitchen or dairy tools 3d, for any stand of household furniture 3d, for every yard of woollen manufacture a farthing, for any stand of wool, meal, butter from 2 to 6d, according to circumstances.

The following are the days on which the several fairs are held: 1st, January 12th; 2nd, February 17th; 3rd, March 28th; 4th, May 17th; 5th, July 8th; 6th, August 17th; 7th, September 27th or 12th; 8th, November 17th. Commodities are brought to these fairs from Londonderry, Newtownlimavady, Coleraine, Kilrea, Dungiven, Feeny, Gortin and Garvagh.

At Park a fair, toll free, is held on the second Friday of every month. This has succeeded one which was formerly held at Stranagalwilly. The commodities exposed to sale here are horses, cows and pigs of every age and price, asses, goats, butter, fowl, eggs, farming untensils, kitchen and dairy furniture, household furniture, frieze, serge, linen, hosiery of every kind, silks, calicoes, hats, shoes, leather, nails, brooms, salt herrings. No webs are exposed at either of the above fairs, as they are always brought to the Londonderry market. The stroke of Upper Cumber contains 9 stones.

Rural Economy

The quantity of arable land in each of the farms is

usually much smaller than the apparent size of the farm in this list. They are let in an undefined manner, and not by the acre but by lots, containing a portion of arable with some mossy or mountainous ground attached. A large portion of the townland is frequently a common for the use of all the tenants indiscriminately. A considerable number of the parishioners are at present without leases. The usual lease is for 21 years and 3 lives, and there are but few middlemen. From the undefined nature of the holdings it was found difficult to ascertain precisely the average rent by the acre of land of the best, middling or worst quality, but it appears to be everywhere wholly paid in money, except on the churchland held by J. Browne Esquire.

The only holdings that are not farmed wholly for subsistence are the large ones and those belonging to Messrs Beresford and Browne.

The quantity of land let in conacre is very trifling. The fields and enclosures are the best shaped on the Fishmongers' proportion. Although they vary very much in size, the ground is never anywhere so cut up with fences as in the highlands of Tamlaght Finlagan. The fences themselves are in general not remarkably bad. The parishioners do not as yet place confidence in them, as appears from their anxiety and care to tether or watch every description of livestock. In some parts of the parish fields may be observed fenced on all sides except that which is next the road, which shows that the proprietor of the field was more disposed to consider fencing as a demarcation of property than anything else. The fences are also variable in their nature, some being of loose stones, some of irregular rows of bushes.

It may be said that there are no model farms: some well cultivated farms there are, but they do not appear to be objects of imitation.

Manures

[In a different hand: The manure chiefly used is a compost of lime, which is to be obtained in all parts of the parish, rotten bog (unfit for fuel) and animal manure, for neither in the reclaimed nor any parts of the parish is there a good subsoil of clay or loam; and when the deep bog is removed, a wretched unproductive till of hungry gravel usually appears, which only after potatoes can return a tolerable crop of oats, while high on the hills flax will not grow].

Implements of Husbandry

There are not so many improved implements of husbandry as in Clondermot. Slide cars are frequent and appear better adapted than any other to small farms and rugged, steep ground. There is a kind of spade for cleaning turf ranges and cutting scraws for the roofing of houses called a flagger. [Insert note: Scraws are the sods peeled off the surface of dried pasture grounds, and used for placing on the roofs of houses a sufficient covering under the thatch]. The form of the shaft or handle is like that of a cross cutting saw [drawing of implement].

There is a threshing machine at Learmount.

Crops

The usual crops of the parish appear to be potatoes, oats, barley and flax. The barley is consumed to a considerable degree in private distillation. Wheat is gradually introducing itself; has been sown to an unusual extent in the present year (1834).

Land and Crops

[In a different hand: The quality of the land is much inferior to that of Lower Cumber, and though in very good years it will yield equal crops of oats, barley, flax, in wet and cold seasons the crops suffer much and produce a much smaller return. There was formerly a large proportion of each farm under flax, and to this the tenants look to pay their rent; but at present a quantity sufficient only to give occupation to the family is raised.

An acre of oats will produce on the average about 7 barrels. The value of an acre of oats on the ground is from 3 to 6 pounds; the value of an acre of barley on the ground is from 5 to 8 pounds; the value of an acre of flax on the ground is from 10 to 12 pounds; the value of an acre of potatoes on the ground is from 10 to 12 pounds. The quantity of potatoes raised depends entirely on the number of the family to be supported: it generally averages about 1 acre to 10 arable.

Markets

Londonderry is the nearest and most certain market for this district, and in consequence of the great exportation of grain to Liverpool the farmer meets with a ready sale for his oats].

Grazing and Drainage

There does not appear to be so much grazing in this parish as in Banagher. Drainage is not much attended to, as may be seen where crops are growing on cut-away bog, so saturated with the

Parish of Cumber

undrained moisture that the enclosure might be almost termed a floating field. The ground is almost everywhere very well adapted for it.

Farm Wages

Farm labourers in the employment of the rector receive for the summer half-year 11d ha'penny a day and for the winter half-year 9d ha'penny, without diet and throughout the year. Those in the employment of farmers receive in summer half-year 10d a day and for the winter half-year 8d. Gentlemen's labourers are not dieted by them at any season. Those who have constant employment with farmers, when dieted by them, have 5d ha'penny a day. Those who are free to work for whom they please receive in the harvest or turf-cutting season 1s a day, with diet; putting out the crops in spring and digging out the potatoes in autumn 9d a day and diet. If not dieted they receive 1s a day in all working seasons.

Employment of Children

2 adults alone are employed as herds, who receive throughout the year 10d a day, including Sundays. Herds are partially employed, young males and females indiscriminately, who tend the cattle in the summer in the moss and mountain farms. They are from 10 to 16 years old and are paid for that half-year from 15s to 21s. In the winter they return to their parents, who are burthened with their support from November to May. In many instances the boy thus employed in the summer is sent to school in winter and as many as possible of the females are sent out to some kind of service. They receive for the season from 3s to 8s for nursing, assisting in kitchen work etc. If no service can be procured, they either go to school or stay at home to spin.

Family Labour and Earnings

The average sum which a labourer can realise by constant employment, embracing all chances of harvest, turf-cutting, spring labour, roadmaking, from the beginning of April to the middle of November is from 7 to 8 pounds 10s. There is little task work to be had at any season, except cutting or drying turf, or fencing. The only way in which the taskman can profit by his contract is by employing such of his family as can assist him in fencing or turf-cutting. The other members of the family perform all the successive processes after the turf is left out on the bank, thus enabling the cottier to meet any other demand for his services by relieving him of constant attendance on his task work.

The following is a statement of the average annual income and expenditure of a cottier, assisted by his wife and 2 children, 1 of each sex, and each under 16 years of age: cottier, working 200 days at the average rate of 8d a day, 6 pounds 13s 4d; cottier's wife, 200 days at the average rate of 2d a day, 1 pound 13s 4d; boy, working 180 days at the average rate of 3d a day, 2 pounds 5s; girl, working 200 days at the average rate of 1d a day, 16s 8d; total average annual earning of husband, wife and 2 children 11 pounds 8s 4d.

Expenditure: house rent 1 pound 10s; diet, consisting of potatoes and buttermilk for the above at 6d a day, 9 pounds 2s 6d; total 10 pounds 12s 6d; balance for clothing and contingencies 15s 10d.

Livestock

5,160 black cattle and 2,400 sheep. They are of a mixed Irish breed, many having been brought from Connaught. The parish has been noted for cattle jobbing during the last 40 years. There are 13 of this calling, besides casual dealers. They frequent the English markets and also those of Londonderry, Newtownlimavady, Coleraine, Cookstown, Dungiven and Garvagh. The price of a cow varies, according to state, age and condition, from 3 to 8 pounds. The sheep are never of a very high quality; they vary in price from 12s to 36s.

Uses made of the Bogs

The bogs are grazed in summer. The bog stuff is mixed up in some composts and the bog wood for fuel, roofing of houses and as torches to spin by on winter nights. The last bogs for turbary are those in Dungorkin, Claudy, Lettermuck, Ballyartan, and Upper and Lower Alla. The remainder are thin mountain bogs, best adapted for grazing. All the turf cut is consumed within the parish.

Drainage

Some attempts have been made by the Fishmongers to drain the bogs, some also on the churchlands. They do not, however, appear to have been followed up.

Planting

Tree plantations require thinning and pruning, particularly those in the neighbourhood of Claudy. There is no nursery for young trees nearer than Knockbrack. The plantations of Learmount were commenced nearly 40 years ago and some trees are still occasionally put down. The situation is good, and some of the trees very large.

Fishing

The Faughan contains trout, salmon and eels, but by no means so much as formerly. The failure is attributed to the many weirs which have been built across its bed.

General Remarks on Economy

There is still room for improvement in the cultivation of this parish. The highest elevation to which cultivation has been carried is about 850 feet. This occurs in Ballymaclanigan and Kilgort. There appears to be everywhere a facility for draining or irrigation. The banks of the Glenrandal, from the hamlet of Stranagalwilly upwards, seem to be well adapted for planting. There is also an abundance of water power and of fuel, but the roads and communications are not very well adapted to an improving district. There is a point in which the parish at large appears to be capable of much improvement: the village of Claudy. It stands nearly in the centre of the district formed by the parishes of Upper and Lower Cumber, and on the high road between Dungiven and Londonderry. Its situation, upon the whole, appears to be more advantageous than that of Dungiven, and it will perhaps in time come of nearly equal importance.

Office Copy of Memoir by J. Stokes

Social Economy

Progress of Improvement

At the Plantation the greater portion of the parish fell to the Grocers' Company, but the native Irish, being allowed to remain on the property, constituted the chief part of the population until after the civil wars of 1641, when the parish became more extensively peopled with Scotch and English settlers.

The late John Acheson Esquire, who settled in the parish about 50 years ago, contributed much to its advancement by erecting houses and bleach works, and making other improvements.

Obstructions to Improvement

[Insert addition: The annual drain by emigration is an obvious obstruction to improvement, especially as many of the emigrants are respectable farmers. Gavelkind, although it still exists, is on the decline. A great part of the parish is held under old leases, and renewals will speedily be granted to a considerable extent. There is some apprehension as to the result].

Local Government

There is no resident magistrate nor any police whatsoever, but the people attend the petty sessions of Claudy in Upper Cumber.

Insurance

[Insert addition: Insurances of whatever kind are nearly confined to the higher classes].

Physical Instruction

There is no establishment for physical instruction in the parish.

Intellectual Instruction

There are 6 schools, confined to such intellectual instruction as is suited to the wants of the poorer orders of the community. Of these, 4 are public and 2 private.

Moral Instruction

The moral instruction of the parish is superintended by the clergy of various persuasions, consisting of the Protestant rector, his curate [insert marginal query: is there one here; these are conflicting statements?] and the curate of Learmount church, a part of whose cure is in this parish, the Presbyterian minister, the Covenanting minister of Clondermot and the Catholic priest of Clondermot and Upper Cumber.

With regard to Sunday schools: [insert query: are there any?]. [Insert crossed out addition: There are 2 Sunday schools in the several townlands of Ervey and Killaloo].

Religious Denominations

[Table contains the following headings: religious persuasions, population, extent of accommodation and place of worship, average attendance and place of public worship, periods at which divine service is peformed, state of the congregation, number of clergymen].

Protestants: [first] 656 people, accommodation for 160 in the parish church, average attendance 130; divine service twice on Sundays in summer and once in winter and on the usual

Parish of Cumber

holidays, congregation increasing, 1 resident clergymen; [second] 50 people, in Lower Cumber, average attendance 50 at Learmount church; divine service once every Sunday and on the usual holidays, congregation increasing; clergymen 1, the perpetual curate; this perpetual cure comprises part of the parishes of Upper and Lower Cumber and Banagher.

Presbyterians: 2,567 people, accommodation for 680 in the Presbyterian meeting house, average attendance 550; divine service: one every Sunday, once in winter, twice in summer and on a few days previous, and half-yearly sacrament, congregation increasing; 1 clergyman.

Roman Catholics: 1,739 persons, accommodation for 700 people in the Roman Catholic chapel, average attendance 500; divine service once every Sunday and on the usual holidays of the Roman Catholic church, congregation increasing; 2 clergymen, who also officiate in a church in the perpetual cure of Clondermot.

Income of Presbyterian Minister

From Fishmongers' Company 10 pounds, from Grocers' Company 10 pounds, from Skinners' Company 10 pounds, from stipend 75 pounds, from royal bounty 100 pounds, total 205 pounds. [Insert note: See manuscript remarks of Lieutenant Downes].

Summary of Education

It appears from the parliamentary returns that in 1821 there was no return of pupils from this parish, but that the number of children at school was 249, and in 1834, 291. And by reference to the tables of population, it will be seen that the number of children receiving education has increased in a ratio considerably higher than that of the increase of population.

Summary of Religion

There are in this parish about 600 Protestants, about 640 families of Presbyterians, each containing on an average 5 persons, and 607 Covenanters. According to the census of 1831 there were then 3,206 Protestants and 1,378 Roman Catholics. The Presbyterians are attached to the Synod of Ulster.

Establishments for the Indigent

There is no provision for the poor, the aged or the infirm, except casual charity. [Insert addition: The cottier's tax is 6 guineas a year and 4 days duty work for a house, garden, grass of a cow, 1 rood of flax ground, potato ground to any extent and as much turbary as 2 slanesmen can cover in one day, which is here called 2 darks or 50 cart's load of turf].

Poor Shop

A poor shop was established in February 1832. In 1833 there were sold: handkerchiefs 45, gowns 57, frocks 49, beds 22, bolsters 20, shawls 109, shifts 148, shirts 119, sheets 68, pairs of blankets 61, petticoats 116, quilts 34, flannel vests 32, aprons 37, slips 16, pairs of shoes 21, pairs of drawers 20; amount of sales 115 pounds 6s 3d ha'penny.

In 1834 defaulters, i.e. persons who paid irregularly, became very numerous. Actual dishonesty is rare. The wives of weavers are said to pay best and unmarried persons worst. The regularity of payment is rather increasing; this is partly accounted for by the low price of yarn, which renders it more profitable for the farmer to sell the flax than to give it out to be spun. Few women can spin finer than 3 hanks out of a lb of flax, which costs 9d; consequently 4 hanks, which constitute a spangle, take 1s worth of flax, for which spangle they get 1s 6d; and as 1 hank is a good day's work, the profit of a day's labour is just 1d ha'penny.

Establishments for Mental and Bodily Diseases

This parish is within the district of the lunatic asylum at Derry. There is a dispensary in Tamnymore, open on Tuesdays and Fridays. A part of the parish is also within the district of that of Faughanvale. [Insert addition: Whether the health of the people has been improved by the dispensary, it would be difficult to ascertain, as no register of diseases has been kept previously].

Dispensary Table

Report for year ending April 1834.
Dyspepsia: 214 patients recommended, 150 cured, 60 relieved, 2 died, 2 incurable.
Fever: 133 recommended, 130 cured, 3 died.
Pulmonic complaints: 235 recommended, 155 cured, 76 relieved, 4 died.
Cutaneous disorders: 304 recommended, 230 cured, 68 relieved, 6 incurable.
Injuries: 72 recommended, 70 cured, 2 died.
Measles: 55 recommended, all cured.
Nervous complaints: 80 recommended, 50 cured, 30 relieved.
Dropsical affections: 22 recommended, 20 cured, 2 died.

Influenza: 146 recommended, all cured.

Diseases not referable to any of the above: 536 recommended, 375 cured, 155 relieved, 6 died.

Total number: 1,797 recommended, 1,381 cured, 389 relieved, 19 died, 8 incurable. Signed John Semple, surgeon.

[Insert addition: Supported partly in the usual manner by subscriptions and partly by the Grocers' Company].

Dispensary Return

A return from the dispensary of Lower Cumber, extending over the parish of Lower Cumber and a considerable part of Upper Cumber.

[Table contains the following headings: year, income and expenditure, relief afforded, number of governors].

1829. Income: subscription 31 pounds 15s, county grant 30 pounds, total 61 pounds 15s; expenditure: salary of surgeon 30 pounds, medicine 29 pounds 11s 4d, other expenses 2 pounds 10s 6d, total 62 pounds 1s 10d; 1,488 patients recommended, dispensary open 2 days each week, average attendance 2 hours, 10 governors.

1830. Income: subscription 40 pounds, county grant 30 pounds, total 70 pounds; expenditure: salary of surgeon 30 pounds, medicine 28 pounds 14s 2d, other expenses 4 pounds 16s 11d, total 63 pounds 11s 1d; dispensary open 2 days each week, average 2 hours attendance each day, 10 governors.

1831. Income: subscription 40 pounds, county grant 30 pounds, total 70 pounds; expenditure: salary of surgeon 30 pounds, medicine 41 pounds 10s 4d, other expenses 2 pounds 13s 6d, total 74 pounds 3s 10d; 1,368 patients recommended, dispensary open 2 days each week, average attendance 2 hours each day, 10 governors.

1832. Income: subscription 40 pounds, county grant 40 pounds, total 80 pounds; expenditure: salary of surgeon 30 pounds, medicine 50 pounds 11s 2d, repairs 4 pounds 5s 9d, other expenses 3 pounds 2s 1d, total 87 pounds 19s; 1,506 patients recommended, dispensary open 2 days each week, average attendance 2 hours each day, 10 governors.

1833. Income: subscription 41 pounds, county grant 41 pounds, total 82 pounds; expenditure: salary of surgeon 30 pounds, medicine 35 pounds 14s, other expenses 3 pounds 5s, total 68 pounds 14s 5d; 1,430 patients recommended, dispensary open 2 days each week, average attendance 2 hours each day, 10 governors.

1834. Expenditure: salary of surgeon 30 pounds; 1,797 patients recommended, dispensary open 2 days each week, average attendance 2 hours each day, 10 governors.

1835. Expenditure: salary of surgeon 30 pounds.

[Overall totals]: income 363 pounds 15s, expenditure 356 pounds 2d.

Benevolence: Establishment for the Indigent

[Table contains the following headings: name, object, management, number relieved, funds, annual expense of management, relief afforded, when founded].

4 schools partly supported by benevolence; object: the removal of ignorance; sundry management; 228 pupils receiving instruction; relief afforded: instruction; [situated in] Ervey, Tamnaherin, Tamnymore, Tamnyreagh.

Places of worship; object: the relief of poverty; management: the churchwardens and others; number relieved variable.

Residences of the gentry; object: the relief of poverty: management: the gentry; number relieved variable.

Poor shop; object: the relief of poverty by selling bedding and clothing cheap; relief afforded: in 1833 the relief afforded was the difference between 115 pounds 6s 3d ha'penny, the amount of sales, and the prime cost of the articles, [blank] pounds. [Insert query: How much in 1834?].

Establishments for Mental and Bodily Disease

Dispensary: 1,797 relieved in the year ending on the 1st April 1834; funds: from the Grocers' Company [blank] pounds, subscription [blank] pounds.

Dispensary of Faughanvale; management: see parish of Faughanvale; number relieved: query, how many from this parish were relieved in the dispensary year ending in 1835?

Justice

There is no establishment of preventive justice in the parish, nor is any such required. The number of the outrages is not increasing. They consist chiefly of attempted rapes, drunken quarrels and cow or sheep stealing. Illicit distillation, although it exists in the more mountainous parts, is on the decline and smuggling is comparatively unknown.

Trade

There is no trading establishment in the parish.

Population Table

From a comparison of parliamentary documents,

Parish of Cumber

the gradual increase in the number of parishioners will be traceable for the last 14 years.

Lower Cumber, 1825: 787 inhabited houses, 6 uninhabited; 826 families, 2,122 males, 2,282 females, total 4,404 persons; 678 persons chiefly employed in agriculture, 1,447 chiefly employed in trades, manufactures or handicrafts, 170 persons occupied and not comprised in preceding classes, 2,295 total persons occupied.

1831: 840 inhabited houses, 21 uninhabited, 2 building; 863 families, 2,212 males, 2,372 females, total 4,584 persons, 1,076 males 20 years of age; 537 families chiefly employed in agriculture, 204 in trades, manufactures and handicrafts, 122 not comprised in 2 preceding classes.

1834, as shown in the first report of the Commissioners of Public Instruction. 1831, as shown in the enumerator's return: 714 Established Church, 1,672 Roman Catholics, 2,468 Presbyterians, 12 other Protestant Dissenters, total 4,866 in the parish; 1834, as determined by the commissioners: 706 Established Church, 1,739 Roman Catholics, 2,567 Presbyterians, 12 other Protestant Dissenters, 5,024 total in parish.

Habits of the People

The general style of the cottages is very superior. Comfort and cleanliness prevail, especially on the line of country between Oaks and Muff in Faughanvale. The food is simple, the fuel good and the dress plain but respectable. There are no remarkable instances of longevity. [Insert query: Is this likely, they being numerous in Faughanvale?]. The usual number in a family is 5, and early marriages are infrequent.

Amusements

The amusements and recreations are few. Harvest home is celebrated by an entertainment called a *churn*. Shooting at marks is practised on Christmas Day and other festive occasions. There are neither patron nor patrons' days. Fires on St John's Eve have been discouraged by the local authorities, as affording an opportunity for party quarrels; however, they are not yet wholly abolished.

The youth of every religious profession used formerly to amuse themselves on Sunday at the Sentry hill in Kildoag. The love of amusement, however, appears to have declined in this as in other parishes, and the Sentry hill has been at length deserted, although dancing and football were practised at it until within the last few years. It is considered to have been used as a look-out station during the rebellion of 1641, either by the military on one or both sides, or, which is more probable, by some band of fugitives who had taken refuge in the neighbouring glen.

Tradition

The following tradition is current in the parish. About 2 centuries ago a man named Lewis, who had emigrated from some other country to Ireland, settled in the lower part of the then parish of Cumber, where he became possessed of a large tract including Oughill, Lettershendony, and choose a site for a castle in the former townland. On a rising ground near the spot called Gortycross <Gorticross> stood a large stone crucifix, at which the neighbouring peasantry used to assemble on the sabbath. This and several other large stones were removed by Lewis, as materials for building the meditated edifice. As he was possessed of much wealth and influence, the insulted peasantry thought it useless to remonstrate, but bound themselves by the most solemn oaths to take vengeance on the first opportunity.

In process of time that opportunity was presented by the rebellion of 1641. The habitation of Lewis was attacked one autumnal morning by a large party, who destroyed many parts of it and killed the servants. He escaped himself by a back window and secreted himself in a marsh near the bog, where a *scrag* or covert of matted trees and brambles appeared to offer a secure shelter. However, owing to a heavy dew which lay on the grass, his enemies succeeded in tracing his footsteps to the scrag. Having drawn him out, they murdered him and thrust his body into a *sheskin* or quagmire, which immediately closed over it; some even believed that he was forced in alive. [Insert marginal note: This was an ancient northern punishment; see *The Serkorgs in England* by Atherstone].

It is also believed that Lewis, although in alarm, did not expect so early an attack, and had only commenced his preparations on the preceding night by burying all his gold; and in order to effect this with the necessary secrecy, it is stated that he intoxicated every inmate of his dwelling, except 2 confidential persons.

Emigration

Between January 1833 and August 1834 about 170 individuals of both sexes, and mostly youthful, emigrated to various parts of America. Great numbers continue in the country for want of means to leave it.

From 80 to 100 persons have migrated to the harvest in England and Scotland within the last year. [Insert marginal note: Not last, nor in 1838]. They were chiefly young cottiers, of both sexes. The season for putting down their crop and cutting their winter firing is over before they go. They leave the care of their places and families to the older children, or to some neighbour, until their return.

There are very few instances of persons going to harvest to the southern or western parts of Ireland, although artisans and others have occasionally gone to all parts of the island in quest of employment.

Letter from an Emigrant to Canada

[Insert marginal note: Sufficient to give the substance [of the letter]. (Copy by permission).

St John, New Brunswick, 17th August 1834.
Dear Father,

I arrived here on the 10th May, my sister Mary and me in good health thank God, and trust in the Almighty that you, my mother and my loving sisters are in good health also. My sister Mary is in Frederickstown, distant from here about 65 miles. She is in place there at 20s per month. I am now employed as second steward <stewart> of the Woodswick Steamboat, who plies from here to Frederickstown, at a salary <sallary> of 40s per month.

I found I was but a few days out of employ after my arrival here. I intend to go home again in the course of 2 years and I trust you will make no arrangement of parting with your land till then, at which you may be assured I shall return, God sparing me and my health and spirits.

Dear father, tho' I have no reason to complain since my arrival here, but one thing I must observe to you and for the information of all friends, that there is a long tedious winter here to what our countrymen at home is not used to, and that it takes great management to provide for the wet day.

However, all who take the journey upon them endeavour to get through pretty fair. This country puts an Irishman to his wits, every man to his fancy. I will neither advise persons of my own or any other family to come out, or yet stop. One deviation I must suggest that I would feel happy that my cousin Mary Kelly would endeavour to get coming here, as I have every reason to believe she might do very well here.

Dear father, I pray you will present my love to James Hassan and family, Uncle Michael and family and Rich Gamble and family, John Kennedy and family, my Uncle Denis O'Kane and aunt and Patrick Ward and family. I would advise cousin James Kelly to remain at home for some further time. I perhaps will be better able to apprise him when he might better suit him.

In order to inform you how provisions rate here, I will give you a very brief detail: first, boarding and lodging for a single man from 12s 6d to 10s per week; general wages of labouring class from 3s 6d to 4s per day; beef from 4d to 4d ha'penny and 5d; mutton much the same; potatoes (new) 4s per bushel, say about 4 stone; old potatoes 2s to 2s 6d; pretty good butter 8d, 9d; and salt 1s by retail. Flour 19s 6d: the super fine 40s per 196 lbs, and in some cases 35s; oatmeal 17s 6d per cwt; rye <ry> flour 22s 6d to 23s; Indian meal 20s to 21s per barrel, each 196 lbs; tea 2s to 2s 6d and 2s 9d and 3s per lb; sugar 4d ha'penny to 5d per lb; milk 3d per quart. Clothing in general very high, shoes in particular: if made by agreement, 11s to 12s 6d per pair; cottons, not to say, out of the way.

Dear father, since my arrival here I have met a number of very respectable acquaintants, [of] which I am happy to inform you. William Carlin is in St John and in good employ, and well liked by his employer, and his son George is in the employ of Mr Gilbert, a member of parliament, about 40 miles from here, and doing well and well liked by him. William Carlin sends his best regards to John Kennedy and family.

So I conclude, dear father, with my best love to you and all my loving friends and acquaintances, and trust in God to see you all again in 2 years, God willing, and remain your loving son till death, [signed] James Ward. I hope you will not omit sending an answer to this.

To Bryan Ward, Comer near Claudy. To the care of Mr Thomas Handcock of Cregg, Londonderry].

Draft Memoir by J. Stokes, 1834

MEMOIR WRITING

Letter concerning Monuments

October 18th 1834,
Dear Sir,

The antiquities which I spoke of to you yesterday are a graveyard and an adjacent standing stone in the townland of Cregg [insert crossed out query: at Templemore, or is it at Cregan in Faughanvale; and if so, identical with Dergbrough? Cregg in Upper Cumber?], in Mr Hugh

Parish of Cumber

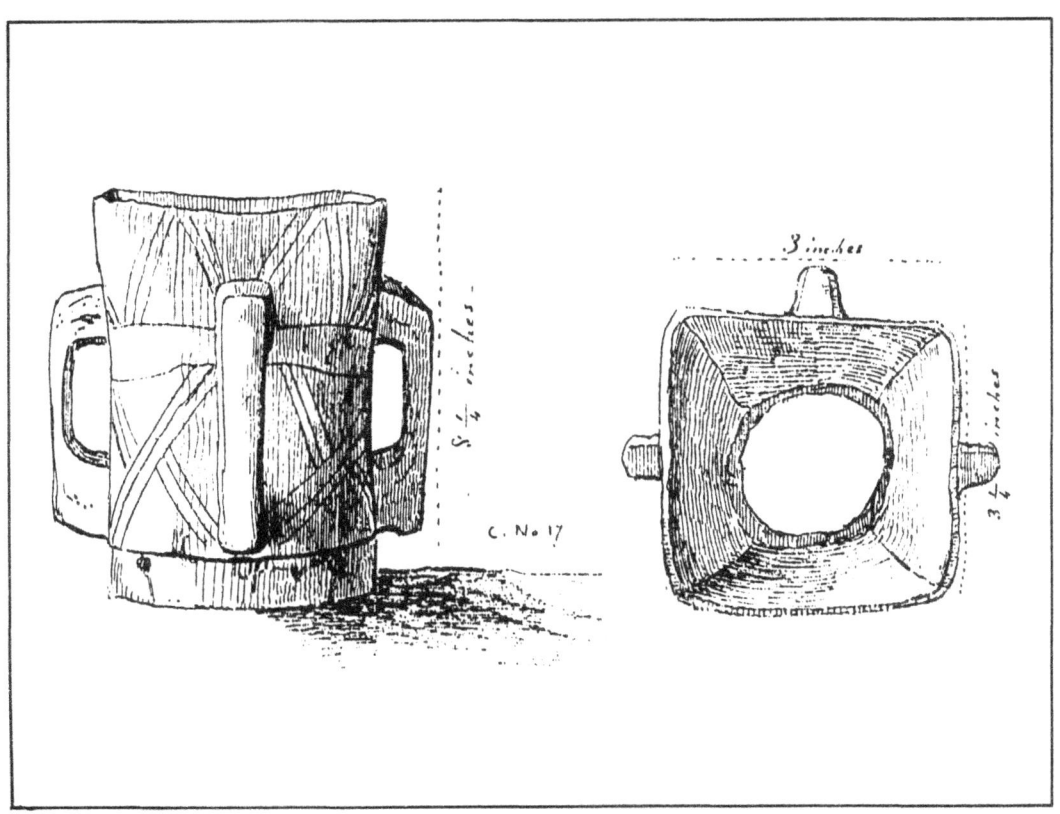

Mether from Dungiven

Handcock's farm. The standing stone is more than 6 feet high and made of a block of quartz, which gives it a very singular appearance. I am not a good geologist but I think it is quartz. At the distance of 32 yards behind it, and to the north, there is a small graveyard 56 feet square and lying very nearly east and west. I saw the foundations of a church in it. [Crossed out: The roof made by thin flags as usual. Yours truly, J. Stokes. The well is about 3 feet deep and to the east corner of the corner.

The little carn at Killaloo (Lower Cumber) is about 16 feet high].

ANCIENT TOPOGRAPHY

Pagan Remains

There is abundance of these. Not only graves, mounts, forts are regarded with fear, but also many little spots and localities are so regarded, they being remembered by the traditions to have been favourite places with the former inhabitants for holding meetings or erecting residences.

Cromlech in Barr Cregg

This monument [drawing] is situated in the townland of Barr Cregg, in a boggy hollow near the Burntollet. This monument was evidently once entirely covered by a carn or heap of stones since removed, most probably by treasure seekers. The stones of its base and circumference still remain and form an irregular oval 56 feet long. At one end of this oval or ellipse is the cromlech now apparently overthrown. It covers a receptacle first formed by stones placed parallel to one another and is 4 feet long by 3 wide and about 3 feet deep. At the other end there is a standing stone having a thin flag set perpendicular to the axis of the oval. It forms part of the circumference of a small enclosure of an irregular form made of stones set on edge.

Miscellaneous Discoveries

In Altahoney there have been found glass vessels of a peculiar form and also some peh pipes. An ancient Irish ploughshare too was dug up in 1834 from Drimnacrush bog.

At an angle of the Fore Glen river near Mulderg church, and called Stranalooby, some ploughshares and several horseshoes were lately obtained. The latter were clumsy and from their form encircled the frog and checked its growth.

Graves

A large grave of a modern form was opened by a farmer called Nutt in Gortnassey, who held the land on which it stood. On taking off the earth from the top they found a large flag supported on small thin flags ranged along the sides and at the end. The top or tombstone was 8 feet by 5. Beneath this there was found a large skeleton which was immediately interred again in a very deep grave dug for the purpose. There was only one-half of the skull.

In the townland of Ling there is another, at present very much disfigured by many small stones thrown on it from the surface of the field. It is oblong and built round in a ring of large stones laid side by side. The interior is concealed by much rubbish but appears to have been 30 feet long in its longest part. In the centre the large flag which is at present thrown on one side formerly stood on 12 short supports and contained under it a quantity [of ashes]. The discovery of these ashes produced a fear which has acted in preventing any further destruction. It is in the farm of a man called Hasson and is believed to have been the "burial place of a giant."

In Park Tireighter a very remarkable one is situated, but it is also disfigured in the same manner, looking at first sight much like a heap of rubbish. It is 26 feet long and 17 feet 3 inches broad. The tradition about it is that it is the grave of a female called Doonan or Mna-yesh, who spent the close of her life here in acts of charity. Close to this grave there was found a small wooden vessel full of bones. It was within a few yards of the grave and on being discovered was buried again. It was also found enclosed within flags, 4 at each side and 1 at the top and bottom. The grave itself is set round with large upright stones.

Standing Stones

The parish contains several standing stones. A very remarkable one, evidently for the same purpose but made not of stone but of wood, stood on the summit of Cruckdooish until a short time ago, when it was pulled up and found to have been supported around the lower ends with stones. It was of oak.

Discoveries in Altahoney

Much arable land in Altahoney has been formed by cutting away and cultivating the little bog of Drimnacrush. Accordingly there was there discovered a Danish fence made partly of clay and partly of stones laid side by side together. It connected 2 standing stones in the manner represented in the margin: [drawing entitled "ancient fence in Altahoney," height of larger standing stone 3 feet]. It came to the side of the Glenrandal and passed on in former times as far as the northern end of Kilgort, but has been there long ago destroyed. This portion in Altahoney is very short and very much dilapidated, the stones at present not at all resembling the drawing, but scattered in some degree. Between the other standing stone and that which is situated in Kilcluggan there is a third exactly intermediate.

Near the fence there was formerly a grave. Around it there have been many situations and spots in which the remains of fires have been found, exhibiting ashes, fragments of charcoals, blackened stones. 30 of these spots have been found and more are discovered almost every season. They were each small and circumscribed, and generally situated at the fence, and were first seen in 1829.

This bog contained also much bog tallow, great quantities of which have been found from time to time and used for household purposes or for making candles. A particular spot now cut away is still shown where it was found most abundantly. It was sometimes in wooden vessels, sometimes in large lumps with marks on the exterior, as if impressed by the wrinkles of cloth. One wooden vessel appeared as if hollowed from the trunk of a tree.

Coins

Many coins have been found in the parish, of different dates, now in the possession of A. Ogilby Esquire, as also a sepulchral urn from Carnanbane.

Remarkable Fort

The most remarkable fort next to Dungorkin is in Carnanreagh. It is situated on a high knoll but greatly dilapidated. In its neighbourhood, in Dunady, an urn of ashes was found within a sarcophagus of 6 stones.

Stone Pillars

In townland of Killycor there is a stone pillar. It is on a small hill composed of granite, flat at the top, abrupt on one side, sloping on another and joined to the higher ground by a narrow neck of land. It is situate at the side of the Faughan and rises to more than 50 feet above its level.

In 1770 2 others were standing at a few feet from this and higher, so as to form with it an

Parish of Cumber 31

equilateral triangle. There was also a surrounding fosse which ran at the edge of the flat ground.

The remaining pillar is situated at a few feet from the abrupt edge of the hill that falls towards the river. It is 10 feet high, at an average 1 and a half feet thick.

There is no rock of a similar kind to be found either in the neighbouring small hills or in its own. It is apparently an unhewn slab. Many fragments lie at its base and among them there is a second slab prostrate and about half the length, twice the thickness of the other.

In 1770 a party from Strabane in one night overturned the 3 pillars, being stimulated by an expectation of treasure. The then landlord erected them again. They were thrown down a second time. He again attempted but was unsuccessful, and one remained prostrate and was partly reduced to fragments, partly carried away to make slabs. The second broke in the raising and the third was re-erected. [Drawing of standing stone on top of a hill].

In 1810 this hill was cut up with fences for cultivation. They were ran in different places across the circular fence and the following results were produced.

At the depths of generally 3 feet below, and in the line of the bottom of the fosse and disposed at regular distances, there were found small chambers or receptacles of stone, formed each of 6 square slabs arranged to form a hollow cube, and each nearly the area of a square foot. These receptacles, of which there were 9, lay under that part of the fosse which overhung the most abrupt declivity of the hill. In each was a small urn formed of burnt red earth and filled with ashes. Shape of urn: [drawing], capacity about a quart. Shape was ascertained by exhibiting various forms on paper to the old man who gave the information, and who seemed to be both intelligent and well informed.

None of these particular urns, or crocks as the country people call them, are to be found, being all broken, but there are 2 crocks of the above form and of burnt red earth in the possession of Alick Ogilvie of Kilcaltan.

It is the opinion of the old man that from the appearance of some imbedded stones at the base of the pillar, that there is under it a larger chamber.

There were formerly many other huge slabs standing upright throughout the adjoining country. They are all at present prostrate, but under one there was found a chamber and urn filled up with ashes; another chamber found in Kinneady.

These urns are frequently found in the bog, without any such protecting receptacle. One was formed of wood, of the adjoining shape: [drawing, cylindrical shape, with centre encircled].

Drawing

Vessel of burnt earth found in Carnanbane, Upper Cumber, in the possession of A. Ogilby of Kilcaltan [drawing, shape of a bowl, breadth 5 inches, depth 6 inches].

Ecclesiastical Remains

At the village or hamlet of Stranagalwilly, on the top of a high knoll on the opposite bank of the Glenrandal, there are the foundations of an old church called Kilcluggah with a small graveyard, in one part of which there is a standing stone. The foundations form nearly a square 26 feet every way, except on the fourth side which is 28. This side contains the door and also a circular foundation 12 feet broad. They are in all parts covered with the green sward and consequently indistinct except in one place. The stones appear here not lying horizontally but in a sloping manner resting back to back. No mortar is visible. What cement there is crumbles to the touch. Traces of Kilcluggah church: [ground plan, main dimensions 28 by 26 feet, rectangular shape; section of wall 2 feet high, with orientation].

The churchyard contains graves but no tombs. It is about a rood in area and is still surrounded in part by a wall which, at the eastern part, is shrouded by old bushes. Among these, and almost entirely concealed from view, is the standing stone. The last burial in this yard was of a man called Kane 4 generations ago.

The wall is merely of stones piled loosely together. There are no adjacent crosses. Tradition reports that in the "wars of Ireland" a party of friars were massacred at the opposite bank of the river and their bodies interred at the graveyard. They were flying from Dunemanna and were in hopes of finding a refuge at Kilcluggah, but on coming to the bank they found the river in such high flood that they were unable to cross and, being overtaken by the hot pursuit of the enemy, were all killed. The place is still pointed out.

Graveyards

There were formerly 2 other graveyards in the village, one in Altahoney and the other in Stranagalwilly near Inver bridge, about half-way in fact between it and Straw. They have, however, been broken up and cultivated.

The mountain Cruckdooish rises abruptly from

behind the graveyard of Altahoney, which appears to have been larger than that of Kilcluggah. It is said formerly to have had a "place of worship." It still contains a large stone crucifix.

Church in Mulderg

In the townland of Mulderg, on Devine's farm, there are the foundations of a building which has no distinguishing name further than being still called "a church." It is 20 feet long by 13 wide and appears to have been built in the same manner as Kilcluggah, in the disposition of the stones which remain.

There is some cement which appears to have been merely clay and pulverises between the fingers. It is surrounded by a very small enclosure not more than twice the area of the building. In this children are still buried occasionally. Within the last 2 generations the walls are much higher, but were torn down for making fences and ditches. Cross at the yew trees: [drawing of cross, height 8 feet 8 inches].

Military Remains

There is at present no building of any military nature in the parish.

Fort in Dungorkin

[J.B. Williams] On a flow, or nearly flat, bog in Dungorkin, and on the north east of Claudy, is a curious fort. It is situated in a circular island about 60 yards in diameter, surrounded by a ring or trench of water averaging 20 yards in breadth. On the eastern parts of this ring there was formerly a platform of oak, which served as the entrance of the fort. About 40 years since this timber was raised, and it is supposed that none now remains.

The situation of this passage, by which alone there is access to the island, is marked by an accumulation of weeds and bog. The island is covered with stunted birch and completely overgrown with bog, but so as to leave some traces of a circular ring raised above the general level, as shown in the accompanying plan: [section from south to north, scale 40 yards to the inch, with annotations: a, the part of the fort in which the timber was found; b, the circular ring of water; c, the island; d, the circular ring raised above the level of the island].

Tradition concerning O'Mullins

A very remarkable tradition of this parish is that the clan of the O'Mullins were massacred and at length extirpated from the neighbourhood. The remainder were driven down in a party and hanged on a tree in Learmount. This is mentioned because the tradition as it is related includes the existence of a chieftain at Learmount. [Insert query: Where was his castle]?

Tradition regarding Doonan

The story of Doonan is that she was exceedingly beautiful, but choose to remain single. She resided not far off and at her grave the remainder of her effects were distributed around to the mourners. It is still called [?] Lunby-na-disha.

Manuscript

An old tenant of Gortnaskey, Mrs Lemon, has lately it se   "found a manuscript at a place called Tods rock, from its having been formerly the den of a fox."

Drawings

[View of the home of Shane Crossach the robber, from an adjacent standing stone, in Carnanreagh, Upper Cumber].

[Mether of yew, parish of Dungiven, in the hereditary possession of the Bonds of Bond's glen, parish of Upper Cumber, 8 and a quarter inches high; view of the interior, 3 and a quarter by 3 inches, depth 8 and a quarter inches; thickness of bottom a quarter of an inch].

Forwarded to Lieutenant Larcom, 14th May 1835 [signed] R.K. Dawson, Lieutenant Royal Engineers.

Office Copy of Memoir on Modern Topography

MODERN TOPOGRAPHY

Towns

There is neither town nor village in the parish.

Public Buildings

The public buildings are as follows: the Protestant church, the Presbyterian meeting house, the Roman Catholic chapel and 4 schoolhouses, one of which contains the dispensary.

Church

The Protestant church stands near the point where the coach road between Derry and Dungiven

Parish of Cumber

enters the eastern boundary of the parish [insert addition: in the townland of Killaloo].

According to the *Third report of the ecclesiastical revenue and patronage in Ireland* (1836), it was erected in 1796, by means, as far as the incumbent can ascertain, of a gift of 461 pounds 10s 9d farthing British, granted by the late Board of First Fruits. [Insert addition: It is a plain structure, kept in good repair]. It is capable of accommodating 160 persons. It stands east and west, and is lighted by 4 windows with circular arches, of which the southern side is furnished with 3 and the eastern gable with 1. At the western gable there is a square tower which, being too low, disfigures the church. [Insert marginal query: Dimensions of church].

Presbyterian Meeting House

The Presbyterian meeting house stands in Brackfield, on the side of the coach road between Derry and Dungiven. It is a plain substantial building in the form of the letter T. It is said to have been erected about 85 years ago at an expense of nearly 1,000 pounds, and to have superseded the original meeting house built in 1730. The interior, including 3 galleries, affords convenient accommodation for 680 persons. Neither pews nor galleries are painted. [Insert marginal query: Dimensions of meeting house? The information here interlined is from the Revd James Allison and differs widely from a former statement, which says the meeting house was built about 1784 and cost 3,200 pounds. Further inquiry would be desirable].

[Insert addition: It was erected at a cost of about 3,200 pounds. Insert query: Can this be so much? The building does not appear as if it cost more than 800 pounds. Revd Mr Allison <Ellison>, the minister, does not know how much it cost, nor neither can he tell where it could be found out].

Roman Catholic Chapel

The Roman Catholic chapel, which stands in Mullaboy, was built in 1826 by subscription and has cost 260 pounds.

The following are among the contributors: the Grocers' Company 50 pounds, George Dawson Esquire, M.P. 20 pounds, the Lord Bishop of Derry 10 pounds, [blank] Stewart Esquire, M.P. 10 pounds [insert marginal query: Christian name?] and William Hamilton Ash Esquire 5 pounds. It is a very plain rectangular building 63 feet by 24 [insert marginal query: height?] and lighted by 3 square windows on one side and 2 on the other. At present there are 2 galleries in progress of erection which are to be furnished

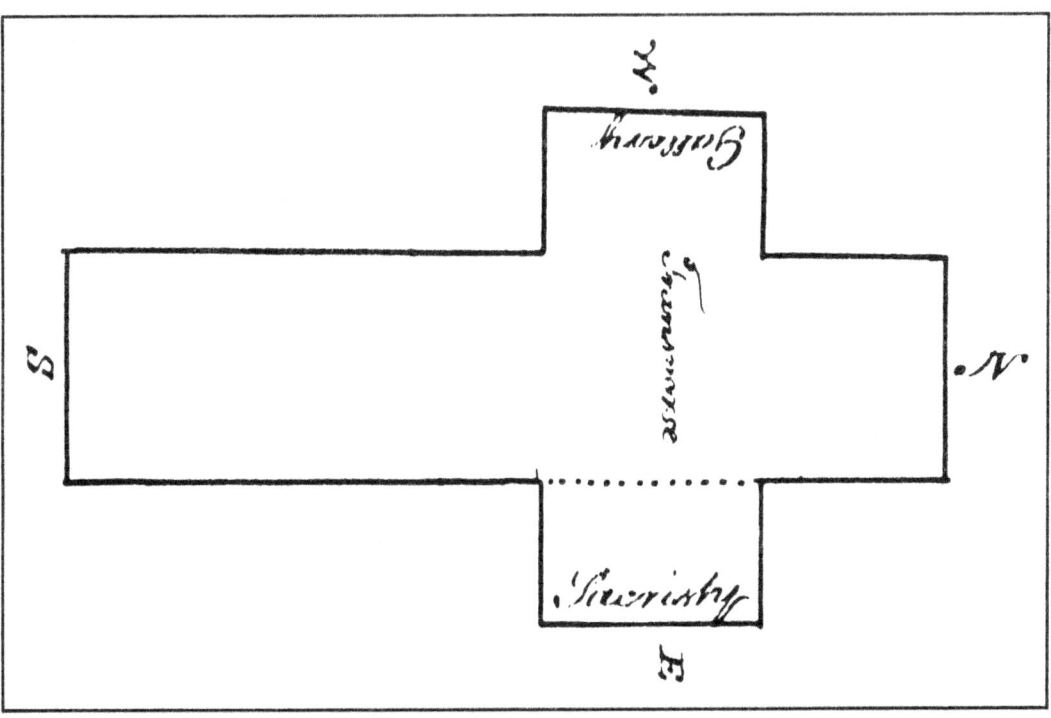

Catholic chapel in Mullaboy

Schoolhouses

The schoolhouses of Tamnymore, Tamnyreagh and Ballynamore were all erected partly by grants from the Kildare Street Society, partly by private subscriptions. [Insert marginal query: Could the various contributors to the building of each school be ascertained?].

The schoolhouse of Tamnymore includes the dispensary. Its site is more romantic than its destination, being on a rock shaded with trees near the Burntollet bridge, on the road between Derry and Dungiven. It is handsomely built and measures 54 feet by 20. Although but 1-storey high, it is commodious and contains apartments for the master. The cost of erection was 279 pounds 4s. Among the grants and subscriptions were the following: the lord lieutenant 100 pounds, the Kildare Street Society 30 pounds, the Grocers' Company 24 pounds, the dispensary committee 40 pounds. The remainder was subscribed by the gentry of the parish.

The schoolhouse of Tamnyreagh is a well-built house of 2-storeys high, 27 feet by 20.

The schoolhouse of Ballynamore is 1-storey high and measures 27 feet by 18.

A handsome and suitable schoolhouse was in 1831 built in Ervey by the Grocers' Company. This is recorded on a stone tablet over the door, which also bears their crest, a loaded camel. [Insert addition: Framed drawing, with the year 1831, of Grocers' Company coat of arms]. Besides a room for the school, the master has apartments. The building is 1-storey high and measures 66 feet by 27. This, and a similiar one in Clondermot, cost 1,100 pounds.

[Insert query: "The schoolhouse built by the Grocers' Company in Ervey and a similar one in the parish of Clondermot cost 1,100 pounds." What was the separate cost of each? What are the dimensions of each? (Query of Mr Dawson based on one put to him)].

Gentlemen's Seats

The Glebe House, the residence of the Revd John Hayden, is pleasantly situated on the northern side of the Faughan near the church, and commands fine views of the river in both directions.

Oaks and Oaks Lodge

Oaks and Oaks Lodge are situated lower down the river, at the point where it is joined by the Burntollet, on immediately opposite banks. Oaks Lodge, the joint residence of Mrs Lyle and her son Hugh Lyle Esquire, is on the southern side, and the ground there slopes more gradually to the Faughan and is divided into large green meadows ornamented with planting both natural and artificial. Oaks, the joint residence of Mrs Acheson and her nephew, Acheson Lyle Esquire, on the opposite bank, which is much steeper, has a truly romantic situation and is seen emerging from amongst the rich wood with which it is surrounded. The demesnes and gardens of these 2 mansions are kept in the nicest order, and the peculiarity of their relative situation contributes highly to the beauty of each.

Mr Lyle has erected a handsome suspension bridge of wrought iron across the Faughan, to connect his grounds with those of Oaks Lodge. The roadway is 3 foot 9 inches broad. It is made of boards laid lengthwise and supported by iron bars connecting the upright rails AAA. The large upright bars at A are 1 and a half inches broad both ways and 8 feet high. The small upright rails AAA are a half by a quarter of an inch. The top horizontal rail is 1 and a quarter by 1 and three-quarter inches. The lower rail is about the same size. The chains are made of long bars of iron, joined together by being turned into links at their extremities. [Insert marginal query: Erected by what mechanist?].

[Insert addition: [Drawing of] Mr Hugh Lyle's iron suspension bridge across the Faughan, scale 40 feet to 1 inch, with annotations.

Bleach Green

There is an extensive bleach green on the Faughan at Oaks Lodge. The houses for the machinery are good and substantial. 2 breast wheels are used, one for the rubbing and washing, and the other for the beetling engine. They are each 14 feet in diameter and 3 and a half feet in breadth. The supply of water, being conducted across the river by a dam, is very abundant.

Corn and Flax Mills

In Listress there are a corn mill and a flax mill, both supplied with water from the same stream. The [first] has a wheel 12 feet in diameter and 2 in breadth, the latter has one 10 feet in diameter and 18 inches in breadth. They are both breast wheels and the supply of water is good except for 3 months in summer.

In Toneduff there is a corn mill which belongs to Alexander Ogilby Esquire. It is fed by the stream that runs through Bond's glen and worked by a breast wheel 12 feet in diameter and 22 inches in breadth. The interior works are very old, and the banks of the mill-race want repair. In dry weather the supply of water is scanty.

Tannery

There is a tannery in Ardground which does a good deal of business].

Communications

The mail coach road between Derry and Dungiven runs for 3 and a half miles through the parish. On entering its western extremity it is 30 feet broad clear of ditches and fences; however, after passing the meeting house, a distance of nearly 3 miles, its breadth increases to 21. It was intended that this road should follow a more direct line between the meeting house and Dungiven, in consequence of which its breadth from Derry hither was extended to 30 feet. [Insert marginal note: The consequence is not apparent, as a width of 30 feet exceeds that required by law].

2 good roads branch off from the coach road to Muff. One leaves it at Oaks, the other at three-quarters of a mile from it in Crossballycormick. The former lies for 5 miles through the parish, and the latter, after running 4 miles through it, merges in the former. All these roads are kept in good order, materials for the purpose being abundant. These consist of quarried and field stones, with gravel from the Faughan and from pits. They are all well laid out, and made and repaired at the expense of the county. Their average breadth is 21 feet clear of fences and ditches.

On the opposite side of the Faughan there is a good road which is connected with the mail coach road by a wooden bridge at Oaks Lodge. It runs through the parish for above 2 and a half miles, throughout which it keeps near the course of the Faughan. Another road branches from it which leads through Bond's glen to Strabane, and of which 4 miles run through the parish.

[Insert addition: There are an abundance of crossroads which are also kept in good repair].

Bridges

There are 2 good public bridges, one of stone, the other of wood. The stone bridge [insert addition: on the mail coach road between Derry and Dungiven] which crosses the Burntollet is handsome and extremely well built. Its single arch, which is semicircular, has an elevation of 18 feet above the water and a span of 39.

The wooden bridge, which crosses the Faughan, is in good repair. It is formed of 5 logs of timber stretched across the river and supported by braces from the 2 sides. It is 54 feet long and 13 broad.

There is also a private suspension bridge (see Gentlemen's Seats).

Several smaller bridges are thrown across the streams by which the roads are intersected.

General Appearance and Scenery

The natural beauty of the parish, with the bold and picturesque features of the environing mountains, compensates a deficiency in cultivation and objects of art. The prospect down the valley of the Faughan from the eastern extremity of the parish, vide the road from Derry to Dungiven, is very fine, extending along the richly wooded banks of the unseen river, interspersed with dark green verdure, to the slope of Clondermot hill, beyond which rise similar elevations, overtopped in the extreme distance by the bold and rugged mountains of Donegal.

From the same point of view there is a prospect up the pass called Bond's glen, along the dark and rough sides of which the eye is led until it rests upon the summits of the mountains of Tyrone. The Glebe House also commands delightful prospects down the river, its reaches alternating with the wooded projections of its banks, until its final disappearance. The left bank is surmounted by small green hills of peculiar shapes, and in the extreme distance the Donegal mountains appear with great effect.

The prospect up the river is similar, but is intercepted by the picturesque bridge of Toneduff, and the whole is suddenly closed by large bold hills. On entering the glen of the Burntollet, about a mile from its junction with the Faughan, its steep and wooded banks are so far asunder as to leave a considerable level space. This is divided into cultivated fields, among which the river meanders beautifully. On tracing the river upwards, the banks, which become closer and more abrupt, exhibit a rocky front. They soon, however, open again, and leave on the left a verdant level which forms a good contrast to the dark foliage around. As the right bank recedes, it becomes higher and more precipitous, but its marked outline is somewhat softened by trees which cover it throughout. Beyond the small pathway, hitherto pursued, leads through a deep shade of fir trees, beyond which the sides of the glen are still much closer than before and present 2 faces of solid rock.

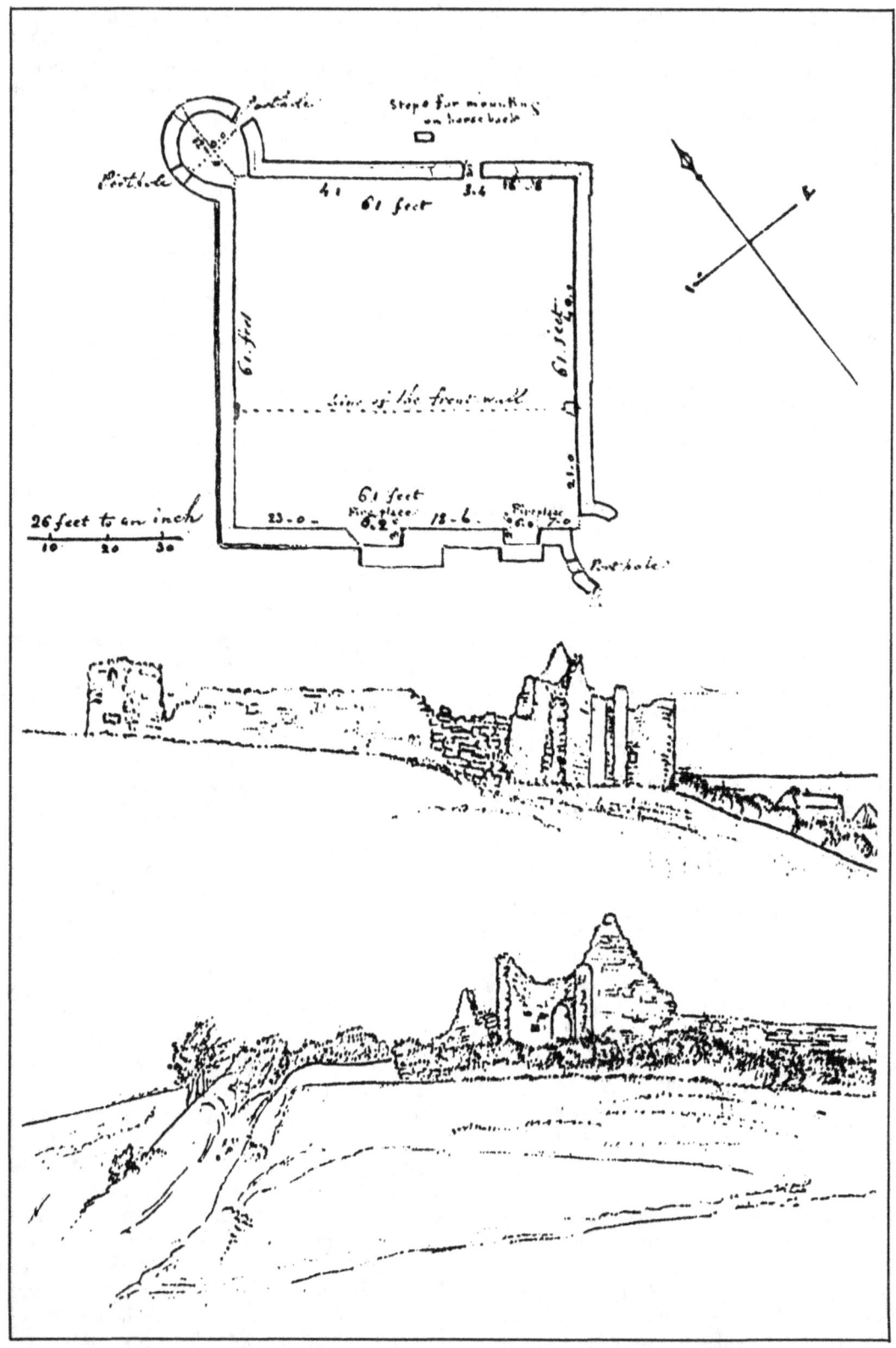

Brackfield Castle

Parish of Cumber

The bed of the river is here encumbered with large masses of stone. A large jutting rock conceals the fall from sight, but a rugged path on the left leads to a point high above the river, from which it appears to great advantage. The river has worn a deep channel for itself through the rock, and the fall must once have been twice as great as now. The water in 2 leaps makes a descent of about 30 feet, reposes a little in a pool beneath, and then rushes to join the steep course of the river.

The crooked oak and shining birch have found space enough to grow on the small ledges and in the fissures of the rock, and these, with a few holly bushes, some ivy and other creeping plants, give a finish to the scene which is still improved by a strong contrast of light and shade.

Memoir on Ancient Topography by J. Stokes

ANCIENT TOPOGRAPHY

Drawing

[Trace of Sampson's map, showing cromlech of Slaughtmanus].

Ecclesiastical: Cross in Oughill

The mutilated stone cross in Oughill, in James Lamrock's garden, is 8 feet long, 22 inches broad and 9 inches thick. The arms are completely broken off. It is lying prostrate in the middle of a fence and overgrown with weeds. In a field a short way off a square stone of a peculiar form is recollected, but it has long ago been destroyed. There was also at a short distance the foundations of a building discovered.

There are no holy wells in the parish.

Military: Brackfield Castle

The greater part of the stones of the castle of Brackfield seem to have been merely carried from the face of the country. The mortar has not that flinty hardness usual in old buildings, and in one of the portholes a few bricks are visible. The local traditions respecting this edifice is that it was built by the O'Cathans.

Nearly the whole of the south eastern and about half the height of the north western flanking tower has fallen down. In the latter there are marks of a second floor. The gate, originally much broader, is now built up and contracted into a narrow door sufficient for the entrance of cattle to be confined in the courtyard. There are marks of a second floor in the house itself and also indications of fireplaces. The lower storey appears to have been 1 room without any partition.

The well which supplied the castle with water is still shown. The situation of the building is commanding and picturesque.

Old Building in Killennan

The foundations of the old building in Killennan is believed by the parishioners to have been that of Lewis' Castle or House (see Habits of the People).

Bell Stones

The cromlech in Tamnyreagh, on Robert Steele's farm, is very remarkable. It stands nearly on a summit of a hill and has on each side an upright stone, one of them 5 feet 3 inches high. The interior of this monument is at present filled with loose stones thrown in from off the surface of the field.

In one part of the south eastern edge of the great altar stone there are 3 curious holes evidently perforated by artificial means, contemporary with the erection of the monument and made for the insertion of the machinery that raised it; see drawings [diagram of method of raising stones].

May not the larger holes have been intended for the insertion of long levers by which the altar stone was removed from its original to its present situation? The concentrated and combined force of a multitude of men acting at one instance at the extremity of a lever through the medium of a rope may have been applied as in the above drawing. As soon as the stone has gained the position AB it will fall over, and it would then be only necessary to drag the levers backwards, their extremities describing a circle and regaining their former position, to be again raised upwards. The most difficult part would be in raising the stone off the ground as in the figure B.

[Insert note by Dawson: I do not agree with Mr Stokes as to these holes having been "perforated by artificial means," but should rather consider them to be of natural occurrence, by the action of the weather or other means. At all events they do not appear to be deep enough to bear out the conjecture below. The stone is of a coarse slaty nature and the holes occur in the direction of the cleavage].

It is related by the country people around that there was formerly a stone at a part of this monument which emitted a hollow ringing sound on being struck. No such part is at present perceptible. It is said to have been a rocking stone and that it chimed like a bell on being moved. It has at all events given its name to the monument, which is known to the neighbourhood by the name Bell Stones.

[Insert note by Dawson: The stone here spoken of stood at the point A upon 2 uprights B. These, with 2 other uprights which stood at C, have long been removed].

Monuments

A few fields distant, and in John McNaught's farm, there is another monument of a singular appearance and in perfect [insert correction by Dawson: good] preservation. It appears to have been of the class vulgarly called giant's graves. It contains at the lower (northern) end what seems to have been a rocking stone capable of vibrating to the touch. With this there are several others connected, and depending on each other in such a manner as to suggest the idea that the whole group must have been a rocking series moving to and fro at every motion of the first stone. They are at present firm, but that can be accounted for by the fact that there has been much rubbish thrown among the interstices of the monument and the probability that a decomposition of the surface of the several stones has occurred.

[Insert note by Dawson: This conjecture, as to the "rocking series," is very ingenious and may be correct, but I cannot trace such evidence in the marks on the stones as should satisfy my mind of its accuracy. The monument appears to me to have been nothing more than a cromlech in which the 2 stones (F and G, nos 10 and 11) were slabs (and D also perhaps) supported on upright stones, of which some still remain; see drawings].

In drawings, the group which consists of the 3 stones marked D E F is represented. The point of view was selected so as to exhibit best the manner in which they rest on each other. The drawing on the margin shows more clearly the principle on which it is supposed that the original builders of the monument acted.

They selected stones approaching as nearly as possible to the annexed forms: [drawing with strategic points indicated]. The stone A resting on the stone D and rocking on it. By its motion the stones B and C were activated. In drawings, the stone D corresponds to A and the stones E and F

Giant's grave in Tanmyreagh

to B and C. It is remarkable that in the original monument there is at the point of contact between A and D a little pebble supporting the whole weight and on which most probably the vibration took place. In the monument also a stone C at its point of contact with B rests in a socket thus: [drawing of interstices of stones] and the whole face is carved over with the sockets. The corner only of the larger stone is inserted. From this it would seem that there had been a trade or profession for making these stones for these peculiar monuments. For the whole face is sculptured over with sockets, although one only was necessary, as if the artist could not foresee what combination his work would be called upon to suit or where it was intended that the point of contact should be.

At the corner of almost every stone there is a rude attempt to carve or make a figure represented in drawings. Many parts are notched and excavated artificially. They are marked in the ground plan of the monument by the letter X. A great variety of carved places apparently without any design or meaning present themselves through the entire monument.

At the lower side of the stone B in drawings there are marks resembling broad arrows. The edge of the stone B is ribbed like the drawing of the margin [drawing]. [Insert note by Dawson: I should take this to be only the natural feature of the stone and the ribbed surface and marks like broad arrows to have been produced by the action of the weather on the coarse slaty stone].

May not these whimsical carvings and cuttings have been performed merely for the purpose of giving the monument a sacred character? The only instances of mechanical design are in the sockets and a couple of very small holes at the edge D of the stone B, made in the same manner as the holes of Robert Steele's monument, but much smaller, being only capable of admitting a thin pencil. If conjecture is allowed to go further, we might imagine that some artful device of priest craft had exerted itself from an adjoining cavern and, pulling a secret cord, had set these rocking stones in motion on every occasion in which it was advantageous to deceive the people.

At a few fields distant there is a small grave (alias) giant's grave, but it is almost entirely concealed in what seems to have been an ancient fence. It is small and its traces are about 4 feet every way. There are also 2 standing stones, one in the midst of a fence, the other separate. There are many parts of the adjacent fences apparently of an ancient construction, but from their having been mixed with modern work it is impossible to decide with certainty.

Fort with Ancient Fences

In the townland of Killennan, on Robert Thompson's farm, there is a fence about 14 perches long which he still makes use of. It is an ancient Irish fence in perfect preservation and topped with a good hedge of prickly gorse. The masonry is singular and characteristic, see drawings. It contains 3 of the usual "standing stones" of the country, one at the part which turns up to Thompson's yard and the other at the highest part of the hill, down the face of which the fence runs. It is made by huge blocks of stone placed in a line and the intervals filled up by carefully fitted dry stone masonry which, unlike any ephemeral modern dyke or ditch, has lasted for centuries and will last for centuries more. In one part some of the stones are arranged in a curious vertical manner totally unlike the present horizontal manner of building; see drawings. [Insert note by Dawson: Most probably accidental].

One-fourth of the fence by that part of the farm which immediately adjoins the house is either of this old Irish architecture or of the same, almost wholly repaired by the present holder. However, he has never made any repairs except where it was imperatively called for by the dilapidation of the ancient line. The fence which we have described above has never required any repair and is in precisely the same state with respect to the stonework as when it was first erected.

Thompson was the first farmer in modern times of the ground occupied by these fences. When he took the land he found it wild and uncultivated, filled with these ancient fences which branched in various directions from a large fort or rath. In this rath he determined to build his farmhouse. In digging downwards he discovered the foundations of an ancient building. At the brim of the fort (which contained upwards of half an acre) he relates that he found a skeleton. This, in obedience to the usual feeling of the country, he built up carefully in the heart of a dry stone wall or fence at about 3 feet distant, not caring to remove it to a graveyard or bring it to any considerable distance from the spot in which he first found it, for fear of offending "those whom he could neither hear or see."

The heart of the stone wall he conceived to be the most appropriate place, it being a place of safety and also analogous to a tomb. In obedience to the same feeling he drew this farmyard wall along the edge of the fort and never in any of his improvements altered any ancient line. He also erected his gates only where he observed an interval or intervals in the ancient lines, and considered himself well repaid for his forbearance when a witch of Clondermot signified her approbation of his conduct. His farmhouse and comfortable offices are now within the ancient circle of fort.

Ancient Fences

The parish contains many of these ancient fences. They occur in the townlands of Gosheden, Slaughtmanus, Highmoor, Ballygroll, Mullaboy. [Crossed out: In the townland of Ballygroll there is, on a part of the mearing between it and Highmoor, a corner of an ancient fence which is altogether constructed in a singular manner, with stones laid vertically. The bog has been cut away from one side of it so as fully to expose its height. On the other side the heath and turf rises high and the fence appears to be concealed. [Drawing of ancient fence and 2 standing stones].

It is most probable that the way in which the ancient stones were generally constructed was first by putting down a series of standing stones as landmarks, secondly by connecting them with lines of smaller stones laid vertically on each other in the manner represented in the above drawing. This it is assumed was the general principle. Variations of course occurred according to circumstances].

[Insert note by Dawson: This occurs at the salient angle of a turf ditch which is the mearing between 2 townlands, and upon a further examination of it Mr Stokes agrees with me in thinking it to be no more than a collection of stones piled up to protect the angle of a ditch, or else that it is part of a conical pile of stones which marked the angle of the mearing before the top ditch was built].

When, in the course of time and the destructive marches of contending armies, these old divisions of property became dilapidated, the great standing stones (which are always sunk into the ground to a considerable depth) were found too heavy and immovable, and accordingly they remain scattered over the whole country as monuments of former ages.

In many cases the fence was low, hence those which still remain are almost wholly concealed by the bog and heath which have grown over them, and they can only be traced by the frequent peeping of a stone above the surface.

Ancient Irish Houses

Great numbers of these occur in the townland of Slaughtmanus, on the western and south western flanks of the Loughermore mountain. They are delineated in drawings. They are occasionally varied by a standing stone or a little "slaught," which is a term given to those monuments that are rendered unintelligible by a growth of bog. Some of them are connected with the foundations of 2 ancient Irish houses, the appearance and situations of which are very interesting. The wild and desolate character of the surrounding scenery associates well with the idea of the many changes that have taken place since they were inhabited. A small sheep-fold stands near and it is instructive to observe the differences in the character of the masonry. The houses stand nearly at the foot of the mountain and there is nothing around but the dreary moor; see drawings.

The most western house is 23 feet 6 inches by 13 feet 6 inches, with a very narrow doorway not broader than the breadth of the body. At the distance of a few feet to the south there is a small enclosure or giant's grave. The ancient fence joins the back wall and precedes up the hill until it is crossed by another. The wall of the house is about 2 feet thick, composed of stones carefully laid on each other without any mortar, and it is remarkable that they seem to have constructed the wall on the same principle as the fence. The ungainly corner stones represented in the drawing are quite similiar to standing stones.

Higher up the hill, but at a short distance, there is another house. It seems to have been a more important one than the other, at least from the superior thickness of the walls. There was apparently a greater attention to comfort, for a dry stone wall, unless when thick, is always cold and admits the air.

[Insert note by Dawson: The upper house: this ruin appears to be curious, on account of the circular end of the house, as shown in the plan sketch. The building appears also to have been surrounded by a circular stone wall 80 feet in diameter, of which only very slight traces now remain, but enough, in my opinion, to determine it. It is mostly overgrown with heath, but stones are to be traced here and there as shown in the sketch. Little more than the foundation of the house is to be seen now, 8th December 1834].

At 40 feet another giant's grave appears. About midway between the 2 houses there are the foundations of a third, but they have been so defaced that they are quite faint and very unintelligible. In fact there seems to have been a hamlet hereabouts, surrounded by well-marked divisions of property.

It was interesting to observe how in many places these fences were indicated to the eye by a line of thicker heath running exactly over them. The most conspicuous and uncovered part is at D and it can easily be found by crossing the top of the mountain from the east, passing by the Slaughtmanus and crossing the end of a half-decayed modern ditch.

Slaughtmanus

The Slaughtmanus, see drawings (from which the townland takes its name), is a curious little vault 12 feet by 3, lying nearly north and south, and roofed by several great stones overgrown with heath. The door looks to the east. If we consider the lower part of the section A B C to be the door, it is only 8 inches wide, but if the upper, it is 2 feet. The interior, when not entered immediately after floods, is dry. It is pretty near the summit of the hill.

Houses in Brockagh

In the townland of Brockagh there are ridges, marks of cultivation and foundations of old houses, but although they are evidently not the remains of modern cabins, for the ground around has never been cultivated since the wars of Ireland, yet they can be seen at a glance to be youthful in comparison with the Slaughtmanus houses. There is a complete village of them here, with one larger and with thicker walls than the rest, resembling the foundations of a public building.

Tradition is silent as to the history of these ruins, but the opinion of the neighbouring inhabitants refers their dilapidation to the "wars of Ireland." We may conclude that this village was destroyed in the rebellion of 1641. Its remains are at a short distance to the south of the road into Monehanegan and on the eastern flank of the hill.

There are a few more foundations scattered at irregular distances, but being of a modern date they do not require further notice than to state that they appear to be contemporary with the village. They are in the midst of scenery wild and secluded.

Standing Stones

The range of low dry hills on which this village is situated continues without interruption to the townland of Highmoor where, nearly on the top of the hill, a standing stone suddenly appears, succeeded immediately by an ancient Irish fence, in the midst of which there is one still larger. [Crossed out: Further on the vertically built corner appears, presenting a very whimsical appearance and instantaneously attracting the stranger's eye and attention. It is represented in drawings. At the right there has been added the remains of a wretched shed, set up by a maker of besoms and intended for his convenience while preparing his heath].

Monuments in Sliebhgore

After passing this by, still preceding down the ridge of the hill and entering into the townland of Mullaboy, a few little "slaughts" appear on the right hand side. Presently a great many groups of old stones are visible, with a giant's grave at some distance to the left. This is represented in drawings. At about 5 chains to the north east of it there is a small cromlech which has evidently been once surrounded by a large cairn. The whole monument has been greatly dilapidated but enough remains to show that it had been once a cairn 20 feet wide. The cromlech itself is merely a slab supported on 2 very low stones about a foot and a half high. Although this monument appears to have been formerly covered with thorn, yet there can be still observed a method and arrangement in the stones which remain. [In the drawings] is an attempt to represent it.

At a few yards to the north east of this cromlech there is a very small giant's grave and also traces in the sod and heath of a small vault, like the Slaughtmanus. It has been altogether covered up and overgrown with bog, but there is still a small depression indicating the entrance and some of the stones of the roof can still be perceived.

Scoby's House

These remains are situated on the south eastern flank of the hill. At its foot there runs a stream separating the townland of Mullaboy from Listress. Following its course will lead at length to Scoby's House, a circular foundation 16 feet in diameter with a door to the east of the usual size, and a wall about 2 feet thick appears in a small grassy hollow on the steep side of the ravine. When the country was wooded it must have been a site of singular beauty.

Tradition is silent as to who Scoby was. The neighbouring inhabitants merely hand down from generation to generation that this is Scoby's House. The name is most probably a corruption from some Irish word, for it is more probable that an early English settler would have made the foundations of his house square instead of round. The character of the masonry in the wall cannot now be discovered, as they are overgrown with heath.

Ancient Remains

Leaving the stream and going up again to the top of the hill, the groups of old stones before alluded to are again seen, and they are found scattered in all directions through the heath and bog. 2 foundations tolerably distinct, with 6 more or less dilapidated, stand up on this hill with many ancient Irish fences branching off in all directions. They extend over the whole southern end of the hill. [Insert note by Dawson: Among other remains is a double circle of standing stones 4 or 5 feet apart and the outermost 80 feet in diameter. It is almost entirely overgrown with heath now, but may be traced on the ground as shown in drawings].

At a very short distance the Ness waterfall passes in solitary beauty. It adds an ornamental feature to the site of these remains.

Cairn on Sliebh Boe

Close to the mearing between Mullaboy and Ervey there is a circle of stones represented in drawings. [Insert note by Dawson: no drawing]. At one part there is a group of large shapeless stones tossed and arranged in a very irregular manner. They are on the north western portion of the circle and from there being no appearance of any design in their arrangement, it is more than probable that this has been a vast cairn long ago destroyed and leaving only the fence as it were, which was made by the builders round the bottom to keep the structure, while they were erecting it, from rolling down. At the bottom of all cairns something of this sort is visible. The circle is 37 yards wide, i.e. in diameter. At a short distance there is a very large standing stone 7 feet high. It stands towards the north.

Standing Stones

None of the standing stones of this part of the country, except a few in Upper Cumber, are arranged symetrically or in a line. It may be stated with certainty that they are ancient Irish landmarks.

Fences

An ancient fence appears at intervals in the boggy parts of the townland of Gosheden. There were formerly great numbers of them on the eastern side of Sliebh Boe, but they have been completely destroyed. Many other monuments with cromlechs have been uprooted by the parishioners at different times. The love of gain has been more destructive to them than the storm and tempest. It is curious that in every such instance the prime mover has been a dream about money.

Wooden Grave

In the farm of Arthur Norris, in the townland of Ballygroll, there was once a giant's grave enclosed as usual by flagstones. It stood unmolested until Norris, having heard that there was a treasure in it, dug it up about the year 1816. On removing the flags by which it was enclosed, and digging up a quantity of sandy soil from the interior, he discovered at the head, foot and sides well-shaped logs of black oak set down as a fence or protection. These he removed to his dwelling house and converted them to many uses. One of them he placed as a lintel over the door of his cowshed, where it still remains. This timber was regularly formed and chipped to answer the purpose for which it was intended, and when raised from the pit or grave where it had lain for so many centuries, was found to be quite sound and in good preservation.

The grave stood in the interior of a bog and the soil about it for several feet on all sides was found hard, dry and of a sandy nature, as if brought there for its reception. It was 8 feet in length by 4 in width. There was nothing more discovered in the digging up and demolishing of it than the timber above described, which had all the appearance of being prepared and placed where discovered by a regular artisan.

Crock in Ballygroll

At a short distance Robert Norris of the same townland discovered an earthen crock of moderate size concealed some feet under the surface and secured by large stones. Over the crock or vessel there was a large heavy flag supported by others sunk in the ground. The crock itself was covered by a thin slate flag of a circular form and stood upon another of the same shape. On removing the top covering, and attempting to lift it up, it immediately fell to pieces, being frail and bad. It contained nothing.

Skeleton wrapped in Paper

In the same townland there was also discovered in a bog a coffin containing a small skeleton apparently of a child. The body was wound round with "sheets of paper." The coffin was rudely and clumsily made and sunk several feet down in the moss. Both it and its contents seem to have been imbedded for a long time, as all were in complete decay.

Parish of Cumber

Articles of Household Furniture

Very many articles, of household furniture and of ancient date and form, have been occasionally discovered by persons of the names of Lamrack and Norris in the townlands of Oughill, Ballygroll and the parts of other townlands that ranged with them, such as small pots and dishes and sundry carpenter and farming implements. They were most usually found in the boggy parts.

Sword-Grave in Slaughtmanus

In the townland of Slaughtmanus, and in the farm of a man called Brown, there formerly stood a giant's grave. It is described to have been an enclosure about 25 feet in length and 9 feet in width, and enclosed by stones of prodigious size set in the ground on their ends, and on the top a flagstone weighing upwards of 4 tons. This was supported at the height of about 4 feet by the pillars leaving in the interior a vacant space. This "grave" or rather altar stood at the Loughermore stream, over against another which stands in the townland of Barr Cregg, Upper Cumber.

This monument stood unmolested for centuries, until about the year 1816 several persons dreamed of a treasure being concealed in the interior, but none took courage to try. At length a party of Killaloo men came over the mountain "with a doctor at their head," and all well provided with sledges and crowbars. They proceeded to the monument to raze it to the ground and procure the treasure. After performing the work of destruction they found, instead of money, a great many instruments of a peculiar form, with spurs and a sword. The ruins of the monument remained in the same dilapidated state till the year 1831, when Brown completely removed every vestige and filled up the pit with the soil of the field.

Destruction of Ancient Vessels

None of the ancient vessels occasionally found by the parishioners are ever preserved, except when they are impelled either by avarice or fear. Thus if there is a rich antiquarian at hand the relic, instead of being tossed to the children, is placed carefully on the cupboard to be soon transferred at a profitable price to his shelves. Or if he reverences the "gentle folk," it is immediately re-interred in the place where it was found by the parishioner.

Tirkeeran Fort

The Tirkeeran Fort, from which a few of the parishioners believe that the barony took its name, is situated in the bog of Lettershendony. It is of a small size and exhibits no peculiar features, except that of being in the midst of a pond of water like the fort of Dungorkin in Upper Cumber. The proper and peculiar name of it is Tirkeeran.

Cranagh Fort

Another remarkable fort is in townland of Ardground, at the site of the stream which divides the parishes from one another and in the midst of a flat meadow or holm. It is a steep knoll rising nearly 30 feet from its base [insert marginal query]. It is altogether covered with brushwood and brambles. The hill was selected as a place of strength and scarped. It is represented in drawings.

It is remarkable that on the top a part has been enclosed from the rest by a shallow ditch. A standing stone and part of an ancient fence are at the foot of the knoll. These have the usual insignificant character of the antiquities of the parish, which all require attention and inspection to be properly appreciated. It is more than probable that sportsmen have frequently passed through the ruins of Sliebhgore without bestowing a thought or look upon them.

Coves

In the cove in the townland of Fawney the parishioners relate that there was a well nicely built round with stones and containing a spring of clear water, very cold. It is at present stopped up. There is another cove in the townland of Killennan.

In Lower Cumber there is, in the farm of James Miller, Lettermire, a cove 10 and a half feet long, 4 feet high at the entrance and 18 inches wide at the entrance; also 2 small recesses and a kind of chimney or opening from the roof of the other end of the cove. At 3 feet from the door there is a little well. A great many peh pipes were found; the roof made by thin flags as usual. The well is about 3 feet deep and to the east course <corner> of the corner.

Standing Stones

There are 17 large standing stones in the parish. They are thus disposed: in the townland of Ervey 1, in Mullaboy 1, in Lackagh 3, in Killennan 4, in Tamnyreagh 2, in Slaughtmanus 5, in Highmoor 1, [total] 17. All these are sunk in the ground.

Fort and Cave

In the bog at Gosheden, on the side of the amountain above Knockbrack glen, there is a small fort altogether composed of small stones. It is of the usual form.

The cave in the townland of Fawney was formerly surrounded by a fort now destroyed.

Hillock

In the townland of Killaloo there is a small hillock adjacent to the road and not far from the church. It seems to be a cairn but not certainly. [Insert note by Dawson: The little cairn at Killaloo is about 16 feet high].

Forts

The fort in the bog of Gosheden mentioned above is partly covered with turf. The forts of the parish have been all destroyed but 3. There were formerly more and they always stood sufficiently near one another for the communication of signals.

MODERN TOPOGRAPHY

General Appearance and Scenery

By the manner in which the flanks of the mountains become steeper and more steep as they approach the river, a great variety of scenery is produced in this parish. Exclusive of the wilderness of Slaughtmanus, the River Faughan is the most interesting feature, winding its way between high banks clothed with natural wood and sparkling with waters clean and transparent. At length it is joined by the Burntollet river, coming forth from its own secluded dell, and lower down the current passes under the picturesque chain bridge which connects Oaks with Oaks Lodge. By following the Burntollet river the stranger will arrive at the falls of the Ness, where in a small space he will meet with much variety of scenery, from the flat lawn surrounded by wooded precipices, to heaps of rude rocks and dashing water. There is a pretty cascade in Slaughtmanus near a place called the Blue Brae.

One of the most picturesque views to be had in the parish is from the ground in front of the old castle of Brackfield, looking up the valley of the Faughan. The Craigastuke rocks at the side of the Burntollet river in Slaughtmanus are worthy of the attention of the painter.

ANCIENT TOPOGRAPHY

Drawings

No.1, Brackfield Castle from the west.
  No.2, Brackfield Castle from the east.
  No.3, Plan of Brackfield Castle, main dimensions 61 feet by 61 feet, orientation and annotations, scale 26 feet to 1 inch [insert memorandum by Dawson: To put the scale and writing east and west].

No.4, Plan of the Bell Stones, townland of Tamnyreagh, with dimensions and orientation. [Insert memorandum by Dawson: The original sketch from which this tracing was made has been sent to Mr Ligar by mistake. It shall be forwarded to Mountjoy to replace this tracing as soon as I can recover it. 9th December 1834].

No.5, View of the Bell Stones from the south east, with dimensions.

No.6, View of the Bell Stones showing the holes, with dimensions. [Insert note: Each large hole is about 6 inches deep and pierced into the rock in the form of a wedge. The smallest is shallow and seems to have been made in the wrong place].

No.7, The Bell Stones, giant's grave in Tamnyreagh, on Robert Steele's farm, with dimensions.

No.8, The Bell Stones from the west, with dimensions.

No.9, The Bell Stones, rough sketch to show the position of the ringing stone.

No.10, Plan of the monument in John McNaught's farm, Tamnyreagh, with dimensions, orientation and annotations, scale 8 feet to an inch.

Nos 11 and 12, View of monument in Tamnyreagh from point A, looking south east.

No.13, Giant's grave in Tamnyreagh, on John McNaught's farm, view from point B.

No.14, Giant's grave in Tamnyreagh from the west.

No.15, Giant's grave in Tamnyreagh from the north.

Nos 16 and 17, Views of part of ancient fence in Robert Thompson's farm, 13 perches long.

No.18, Fence in Highmoor, 6 feet 6 inches high.

No.19, Fences in Slaughtmanus with dimensions and annotations, scale 6 inches to 1 mile, plan and section. Plan of the upper house, scale 40 feet to 1 inch. View from point F of the upper house.

No.20, View of lower house in Slaughtmanus, with annotations and dimensions.

No.21, Ground plan of lower house in Slaughtmanus, with dimensions and orientation, scale 1 inch to 10 feet.

No.22, Sketch of upper house in Slaughtmanus, plan of area with dimensions, showing giant's grave, scale 1 inch to 10 feet. 12th November 1834.

Parish of Cumber

No.23, View of Slaughtmanus from the east; section of the door.

No.24, Closer view of the Slaughtmanus.

No.25, Plan and sketch of the remains of a monument at Mullaghboy, with dimensions and orientation. 12th November 1834.

No.26, Ground plan, with dimensions and orientation, of a double circle of standing stones on Sliebh Gore. The walls are from 7 to 8 feet across (out to out).

No.27, Cranagh Fort, plan with orientation, scale 1 inch to a chain.

Sketches of Antiquity by J. Stokes

Drawings

Plan of the Bell Stones with annotations and dimensions, scale 4 feet to an inch. [Insert note: Forwarded to Lieutenant Larcom to replace the tracing already given in with the Ancient Topography of Lower Cumber [signed] R.K. Dawson, Lieutenant Royal Engineers, 15th December 1834. NB The Memoir was sent through Mr Stokes' hand].

Monument in Ervey, view of a [stone] circle 37 yards in diameter from the other side of the [county ?] mearing.

Copy of Memoir Sections by several Authors, including George Downes, J. Stokes and C.W. Ligar

NATURAL STATE

Locality

This parish is situated in the eastern part of the barony. It is bounded on the north and north east by Faughanvale, on the south and south east by Upper Cumber and on the west by Clondermot. Its extreme length in a south easterly direction is about 8 and a half miles and its extreme breadth is above 4 and a half. Its content is 14,463 acres, of which the quantity uncultivated is [blank]. [Insert marginal note: This parish has an insulated townland].

NATURAL FEATURES

Hills

The highest points above the sea are: Slieve Kirk (the greatest elevation of), 1,074 feet; Slaughtmanus, 978 feet; Slieve Buck, 823 feet; Lettermire, 815 feet; Brockagh, 700 feet; Tamnakeerin, 678 feet.

The range of Slieve Kirk has here its south eastern termination and forms the north western face of Bond's glen. It is situated at the southern extremity of the parish and on the southern side of the River Faughan, to which it falls in a northern direction.

Slaughtmanus, Slieve Buck, Brockagh and Tamnaherin are on the northern side of the Faughan and are the principal points in the range of which Legavanan <Legavannon> in Faughanvale is the chief. Slieve Buck is the principal point at the western extremity of this range, which lies east and west, and is bounded on the south by the Burntollet river. Its top is round, but runs off in a long ridge to the south which on the east is steep and falls to a stream, a tributary of the Burntollet, and on the west slopes very gradually to the Faughan.

Lettermire forms the western extremity of a chain which is bounded by the Burntollet on the north, the Fore Glen river on the south and the Faughan on the west.

Valleys

The principal valleys are the valley of the Faughan, Bond's glen and Burntollet glen. The sides of the valley of the Faughan are steep and near the river almost precipitous. Bond's glen is a deep and good pass from this part of the country into the county Tyrone; through it lies a road between Dungiven and Strabane.

Burntollet glen for 2 miles from the Faughan is steep and precipitous; at this distance the sides terminate in a beautiful waterfall called the Ness, above which the glen opens and becomes less interesting.

Lakes and Rivers

Lakes none.

The chief river is the Faughan (see Clondermot). It enters the parish from Upper Cumber and takes a north westerly course [insert superscript: Tirkeerin?] for 2 and a half miles. Its banks, which are here steep, in some places almost precipitous, are clothed nearly throughout with natural woods and plantations of beautiful and romantic character.

The Burntollet, a tributary to the Faughan, is a considerable mountain stream that rises in Bovevagh. Its course is westerly. It flows for 5 and a half miles through the parish and divides it from Upper Cumber for 2 and three-quarters. The general fall, for 3 and a half miles from the point where it enters the parish downwards, is 30 feet to the mile. The supply of water is good for 9 months of the year and more water power might be obtained from it than hitherto.

At 2 miles from its mouth is a fall of about 30 feet called the Ness (see Hills), a name corrupted from the Irish *An Eas* or "the waterfall." It descends in 2 leaps, of which the upper one measures 8 feet, the second 22. The height of 60 feet is assigned to it by Sampson, but the discrepancy between the 2 statements is rendered the less startling by the consideration that the impetuous torrent is continually washing away the rocks at the top of the cascade. Above the fall the valley of the river is broad and uncultivated; below it the sides are steep and precipitous, and richly covered with wood. The spot itself is strikingly picturesque.

The Bond's glen stream or Bond's glen burn, a tributary to the Faughan, is 2 and a half miles long and falls 100 feet in that distance. In dry weather the supply of water is scanty.

Bogs

The bog, considered as a whole, is of great extent in the mountain. It varies from 1 to 400 feet above the sea and from 850 to 250 feet above the Faughan, but there are detached portions in the lower grounds which do not rise more than 250 feet above the sea. On the southern side of that river but little timber is found imbedded in it, but on the northern there is a considerable quantity of fir and oak, with some birch. The trees have been broken at from 1 to 3 feet above the roots and lie promiscuously with the stumps upright. Some have been found charred with fire.

The bog in the lower country and in level places is from 3 to 10 feet deep, but in the mountains it rarely exceeds 8 feet, from which it varies to 2 feet in general, but is occasionally less than 1 in depth. The substratum is blue clay and gravel.

A tract commonly called Ballynamore <Ballynamoor> bog, which extends over a part of that townland and those of Strathall, Crossballycormick, Fawney: and it covers between 150 and 200 acres, and is [blank] feet deep. It is in general [blank] feet above the sea and [blank] above the nearest part of the Faughan.

It is surrounded on all sides but the southern by higher ground. Until the last 5 years great quantities of fir and black oak was raised throughout the bog. The trunks varied in length and thickness, and the roots and stumps which remained upright were detached from them. In many cases there have been 3 logs found one above another. 2 trunks of fir above 70 feet long were dug up a few years ago near the house at Oaks. These bogs are properly called "flow bogs."

A mountain tract commonly called Ervey bog, being mostly in that townland, covers more than 200 acres and is in some places 6 feet thick. Its highest point is 550 feet above the sea. No timber has ever been found imbedded in it.

A range of bog which extends over a part of Killaloo, Oughtagh, Brackfield and Lettermire covers more than 100 acres. It is not so flat as the Ballynamore bog, and its highest part is about 400 feet above the sea and 250 above the Faughan. It is not so flat as the Ballynamore bog. Fir and black oak are thickly imbedded throughout. The trunks are found lying promiscuously and always burnt at the root. A log of oak has been found in it, 40 feet long and 5 round, and one of fir 84 feet long. There are at present 2 trunks, one of oak 18 feet long and 4 round, the other of fir 45 feet long and 3 round. All the trunks are without bark and much diminished in circumference by decay. The bark of its small branches comes off in the hands.

The Toneduff bogs are 3 in number. The largest, which extends also into Ardground, is in general 600 feet above the sea.

There is a small bog partly in Toneduff and Ardground, which covers more than 30 acres. It is 300 feet above the sea and 100 above the Faughan. No timber whatever has been found in it.

The main mountain bog of Toneduff occupies a great part of Ardground; also covers above 200 acres. Logs or branches of black oak and fir are occasionally found here, but a trunk rarely. They lie promiscuously and are various in length and thickness. Being all in a similar state of decay, they are probably coeval in destruction. There is here 1 trunk of black oak, 18 feet long and by 4 round.

The Slieve Kirk bog occupies an extensive range of mountain. Commencing at the mearing of the county of Tyrone it overspreads the western side of Bond's glen with a great part of Legaghory and Gosheden. It covers in all 500 acres and is from 500 to 1,051 feet above the sea. Timber is seldom found here in any considerable quantity. It is always black oak or fir and is met with equally upon and below the surface. It lies promiscuously and is various in length and thickness. The usual charred appearance of the roots suggests the idea of combustion.

The Oughtagh bog, which is mountainous, rises from 350 to 600 feet above the sea and 100

Parish of Cumber

in its lowest part above the level which the Burntollet river has below the Ness. It contains a few roots of black oak and fir, but very few trunks. Within the turf are several layers of branches, one over another. The timber varies in size and seemingly in age, particularly the trunks and branches. It is dispersed equally throughout.

The Listress and Gortnarede bogs, a high and mountainous range covering a great part of Listress, Slaughtmanus, Mullaboy, Highmoor, Tamnierin, Brockagh and Gortinrede: it bears different names according to the townland it traverses, and exceeds 1,000 acres. It is from 200 to 400 feet above the sea. It contains in all parts, and equally dispersed, the usual black oak and fir, every root burnt and the root end of every trunk charred.

The Lettershendony and Killennan bogs cover 50 acres. They are 300 feet above the sea. It is greatly cut away. Fir and black oak have been found here scattered promiscuously but equally throughout. Their roots and trunks had a charred appearance.

One-fourth of the bogs are very shallow, not rising more than 18 inches above the clay bottom. The altitudes here assigned to the bogs are only approximations in round numbers.

Woods

The banks of the Faughan and Burntollet, with many parts of Bond's glen and others, are covered with a natural growth of oak and birch. Near the Glebe House, Oaks and Oaks Lodge it is large and interspersed with artificial planting. This is also the case with the banks of the Burntollet and the Ness, but the old oaks which once adorned this waterfall were cut down towards the close of the last century, and it is merely their shoots, intermingled with fir, that now supply their places. Much of the wood along the Faughan and in Bond's glen, not being protected by fences, continues stunted from the inroads of cattle.

Coast and Climate

Coast none.

The air is mild and healthful, and the variation in the harvest season between the valleys and the mountains depends solely on the time of sowing.

Insulated District

There is an insulated district of 460 acres contiguous to Banagher, which formerly constituted the townland of Teenaght in Lower Cumber, but has been divided into 2 parts, one of which, consisting of 333 acres 2 roods 33 perches, retains the former name; and the other, consisting of 126 acres 1 rood 7 perches, has been transferred to Upper Cumber under the name of Gilky hill. It is bounded on the east and north east by the Faughan, and extends back to the south, where it embraces a flat round hill 450 feet above the sea, an underfeature of Slaboy hill. The base is much broken and varied by small ridges, which form a rather steep bank to the Faughan. This river, in passing round the hill, makes a turn to the north west from a nearly northerly direction and thus washes its base on the east and north east.

This district contains about 20 acres of bog, which does not differ from that of Upper Cumber in general. There is no wood, natural or planted, nor are there any public buildings or gentlemen's seats throughout this townland.

Draft Memoir by George Petrie

ANCIENT TOPOGRAPHY

Sepulchral Remains

Sepulchral and other monuments of pagan times are not uncommon in this parish. On Bollabracken there is an upright pillar stone of quartz and there is a carn of stones, which tradition points out as the sepulchre of a chieftain. In other places there are small mounds which are also evidently sepulchral. Near one of them an urn was lately found within a sepulchral cist <kist>, formed of large flagstones, and similar urns have been frequently found in the parish. They are rudely ornamented and usually hold about 3 pints.

Forts

There are 11 forts. The earthern forts are remarkably numerous, but few of them present any features deserving of particular notice. One of the most uncommon is that of Dungorkin, which gives name to the townland. This is of an elliptical form, and it is 186 feet in its greatest diameter and in its lesser 129 feet. It is surrounded by a [?] wet ditch [?] 84 feet wide, across which there is a causeway of piles, over which cross-beams had been placed first, and on these transverse pieces. Opposite this causeway a spacious gate of oak was dug up in the last century.

The fort in the townland of Lettermuck, near the carn above noticed, is remarkable for its beauty and preservation.

Ancient Church

There are no ecclesiastical ruins now remaining in the parish. The ancient parish church, having become ruinous in the troubles, was rebuilt or re-edified in its present form in the 17th century. It was founded originally in the 5th or 6th century by St Eugenius, Bishop of Ardstraw and the disciple of St Patrick, by whom several other parish churches in the diocese were erected. The situation of the church, on the bank of the [blank] river, is one of much tranquil beauty.

There were no castles of lime and stone ever erected within this portion of the original parish.

SOCIAL ECONOMY

Diseases

There are no diseases peculiar to Upper Cumber, except those resulting from a damp climate. The average number of persons relieved at the dispensary per annum is 1,400. Of these, there were of rheumatic complaints 56, dyspepsia 62, catarrh 80, the rest consisting chiefly of bowel complaints and diseases of children.

Fair Sheets by Thomas Fagan, September and October 1834, and March 1835

NATURAL FEATURES

Bogs in Lower Cumber

The long range of bog runs through and embraces parts of townlands of Strathall, Crossballycormick, Fawney and Ballynamore <Ballynamoor>; is in extent from 150 to 200 acres. There has been great quantities of fir and black oak raised out of those bogs from time to time, varying in length and circumference, and lying indiscriminately in the bog. In many cases there have been 3 logs or butts of trees found one in top of another. Few trunks have been found in that part of the bog in the townland of Ballynamore for the last 5 years.

The large mountain bog principally in townland of Irvey and joining Ballynamore exceeds 200 acres. The turf cut on this bog surpasses in quality that cut in low bogs. Many persons who cut turf in the above bog consider the turf a third degree in quality better than turf cut in flow or low bogs. There is no timber of any kind or of any consequence imbedded in the above bog.

Killaloo bog exceeds 100 acres. It embraces a part of townlands of Killaloo, Oughtagh, Brackfield and Lettermire, though called after the above name. This bog is thickly imbedded in the interior and exterior with fir and black oak, all which timber is found to be most valuable in many instances for roofing, joisting <joicing> and firing, and also permanent in tables, chests and bed-posts. These timbers are found lying in many directions and varying in length and thickness, and in all cases found to be burnt at the one end and greatly layered over each other. There are many heaps of timber cut up in this bog for fuel and other uses. There are 2 trunks, the one of oak, 18 feet long and 4 in circumference, and the other of fir, 45 feet long and 3 in circumference. 16th September 1834.

There is a small bog partly in Tonduff and Ardground called Tonduff bog. It exeeds 30 acres of low bog and productive of no valuable timber whatever. The main mountain bogs of Tonduff embraces a great part of townland of Ardground and is a united range through both townlands. The extent of those bogs exceeds 200 acres and in some cases there are butts and branches of black oak and fir to be met with, but seldom a trunk of any size. Where these are discovered they lie <lye> in all directions and differing in length and circumference, and seem to fall about the same time. There is one trunk of 18 feet long and 4 in circumference in this bog.

That extensive range of mountain bog, commencing at the mearing of the county Tyrone and parish of Donaghedy <Donaughady>, and running through that part of the parish of Lower Cumber called west of Bond's glen, and embracing a great part of the townlands of Lackagh, Killdogues, Ardground, Legahory and Gosheden, exceeds 500 acres; and only in a few instances that any quantity of timber is found in these bogs; and what is found consist of black oak and fir and is found to lie equally in the interior and exterior and in all directions, and varying in length and circumference, and in almost all cases a part of the butt trunk or stem is found to be burnt.

There are large parcels of those bogs reclaimed by Mr Lyle to the extent of 30 acres and is now growing good crops of all kinds of grain. There could be still numbers of acres reclaimed along the edges of those bogs if proper measures were taken for that purpose, and would give employ and bread to many of the working class. 17th September 1834.

Bogs

Oughtagh bog exceeds 50 acres of high mountain bog and a most excellent quality of turf can be got of it. In some instances there is to be met with some butts of black oak and fir, but very few trunks of either kind. There are many layers of branches, one in top of the other, being useful for winter firing but not substantial for other uses. These butts are in all cases burnt at the top. Butts and branches vary in length and seemingly in age, particularly at the stems and branches.

So little is the black oak valued when compared with the fir that only in a few cases the people give themselves the trouble of raising them unless they meet with a good trunk. Those timbers are got equally in all parts of the bogs.

That long range of bogs extending from Listress to Gortnaread, a distance of 3 miles, with little intermission of arable or coarse land and mostly of high mountain bogs, and embracing a great quantity of the townlands of Listress, Slaghmanus, Mallabuoy, Highmoor, Tamnierin, Brackagh and Gortnaread: the bogs bear different names proportionable to the names of the above townlands and is in many parts productive of the timber already described, equally in all parts of the bogs and lying in the same order as in other bogs already mentioned. This range of bogs exceeds 1,000 acres and is used as grazing in the summer months, as well as for turf-cutting.

A great portion of the parishioners of Faughanvale cut their turf in those bogs, and heath brooms are raised [out] of many parts of those bogs, particularly of Sleve Goar and Highmoor, and sold in Derry, Strabane, Dungiven, Newtownlimavady, Omagh and many other towns, and even brought to Dublin for sale, by which employment many persons young and old make a livelihood for themselves and families.

There are many parcels of ground reclaimed along the edges of those bogs, and is now growing most luxuriant crops of all kinds. The moss is so shallow in many parts of those bogs that hundreds of acres could be made good arable ground and give employment and a residence to many poor distressed families that now suffer the greatest privations and left a burthen on the generous public. 18th September 1834.

The range of flow <flaugh> or low bogs embracing a part of Lettershendony and Killinnen exceeded 50 acres, but is mostly cut away and many parts of the edges reclaimed. There have been many parcels of fir and oak got in these bogs, differing nothing in the order and lie of timber in other bogs.

One-fourth of the entire bogs inspected and enumerated in the parish of Lower Cumber is so shallow, including the parts cut away, that there does not appear to be 1 foot 6 inches of turf in depth over the clay surface; and viewing and seeing the abundant crops of all kinds that grow on the parcels of bog and mountain already reclaimed, it evidently appears and is finally believed by many of the parishioners of Lower Cumber, and even the occupiers of those large tracts of moss and mountains, that if proper measures was taken to reclaim and cultivate those shallow parts of bogs and mountain that now lie almost useless, the general crops of the parish could be greatly augmented, employment, bread and a habitation procured for many poor distressed families that are now suffering the greatest privations. 20th September 1834.

SOCIAL ECONOMY

Tradition

History of Mr Lewiss, formerly a resident gentleman. Mr Lewiss was a gentleman believed to emigrate from some other country to Ireland and settled himself in the lower part of the then parish of Cumber, where he became the proprietor of large tracts of land including Aughill, Lettershendony and subdivisions of other townlands in that part of the parish. He is also said to be a man of extraordinary wealth.

He choosed a site in Lettershendony, where he got a splendid castle built and in which he resided many years previous to the war of 1641. In same place, and near the site chosen for the castle, there was a rising ground or little hill called Gortycross, which place was selected and at which place the Roman Catholics of that part of Cumber was for a series of years in the habit of congregating on sabbath days at divine service.

The reason this place was called Gortycross was that in all places of Catholic worship there is a stone cross erected either on the house or, if in the open air, it is erected wherever the altar stands; and in the above-mentioned place of congregating there also stood a large stone cross, together with many other large stones used for different purposes, all which cross and other stones the aforesaid Mr Lewiss caused to be taken down to be used as building stones at the erection of the castle, he being <been> at that time proprietor of the soil and commanding such wealth and influence in the country that the aggrieved Catholics thought it useless to remonstrate with him on the impropriety of destroying their field chapel, but bound themselves by the most solemn <sallemn> affirmation that if ever an opportunity offered, they would be revenged of Lewiss.

The war of the 1641 ensued in some short time after the abolition of the place of worship at Gortycross, and Mr Lewiss, well knowing that the threats <treats> held out by the Catholics would be executed on him, he commenced to make preparations for the threatened attack. 3rd October 1834.

The first step taken by him was to secure his gold, which he possessed in great abundance and kept coffered in his cellar. He set all the inmates of his house intoxicated with liquor, with the exception of 2 persons who were his confidentials, and who, assisted by Lewiss, carried out the immense quantity of gold which was up to that time lodged in the cellar, by hand-barrows, and lodged in a part convenient to the castle, and it remains undiscovered to this day.

The following morning, after the removal of his treasure, he and all his inmates was surprised by an attack made on the house by a large party, who destroyed many parts of the castle and also of the servants. Mr Lewiss got making his escape by some back window on the house, and retreated to a glen or marshy place near the bog and hid himself in a scrag; but there was a heavy dew <due> and mist that morning, it being in autumn, and they succeeded in tracing him to the place where he hid under one of the bushes in the scrag.

They pulled him away from his place of refuge and buried him, or rather forced him down in a sheskin or quagmire in the verge of the bog, and which immediately closed in over his head and never seen or heard of since. Some think they first cut off his head before forcing him down in this place, others think they forced him down alive, but the pit or place where he was put down is visible to be seen at the present time and also the cross and some of the stones which caused the above inhuman act.

Insurances

There is not an instance of any sign or public document in the parish on any mansion or farmhouse or public establishment intimating the house, property or chattels being insured, or any private intelligence of the same yet ascertained.

Emigration to America

From January 1833 to August 1834 there have emigrated to various parts of America from the parish of Lower Cumber 170 of both sexes and of all ages, chiefly young men and maids; and not of the poorest class, as those in narrow circumstances have not the means of emigrating and consequently are obliged to content themselves by awaiting better opportunities, though with reluctance. For certain it is that one-half of the working class particularly are obliged to remain in their native land for want of ample means to take them to some other country, where they could expect to provide better maintenance for themselves and families and relieve themselves from the bondage, oppression and destitution they have so long endured, and believe to be their lot while compelled to remain in this unhappy country.

Migration

Migration to harvest in England, Scotland and other places: from 80 to 100 persons have emigrated to harvest in England and Scotland from the parish of Lower Cumber within the current year. Those persons are chiefly the youths of both sexes and of the cottier class. There are many instances of man and wife, newly married and of the above class, going together to harvest. The process of putting down the crops and cutting their winter firing is over with harvesters at the time of year they emigrate to the above countries, and they leave the care of their places and families to the older members or some neighbour till they return from harvest. 4th October 1834.

There are very few instances of persons going to harvest to the southern or western parts of Ireland from the parish of Lower Cumber, though artisans and labourers and persons in various occupations go to Dublin, Cork, Galway, Belfast, Drogheda and many other seaports and inland towns to procure employment from the above parish.

PRODUCTIVE ECONOMY

Collection of Rents

Rent agents in the parish of Lower Cumber are in some instances paid percentage and in others by fixed salaries as both parties may agree before. Average rent per acre for first quality of land in the parish of Lower Cumber is 1 pound 2s, second quality of land 15s, third quality of land 10s, coarse land from 2 to 6s per acre. For the parish of Lower Cumber rents are paid in money.

There may be some instances of resident landlords giving employment to the men or horses of any of their tenantry who attend them during the hurry of sowing, harvest, turf drawing, road making for farm accommodation etc, for which labour they are either paid on sight or allowed in the

Parish of Cumber

following gale [day] of rent, as the tenant may judge his own circumstances. But as above stated, rents are most commonly paid in money.

Conacre Leases and Size of Holdings

There are very few instances of landholders in the parish of Lower Cumber letting out any quantity of ground in the conacre line for oats, flax, potatoes or meadow, unless in the case of meeting with some disappointment such as loss of cattle, malady or sickness in the family or other casualties, under which circumstances they are obliged to let for ready money to meet pressing demands.

Farms in the parish of Lower Cumber vary in size, but are most commonly from 10 to 20 acres; many holdings higher and lower.

Size of enclosures and fields in the parish of Lower Cumber vary from 4 to 8 acres and are most commonly enclosed or fenced with clay ditches raised from the soil and planted with whitethorn quicks, or fir seed sown along the ditch at half height or on the top; and in some instances, where stones are at hand, they are most partly faced with stones; and where there is abundance of stones to be had, the entire fence is built with stones and no quicks whatever put in; and in other instances, where they are not able to procure stones or quicks, the fields are enclosed by deep drains being made round the fields and the stuff raised forming a part of the fence; and in some cases no fence of any description to protect the crop but guarded by a herd-boy.

Taxes and Tithes

For the last year there is not any other taxes claimed of the landholders of Lower Cumber than tithes and grand jury levy or county cess, and vestry levies for the support of deserted children.

Marle and Limestone

There are some instances of marle being raised in some parts of Lower Cumber but not to any great extent, nor is it considered to avail the soil anything.

Limestone is procured by the parishioners of Lower Cumber chiefly from Ardground, Lettershendony, Highmoor and parts of Grocers' property and Bond's glen, but Ardground and Bond's glen is the principal.

Quarrying and Expense of Burning Lime

Quarrying the quantity of limestone for 110 barrels of lime 5s; cost of carrying the lime 5s; cost of carrying the lime a distance of 1 mile by horses 10s; breaking the same to size for burning 10s; setting the kiln with materials or filling it 5s; vending the contents or repairing it for sale or use 4s; cost of turf sufficient to burn the above quantity 1 pound 4s; purchase of the limestone, if the purchaser quarry them, 10s; total expense of burning 100 barrels of lime within 1 mile of the quarry 3 pounds 8s; cost of attendance on the horses carrying the limestone from the quarry to the kiln, omitted in the above, 5s; total expense 3 pounds 13s.

The landholder whose means enables him to procure lime for his land in the above manner can put it on his land at 9d per barrel; and if purchased at the limeworks ready for use, it will cost him 10d per barrel slack and further expense, depending on the distance to be brought.

Manure

Burning the soil for manure is not very prevalent in the parish of Lower Cumber, but in all instances where such practice prevail, it is the outskirts and mossy mountainous parts of the holdings that are chosen for the above purpose.

Teams of Oxen and Horses

The practice of working with oxen in ploughing, harrowing, caring [carting?] is become very prevalent in the parish of Lower Cumber within the last 10 years, and are found to be very useful for the above purposes. [Crossed out: 4 oxen is a team].

It was a common practice in the parish of Lower Cumber up to 1814 to have 3 horses in a team, but since the introduction of English and Scotch ploughs into the parish, the farmers can dispense with a third horse in a team and can perform the work much better. 6th October 1834.

Rotation of Crops

The crops commonly put down in the parish of Lower Cumber are oats, barley, flax, potatoes and small parcels of wheat. There are also turnips, clover, field peas and broccoli <brockla> put down for cattle feeding.

Seed and Harvest

Quantity of wheat seed per acre Cunningham 16 stone; quantity of barley seed per acre Cunningham 12 stone; quantity of oats seed per acre Cunningham 20 stone; quantity of flax seed per acre Cunningham 36 gallons; quantity of potatoes seed per acre Cunningham 32 bushels. All crops put down for cattle feeding such as clover, turnips, field peas and broccoli.

Average harvest produce of wheat per acre Cunningham 7 barrels; average harvest produce of barley per acre Cunningham 7 barrels; average harvest produce of oats per acre Cunningham 8 barrels; average harvest produce of flax per acre Cunningham 5 cwt; average harvest produce of potatoes per acre Cunningham 240 bushels.

It may appear strange that the harvest produce of the above crops are so near each other, particularly wheat, barley and oats, in weight and number of barrels, but it suffices to say that the prime and best laboured part of the farm is always chosen by the farmer for the growing of wheat and barley, and flax also. Besides, the weight of barrels of oats, wheat and barley differ very little in this part of the country: weight of wheat per barrel 20 stone, barley per barrel 21 stone, oats per barrel 18 stone.

Carriage of Commodities

Almost all landholders in the parish of Lower Cumber have their own conveyances to send commodities to market, but in the absence of such accommodation there are 4s per day paid to a carter for taking goods of any description to Derry, Strabane or Coleraine markets. 7th October 1834.

The landholders of the parish of Lower Cumber send to Derry markets oats, wheat, barley, flax, pork, butter, fowl, eggs, yarn, linen, meal, potatoes, beef, mutton, veal, all which commodities are speedily purchased at the aforesaid markets for exportation and home consumption.

Grazing, Cattle Jobbers and Green Feeding

There are very few instances of whole farms being let out exclusively for grazing in the parish of Lower Cumber, unless mountain farms which are not considered to be good for tillage.

There are only 5 persons known in the parish of Lower Cumber who live exclusively by cattle jobbing, though there are many who deal in the idle season of the year in cattle of every description. The above traffic is practised in the above parish for the last 40 years.

It is become a very prevalent practice among the farmers of the parish within the last 6 years to put down parcels of ground under crops of turnips, clover, field peas and cabbages for the purpose of feeding all kinds of cattle, particularly stable feeding and fattening.

Draining of Bogs

There are some instances of proprietors and landholders running drains through many parts of the bogs in Lower Cumber, but not followed to that extent that it would have the desired effect of drying the surface or interior of the bogs.

Breeds of Poultry

The principal breed of poultry in the parish of Lower Cumber are geese, ducks, hens, Guinea <Guinia> breed and peacock breed and turkeys.

Increase of Fowl

In consequence of the great demand at markets in Londonderry for eggs and fowl of every description since the establishment of steamboats from Derry to England and Scotland, geese, turkeys, ducks, hens and Guinea hens have increased within the last 5 years 400% to what they were previous to that date in the parish of Lower Cumber, and is found to be as profitable and beneficial as any other stock commonly fed on the farm.

ANCIENT TOPOGRAPHY

Krannagh Fort

There stands in the townland of Ardground, and holding of David Mitchel, one of the most extraordinary forts for height, strength, size and curiosity perhaps in this or any other province in the kingdom of Ireland. It is in a valley at the entrance of Bond's glen, at the north east side. It covers upwards of 1 square acre of land and rises upwards of 60 feet above the surface of the stream that divides Upper and Lower Cumber, and runs within a few yards of the outside rim or exterior of the fort. It is enclosed by 3 different rims rising gradually one above the other. When you arrive at the top or summit it is almost a complete thicket of various kinds of old trees and bushes.

On the south side is a pile of rocks forming a part of the mount and rising almost perpendicular and through which there is a kind of passage by which persons can ascend and descend the above extraordinary height. On landing at the top by this last-mentioned passage is a hollow place 4 feet wide, a similiar depth and several feet in length. This is said to be a giant's grave. There are also great sinks in the rocky parts of it. It is on all parts studded with old trees, brambles and old ruins of all kinds of natural wood, and is productive of variety of herbs. On the surface of the soil there are a large quantity of rods cut every year off the above fort, found very useful for making farm potatoes and turf clieves and baskets.

Parish of Cumber

To add to the beauty and antiquity of Krannagh Fort, it is surrounded on either side by ranges of extraordinary rocks and hills, all mantled with vestiges of old native wood and rising to even a greater height than the fort. By standing on either of those hills the fort resembles a pyramid, and the romantic appearance of fort, hills and glens seems a combination of art and nature.

In 1813 Mr Mitchel of Ardground and his son the present David Mitchel, who occupies the farm on which stands the aforesaid Krannagh Fort, was in search of sand or some other object, which led them to penetrate the surface of one side of the above fort, where they discovered at some depth a smith's anvil and one half of a grinding stone, since which discovery they, with many others who heard of the above discovery, are of the opinion that the above-mentioned fort must have been the residence of some of the Danes or ancient inhabitants of this part of Ireland.

NATURAL FEATURES

Old Wood

On that side of Bond's glen in the parish of Lower Cumber, and embracing subdivisions of townlands of Ardground, Killdogues and Lackagh, there is the ruins of a large tract of native oak wood, particularly in townland of Lackagh. The part of the old wood in this townland, and in the holding of Robert Bond, is productive of large quantities of nuts each year, which the said Robert Bond sells in city of Derry, together with many cart-loads of rods cut in the same wood, for which he gets a certain sum, some hundred in number. The neat [net?] product of the above articles is believed to amount to 20 pounds per annum.

This part of the old wood is more anxiously protected from trespass of people or cattle than any other parts of the same range. Particularly during autumn it is watched by night and by day.

PRODUCTIVE ECONOMY

Valuators and Surveyor

Messrs Brassington and Gayle <Gale>, valuators, and Mr Porter, surveyor, are at present employed on the property of Mr Ogilby of Pellapar in the parishes of Upper and Lower Cumber.

MODERN TOPOGRAPHY

General Character of the Parish

The parish of Lower Cumber, though not thickly inhabited with gentlemen's seats, improvements or mansion houses, is possessed of more natural properties, romantic sceneries and antiquities of both art and nature than perhaps many other parishes in the province of Ulster. There is in the south western parts of the parish extensive tracts of native oak woods, lofty mountain, hundreds of acres of valuable bogs, extensive slate, limestone and building stone quarries, most valuable mineral and other springs, black oak and fir imbedded in the bogs, sufficient running streams to accommodate mills, extraordinary glens and ravines, many of those vestiges of antiquities such as old forts and standing stones, and lofty rocks, a very extensive bleach green. The north west and eastern parts of the parish is in many of the above qualities and property superior to the above-described south western division.

There is the beautiful and celebrated River Faughan which divides those and the aforesaid parts of the parish, in sight of which stands the extensive ruins of Brackfield Castle, once the seat of some of the great O'Kanes. At the same place an extensive and ancient Presbyterian meeting house, the rectory, the seat or residence of Counsellor Lyle. Those standing monuments of ancient and modern dates, combined with the planting and improvements made about the 2 last-mentioned mansion houses, the extensive and almost uninterrupted tracts of native oak wood, and lofty rocks and rising ground on both sides of the river, render the site romantic and delightful.

Farther east is the river called the Burntollet, overhung with lofty trees of the native oak and piles of rocks surpassing others in the height and dimensions for a distance of 1 mile, when next appears the extraordinary precipice and tremendous <tremendious> waterfall called the Ness <Nhess>. This immense pit is almost unrivalled and is beautifully ornamented on all sides by plantations of various kinds of forest trees which, combined with the native growth <groth> of oak wood, renders the site at once romantic and delightful and little, if any, inferior to many falls so celebrated in history.

Proceeding northwards is numbers of lofty mountains, extensive bogs productive of best quality of turf, black oak and fir, timber, lime and building stone quarries, rivers and streams to accommodate mills, various monuments of antiquities such as forts, caves, standing stones, giant's graves, old burial grounds, extraordinary enclosures of ancient standing.

Enumerating the aforesaid qualities and properties of which the parish of Lower Cumber is possessed, combined with the advantage of being in the immediate neighbourhood of one of the best seaport towns in the north of Ireland, and surrounded by many inland markets and fair towns affording demand and purchases for every commodity of agricultural produce for exportation and home consumption, that nothing short of absenteeism, exorbitant rents, heavy tithes and other taxes, the want of investments in establishing public institutions and public works, reclaiming bogs or mountains and such other industry as would afford employment to the working class, could render the parishioners of Lower Cumber unhappy. 8th October 1834.

ANCIENT TOPOGRAPHY

Demolished Grave

In the townland of Slaghmanus, and in the farm of a man of the name of McAvraghan, otherwise Brown, there stood one of those giant's graves, a most extraordinary enclosure from 20 to 30 feet in length, 9 feet in width and enclosed by flags of a prodigious size set in the ground on their ends, and on the top a flagstone of extraordinary dimensions believed to weigh from 3 to 4 tons. This top flag served as a canopy and was supported at the height of 4 feet by the aforesaid flags enclosing the grave and leaving the interior a vacant space. This grave stood immediately over Loughermore stream and within a short space of a similiar one which stands on the south east side of the aforesaid stream, and in the townland of Barr Cregg.

The above-described grave, which stood on the north west side of the aforesaid stream, stood unmolested for centuries till some time about 1816 several persons dreamt of a treasure being concealed in the interior of the grave, but dare not go to seek it after night or disturb the monument by night or by day.

About the aforesaid [period] there was a Doctor [blank], who was in the habit of staying some days at the rectory of Lower Cumber, otherwise Glebe House at Killaloo, who, on hearing of the dreams and the treasure concealed in the above grave, mustered many sturdy men, including the rector's labourers and others from the neighbourhood of Killaloo, together on a day, provided sledges, crowbars and proceeded to the giant's grave to have it razed <raised> to the ground and procure the treasure. They succeeded in throwing the top stone to one side and commenced digging up the interior and removing as many of the standing columns as obstructed their progress.

In digging up the part the money was supposed to be concealed, they dug up a great quantity of the interior of the old grave, dislodged the canopy or top stone, together with many of the pillars by which it was supported, and completely destroyed the original form without any success, other than there was discovered a few of the following articles such as chisels, compasses <compises>, hammers, spurs, an old sword, in and about the premises. 15th October 1834.

The ruins of the giant's grave remained in the above dilapidated state from the aforesaid period up to 1831, when Mr McAvraghan totally removed the stones by which the grave was covered and enclosed and removed all vestiges of the old monument, then filled up the pit and brought it on a level with the remainder of the field on which it stood, the quantity of stones by which this grave was built being so great and the stones so large that it took the aforesaid McAvraghan and his labourers many days to remove, sledge and break them.

The above McAvraghan is one of a numerous tribe of that name who inhabit a great part of the west of the townland of Slaghmanus, and have within the last few years changed their name from McAvraghan to Brown.

Concealed Crock

Robert Norris of Ballygroll discovered lately in his farm, a short distance from the aforesaid giant's grave, an earthen crock of moderate size, concealed some feet under the surface and secured by large flags. Covering the crock was a large heavy flag supported by others sunk in the ground. In a circular form beneath this large stone, and immediately over the crock, was a thin slate flag, and under the bottom of the crock was placed a similiar slate flag. On removing the top covering off and attempting to lift the crock, the moment it was put hands to, it mouldered down into dust. Until disturbed this crock remained in its original form, but nothing deposited in it.

Discovery of a Skeleton

In the above townland of Ballygroll in a bog there was lately discovered the skeleton of a child coffined. The inside covering was sheets of paper used instead of linen as a winding sheet. This coffin was made on a rough construction and sunk several feet down in the moss. The coffin and its contents seemed to be imbedded for a long time in the above place, as all appeared in complete decay.

Several Discoveries lately made

There has been several articles of household

Parish of Cumber

furniture, and of ancient date and forms, lately discovered by persons of the names of Lamrock and Norries in townlands of Aughill, Ballygroll and subdivisions of other townlands, ranging with the aforesaid such as small pots, dishes and various other vessels of olden times and make, together with carpenter and farming implements. The above articles was most partly found imbedded in the boggy parts.

Demolished Grave

In the farm of Arthur Norris, in townland of Ballygroll and parish of Lower Cumber, there stood one of those giant's graves so numerous in that part of the parish. This grave was enclosed by flagstones and stood thus unmolested perhaps for the last 1,000 years or more, till the above Arthur Norris, having heard that there was a treasure of some description of coin concealed therein, and in order to find the treasure, he dug it up about the year 1816.

On removing the flags by which it was enclosed, and digging up a quantity of sandy soil where it stood, he discovered at the head, foot and sides of the grave well-shaped logs of black oak set down as a fence or protection. Those logs he removed to his dwelling house and converted them to many uses, and one of them he placed as a lintel <lentle> over a cowhouse door, where it remains to the present time. This timber was regularly formed and chipped to answer the purpose for which it was intended, and when raised from the pit or grave where it lay for so many centuries was found to be quite sound and in good preservation.

This giant's grave stood in the interior of a bog and the soil about it for several feet on all sides was found to be quite hard, dry and of a sandy nature, and appeared by its shape and dimensions as if placed there for the reception of the above grave.

The grave was 8 feet in length and 4 in width, much resembling the shape and size of modern graves. There was nothing more discovered in the digging up and demolishing of this grave than the timber above described, which had all the appearance of being prepared and placed where discovered by a regular artisan. 15th October 1834.

Brass Axe

[Insert addition: There is at present in the house of Elizabeth McElhatten, townland of Slaghmanus and parish of Lower Cumber, a very curious brass axe, lately discovered between 2 fir blocks at a depth of 10 feet under the surface of a solid bank in a bog in the townland of Munnaboy, in the aforesaid parish. Informant John Colgin. [Signed] Thomas Fagan, 26th March 1835].

Fair Sheets by J. Bleakly, September 1834

PRODUCTIVE ECONOMY

Model Farms in Crossballycormick

James Smyth: 48 acres, Cunningham measure; 40 acres under crop, viz. corn and wheat 14 acres, potatoes and turnips 6 acres, flax 4 acres, meadow, rye grass and clover 16 acres, pasture 8 acres. 3 horses, 7 cows and 1 bull (Durham breed) in prime order. Berkshire pigs also in good order. Good implements of husbandry. Fields well formed and very well fenced with good clay and stone ditches, well quicked and some stone walls. Cattle stall fed, good green feeding. Excellent dwellings and office houses, built of stone and lime and slated.

Rotation of crops are: 1st oats, 2nd flax, 3rd potatoes, 4th turnips, 5th wheat, 6th oats again laid down with clover and grass, which is cut 2 or 3 times in the season, then preserved for meadow or let out 2 years for pasture.

There are 5 acres of excellent irrigated meadow, reclaimed from cut-out bog. Annual rent 80 pounds, annual local taxes 13 pounds.

An excellent steamer for boiling potatoes etc. for cattle. The boiler is of cast iron, placed in a furnace. A barrel with holes in the bottom (filled with potatoes) is placed on the boiler, which is filled with water, the barrel covered close at top. Dated 30 August 1834.

Robert Smyth: 40 acres, Cunningham measure; 23 acres under crop, viz. 9 of oats, 5 of wheat, 5 and a half of potatoes, 1 and a half of flax and 3 of clover. Annual rent 20 pounds, annual local taxes 12 pounds 13s 9d. 3 horses, 14 cows, in prime order, good implements of husbandry. Enclosures well shaped and well fenced with good clay ditches, well quicked, green feeding, turnips etc; excellent dwelling and office houses with a very neat garden.

Samuel Smyth: 11 acres, Cunningham measure; 5 and a half acres under crop, viz. oats 2 and a half acres, wheat 1 acre, potatoes 2 acres. [Insert note: Wheat is not a usual crop on this farm]. Annual rent 10 pounds, annual local taxes 1 pound 4s. 1 horse, 3 cows. Good implements of husbandry. Good dwelling and office houses, good gates, good butter. Fields well shaped and fenced with quicks and whins on top of some.

Rotation of crops are: 1st potatoes, 2nd oats laid down with clover and grass, which is cut for 1 year and let out for 2 years for pasture. 5 acres of this farm has been reclaimed by draining, levelling, ditching and manuring. Green feeding are turnips and clover; proprietors Ponsonby and Alexander.

Model Farms in Fawney

Samuel Donald: 35 acres, Cunningham measure; 4 acres of wheat, 3 acres of flax, 9 acres of oats, 2 and a half acres of potatoes, 1 and a half acres of turnips. 20 pounds 16s 8d annual rent, 5 pounds 10s annual local taxes. 2 horses, 5 cows, 2 sheep Irish breed. Fields tolerably well formed and fenced with good clay ditches quicked, some stone ditches. Good implements of husbandry. Dwelling and office houses tolerably comfortable.

Rotation of crops are: 1st potatoes, 2nd wheat, 3rd flax laid down with clover and grass seed. Good cheese and butter; proprietors Ponsonby and Alexander.

Henry Caldwell: 35 acres, Cunningham measure; 6 acres of oats, 1 rood of flax, 1 acre of wheat, 6 acres of potatoes. 2 horses, 6 cows, 4 sheep, Irish breed. Annual rent 12 pounds 6s 2d, tithe 2 pounds 10s, county cess 1 pound 12s. Good implements of husbandry. Fields pretty well formed and fenced with clay pitches quicked with some firs. Dwelling and office houses tolerable. Good cheeses and butter.

Rotation of crops are: 1st potatoes, 2nd oats, 3rd wheat, 4th flax laid down with clover and grass seed. Proprietors Ponsonby and Alexander, middleman John A. Smyth Esquire. 1st September 1834.

Model Farms in Tamnemore

Alexander Noble: 50 acres, Cunningham measure; 20 acres under crops, viz. wheat 4 acres, corn 6, potatoes 5, flax 2 acres, meadow 2 and a half, clover 2 and a half acres. Annual rent 5 pounds 8s, annual local taxes 9 pounds 1s. Good implements of husbandry, good iron and wooden gates, fields tolerably well fenced and well shaped, ditches pretty straight. 3 horses, 6 cows, no sheep. Good cheese and butter. Cattle Irish breed. A large stone roller for bruising flax.

William Brown, Tamnemore: 70 acres, Cunningham measure; 15 acres under wheat and oats, 3 acres of flax, 3 acres of potatoes, 2 and a half acres of meadow. 9 pounds 10s annual rent, 16 pounds taxes. 4 horses, 8 cows. Good implements of husbandry, good fences, good iron and wooden gates. Good dwelling and office houses. Good cheese and butter.

Robert Miller, Tamnemore: 20 acres, Cunningham measure; 7 and a half acres of corn, 2 acres of potatoes, 3 roods of flax, 3 acres of meadow. Good dwelling and office houses. 10 pounds annual rent, 4 pounds 10s taxes. 2 horses, 5 cows. Good butter and cheese. Good implements of husbandry. Good iron and wooden gates, fields pretty well formed and well fenced with clay and stone ditches quicked. 3rd September 1834.

Model Farms in Brackfield

Robert Miller: 15 acres 3 roods 37 perches, Cunningham measure; corn 6 acres, potatoes 2 acres, flax 3 roods, meadow half an acre, total under crop 9 acres 1 rood. Ditches straight and well quicked, fields well formed and clean. Dwelling and office houses in good repair.

Rotation of crops are: 1st oats, 2nd potatoes, 3rd corn 2 crops and 1 of flax. No regular system as the farmer must put in the crops to suit the nature of the soil and the season. The best crop of corn off lea or new ground without manure that has been for many years in the parish is on this farm.

Land requires manure at all times for potatoes. Light soil will not produce good wheat, poor land will not produce good potatoes or wheat. Potatoes, corn and wheat does best on upland. Rye does well on moss; wheat is not a general crop in this parish. Some have tried it this year and appears well. 2nd September 1834.

Annual rent 22 pounds 17s 4d Irish currency, annual taxes 4 pounds 7s 7d Irish currency. Good implements of husbandry. Stock 2 horses, 5 cows, 4 sheep, English, Irish and Scotch breed. NB Short leases are a great obstruction to improvement. Ruins of an old castle in Brackfield.

John Cather: 39 acres 2 roods, Cunningham measure; 22 acres of arable, 6 acres of oats, 3 acres of potatoes, 1 of flax, 1 rood of turnips. 21 pounds annual rent, 2 pounds 12s of tithe, 2 pounds county cess. 2 horses, 5 cows, 6 sheep, Scotch and Irish breed. Fields well formed, about to be improved, new ditches making at present. Houses tolerably comfortable. He obtained a premium for good ploughing. Good butter and cheese.

Model Farms and Tenants in Irvey

James Canning, Irvey: 75 acres; 9 of oats, 1 of

Parish of Cumber

wheat, 3 potatoes, 1 acre and 1 rood of flax. 34 pounds annual rent, 5 pounds county cess, 4 pounds 5s tithe. 3 horses, 6 cows, 9 sheep. Fields tolerably well formed and fenced with clay and stone ditches, some quicked. Dwelling and office houses middling comfortable. Cattle Irish breed. Females chiefly employed by spinning; proprietor Grocers' Company.

Mrs Burnside: 30 acres, Cunningham measure; 7 acres under crop. 2 horses, 8 cows. Good ditches, good implements of husbandry. Fields well shaped and fenced. Good dwelling and office houses, good cheese and butter. Good iron and wooden gates. Annual rent 21 pounds, annual taxes 6 pounds 8s. Cattle English, Irish and Scotch breed.

The tenants are bound in their leases neither to let or sell, which is another great obstruction to improvement. A tax on absentee landlords would be a great good to the county. Obtained from Dr Long, 3rd September 1834.

Model Farms and Obstructions to Improvement

Revd James Allison, Toneduff: 83 acres; 36 arable, 35 pounds annual rent, county cess 5 pounds. 3 horses, 6 cows, 9 sheep, English, Irish and Scotch breed. Good implements of husbandry. Good dwelling houses and office. Fields pretty well shaped and fenced. Crops are oats, potatoes, barley and flax, often let out 4 years for pasture.

Mrs Mitchel, Toneduff: 52 acres, Cunningham measure; 20 acres under crop. 50 pounds annual rent, 8 pounds annual taxes. 3 horses, 14 cows, 8 sheep. Good fences, tolerable gates, fields well formed and well fenced with good clay and stone ditches. Good cheese and butter. Farm well sheltered with large ash and other trees.

The tenants have no lease in Toneduff, which is a great obstruction to improvement in this part of the parish. Subdivision of holdings is another great injury to the country; proprietor Skinners' Company. Information obtained from Revd James Allison and Revd John Hayden.

Model Farms

Revd John Hayden, Killaloo: 52 acres, Cunningham measure; oats 6 acres, flax 5 acres, potatoes 4 acres, wheat 1 acre, turnips 1 acre, meadow 7 acres. Stock 5 horses, 9 cows, 60 sheep, English, Irish and Scotch breed, in prime order, some stall fed. Good implements of husbandry. Fields well formed and remarkably well fenced with good clay and stone ditches, well quicked and neatly dressed. Good iron gates to each field. Good dwelling and office houses in good repair. A regular sheep-walk. County cess 5 pounds per annum, no tithe.

Modern Topography and Social Economy

Church

The church is too small and equally inconvenient for the Protestant parishioners (who are increasing very much) of both ends of the parish, as the church is situated (using the Irish phrase) in the middle of one end of the parish.

Persuasions of the People

The persuasions of the people of the parish are Episcopalians, Presbyterians, Roman Catholics and Covenanters.

There are in this parish of the Established Church about 600 persons, Presbyterians about 640 families, each family on an average of about 5 in number, making the total of 3,200 souls; Covenanters very few, about 6 or 7. [Insert addition: According to the census of 1831, there were 3,206 Protestants and 1,378 Roman Catholics. The Presbyterians are attached to the Synod Of Ulster; tithe 560 pounds]. Information obtained from Revd John Hayden and Revd James Allison.

Dispensary

Dispensary days in Lower Cumber are Tuesday and Fridays; Dr Semple, medical attendant.

Notes on Bleach Mills from William Kidde to Captain Portlock

Productive Economy

Letter concerning Bleach Green at Oaks

Oaks bleach green, carried on under the firm of Lyle, Smyth and Co., contains about 17 acres, Cunningham measure. The machinery and apparatus consist of 3 boilers, each containing 120 webs or 240 pieces of linen; of wash mills 3 pair of feet; of rub boards, 3 double rollers on a crank; 3 souring and 1 large steeping cistern, 2 double engines of 3-piece beams, with drying and airing lofts to correspond. The process may be calculated 12 boils in alkali lye, 1 steep in a solution of muriatic acid, 3 steeps in a solution of vitriolic acid, scalded and blued. The cost of bleaching varies according to the quality of the linen (the finest being most easily bleached) and the price of material; the average may be taken at 4s 6d per piece. The number of pieces bleached about 15,000 annually.

The number of hands employed are as under: 1 foreman, 2 wash mill men, 2 furnace men, 2 rubboard men, 9 field men, 3 loft men, 4 engine men, 2 carpenters, 2 watchmen each night, 4 in lapping room, 1 turf man, [total] 32.

The bleach green is supplied with linen from the markets of Fintona, Omagh, Strabane, Derry, Coleraine and Ballymoney. The markets for consumption are Dublin and the English markets, viz. London, Liverpool, Bristol, Birmingham, Manchester and Nottingham.

Hoping the above statement satisfactory, I am Sir, yours William Kidde, foreman. [To] Captain Portlock, Royal Engineers, Londonderry.

Copy of Grant Deed of Irish Society

History

Grants to Goldsmiths' Company

September 10th 1618: by deed of testament of this date, the Irish Society grants to the wardens and commonality of Goldsmiths of the city of London, and to their successors and assigns forever, all the manor of Goldsmiths' Hall in the county of Londonderry, alias Coleraine, consisting of the several denominations therein treated as comprised in the said Goldsmiths' proportion no.1, according to their lot, a division with the other companies and which lands had been erected into a manor by virtue of his majesty's tithes patent, and called the manor of Goldsmiths' Hall, with all profits and appurtenances to said manor and lands belonging.

October 31st 1730: by deed of this date the Goldsmiths' Company, in consideration of a sum of 14,100 pounds, conveyed to the Earl of Shelburne the said manor lands and premises, excepting the advowson of the church of Clondermot and all other churches, subject to a fee farm rent of 200 pounds a year.

April 10th 1740: by deed of this date executed pursuant to a decree of the Court of Exchequer in Ireland, the Earl of Shelburne, in consideration of 16,000 pounds, conveyed the said manor to Brabazon, Earl of Bessborough, subject to the said rent of 200 pounds.

November 3rd 1753: by will of this date Lord Bessborough devised the said manor to his third son Richard Ponsonby and his heirs forever.

1787: by his will of this date the said Richard Ponsonby devised the said manor to his nephews William B. Ponsonby, afterwards Lord Ponsonby, and George Ponsonby, afterwards Lord Chancellor of Ireland, equally as tenants in common.

December 28th 1803: the said William B. Ponsonby, thus Lord Ponsonby by his will of this date, devised his moiety of the said manor to his second son William Ponsonby, afterwards Major-General Sir William Ponsonby, and his heirs forever.

The said Sir William Ponsonby, having been killed in the battle of Waterloo, the said moiety of the said manor descended to his only son and heir-at-law William Ponsonby.

The said George Ponsonby, Lord Chancellor of Ireland, by his will devised his moiety of the said manor to his son William Robert Ponsonby and his heirs. The said William Robert Ponsonby by his will devised the said moiety of the said manor to trustees upon certain trusts for the payment of debts, in execution of which the said moiety of the said manor was sold under a decree of the Court of Exchequer in Ireland, and Alexander Alexander became the purchaser thereof, for a sum of: [insert marginal note initialled A.L.: I think 47,500 pounds].

The said Alexander Alexander by his will devised the said moiety of the said manor to his brother John Alexander, who has since purchased from the said William Ponsonby the other moiety of the manor, for the sum of 52,500 pounds, and now is the owner of the entire, though subject only by the payment of the said rent of 200 pounds.

From the above statements, some idea may be formed of the great increase of the value of property in this part of Ireland within a short period, as the same property which in the year 1740 was purchased for a sum of 16,000 pounds Irish afterwards produced the sum of 100,000 pounds British.

Notes on Name of Cumber by John O'Donovan

History and Natural State

Origin of Name: Cumber

The name Cumber, the original appellation of the parish now divided and distinguished as Lower and Upper, is not of ecclesiastical origin, being the topographically applicable name of the locality or townland in which the original parish church was situated. The word in Irish, as in Welsh, signifies literally "a meeting of streams or rivers."

Parish of Cumber

[Insert addition: It is translated "alveus" by O'Flaherty in his *Ogygia*].

The Irish write it *comar* and *cumar*, rarely cumbir or combar, and the Welsh cymmer, which is thus explained by the learned Edward Lhwyd "Cymmer, plural cymmere, is the meeting of 2 or more rivers, whence Pont-y-Cymmer near Lhan Trisaint in Glamorganshire and Lhyn-y-Cymmer in the Severn near Lhan Idloes." The name is of common occurrence in Ireland and has been explained confluentia by Colgan, as "comar na dtri nuisce confluentia trium rivulorum" (*Triadis Thaumaturgae*).

Peter Connell in his dictionary states that this is a Welsh word of great antiquity and not Irish; and if by Irish he means Scotic he is probably right as the Irish have another generic word for water not found in the Welsh, namely *uisce*, which is cognate with the Latin aqua. The word is obviously compounded of *com*, cognate with the Latin con, and *bior* "water," a Celtic word of great antiquity now obsolete in Ireland, Scotland and Wales, though retained in several compound formations in both countries.

It is so explained in Irish manuscripts of the oldest antiquity, as in the Leabhar Breac *Bir-an-uisce*, and again in *Cormac's Glossary Bir, .i. tibraid no sruth*, bir "i.e. a well or stream;" and again under the word *bradan* "a salmon," bradan, .i. bir fuid en, .i. en bir ar fud uisce, ar fid bir, .i. ar fid uisce, ut dicitur bir acas inbhir acos tobar: "Bradan, .i. bir-fuid-en, i.e. 'what is in the water;' ar fid bir is the same as ar fid uisce, i.e. 'in or through the water,' ut dicitur bir and in-bhir, and to-bar." Cormac means by this that it was retained in the compound word inbher, "the entrance of one river into another or into the sea," and tobar, "a spring or fountain."

The word is also found in many other Irish compounds as *biorar* "watercresses" and biorrae, "a watery field," hence the Biorra, the Irish name of the town of Birr as explained in the *Leabhar Breac* "Bir, uisci agus rae mag." So also in the British aber, which is explained by Lhwyd as the fall of a lesser water into a greater, as of a brook into a river or of a river into a lake or sea.

For the meaning of the prefixes *in, to,* or *ti* and *a*, in the words inbhear, tobar or tibir and aber, no ancient authorities have been found; and etymological conjecture is of little value except when supported by a high degree of probability, as appears to be the case in the English word river which, though immediately derived from the French, would appear to be in its Celtic radices *rith* "to run," cognate with the Greek *reo* and the Latin ruo, and *bir* "water," making rith-bhir (ri-vir) "running water."

[Crossed out: It has been conjectured by the most learned philologists that the Celtic dwvyr *dabhar*, plural dwvrau, is cognate with the Sanscrit udum, "water," Latin udus-a-um and unda, the Greek *udor*, i.e. fudor or vudor, the English "water," with other cognates in the Indo-European languages; but the analogy will not hold without supposing a transposition of the letters not likely to have occurred, and it seems more probable that *dobhar* is a word compounded like the others already referred to and cognate with the Sanscrit dabra, "ocean." It might indeed be supposed that this word has more direct cognates in the Semitic family of languages than in the Indo-European, as the Arabic bir "wells"].

As this word bir, though now obsolete in its simple form, enters largely into Irish topographical names, it will not be considered improper to endeavour to ascertain its origin by a comparison of its apparent cognates in the languages of Indo-European and Semitic stocks, as such inquiry must be of essential importance towards the investigation of the ancient history of mankind.

From the fact that the Irish had a different word unknown to the Welsh *uisce*, cognate with the Latin aqua and the gaulish eau, anciently written eague, it might be hastily concluded that this word is not of true Celtic or Indo-European origin, and particularly as direct cognates with it are found in the languages of Semitic origin: thus Arabic bir "wells," Persian bar-an "rain," Turkish bar and behr "sea," Hebrew and Venetian bar-an "wells," Malagasy bihar "sea." [Insert marginal note: Make certain [initialled] POK].

On the other hand, however, it will appear that cognates nearly as direct are found in the Celtic and all the other languages of Indo-European origin, as the Armoric ber and bar "sea," the Gaulish and English river, which appears to be in its Celtic radices rith "to run," cognate with the Greek *reo* and the Latin ruo, and bir "water," making rith-vir pronounced ri-vir "running water."

The cognates at first sight less striking are those in which the initial letter b has been softened into m, a change of general occurrence in languages of this stock, as in the very word bir which would make in Irish *o'n mbir* in the ablative case. [Crossed out: From not attending to this fact Mr Lhwyd fell into the error of supposing the compound cymmer to be found from mir and not from bir as it is written in the ancient Irish].

Keeping this fact in view, the connection between the Irish *muir*, genitive *mira*, "the sea" must be at once obvious, as well as its relationship to the various words in all the Indo-European languages expressing ocean, sea, lake and water simply, as Sanscrit mira "ocean, sea," (Pritchard) Latin mare, Germanic meer, Sclav [Slavonic] morie, Dalmatian more, Icelandic mar, Teutonic maere and maere, Cornish mor, Armoric mar, mor and var, French mer, Bohemian more, Slavonic Polish morze, Gothic marisaiv, "a pool," Dutch maras, French marais, English morass "a marsh," Tamoulic mari "rain," Arabic mara, "to spring or spout as water," Arab marakv "a lake," old Saxon mars, merse, mere "a lake," hence Windermere and Mersey, Dutch and Teutonic meer "a pool" (Armstrong).

These analogies are unquestionably striking, yet there are others which, though much less apparently obvious, have been noticed by philologists and are not undeserving of attention. Thus if it were stated that the German wasser and the English water were allied to the words already given, it would probably at first appear absurd; and yet it will be shown that this analogy is far from being improbable.

The English water and the German wasser have been derived with every appearance of certainty from the Greek *udor* i.e. fudor, which appears to be cognate with the Sanscrit udum, and the Latin udus-a-um and unda, but this Greek word is obviously the same as the old Celtic dur "water," with a prefix; and this Celtic word dur is as plainly but an abbreviation for sound's sake of the Irish dobhar or tobar or the Welsh dwvyr, plural duvrau, which is cognate with the Sanscrit dabra "sea;" and in this form the word is preserved in the Irish *dobhar-chu* "an otter" or "water dog" and the Welsh dyver-gi and other compounds.

From these analogies it would not perhaps be too much to conclude that the Irish word bir preserves the root from which so many words have been derived, as unquestionably, if its relationship to those apparent cognate words be allowed, it is obviously the more ancient form of the word; for b has never taken the place of m in such formations, though as already observed b has been constantly softened into m; and as those cognates are found not only in all the languages of Indo-European origin, but also and more directly in those of the Semitic stock, it may perhaps be regarded as not peculiar to either but as one of the primitive words common to the various members of the great human family.

But be this as it may, the question is not undeserving the attention of the learned, and may possibly contribute some valuable light to the history of the formation of language now prosecuted with so much success, as to lead to the most important results in tracing the general history of mankind.

Notes on Townland Names in Lower Cumber by John O'Donovan and George Petrie

Notes on Townland Names

Ardground: "high ground."
 Ballynamore: Baile-na-maor.
 Ballygroll: [blank].
 Brackfield: Gort Breac.
 Brockaogh: Brocach "badgery."
 Clonmakane: Cluain McCathain.
 Crossballycormick: Cros Bhaile Chormaic.
 Ervey: Erveach, Airbheach, Oirbheach "ploughed or furrowed ground;" Ervey or Erveach "cultivatable."
 Fawney: Fanaidhe "declivities."
 Gortinreid: Gortin Reid.
 Gosheden: Geosadan; Sliabh Kirk is in this townland.
 Highmoor: is a high moor, Currach Ard.
 Killennan: Kill Fheannain; see Kill Fhionain, county Limerick.
 Killaloo: Kill Dalua; has a church.
 Kildoag: perhaps Cuil Damhoige.
 Lackagh: Leacain; it is a sloping land.
 Legaghory: Lag-a-choirre.
 Lettermire: Letir Maoir.
 Lettershendony: Letir Seanduine.
 Listress: Liosatreassa; has no "lios."
 Mullaboy: Mullach Buidhe; Sliabh Buck is in this townland.
 Oughtagh: Uchtach is a "rising ground."
 Oghill: "yew wood," Youghall, Eo Choill.
 Slaughtmanus: Leacht Mhaghnais; Carrag-a-stuke is in this townland.
 Strathall: probably Sruthaill, the name given in Munster to those half-cliffs on the banks of rivers; this townland rises rather abruptly over the Faughan.
 Tamnaherin: [blank].
 Tamnamore: [blank].
 Tamnareagh: this appears to be mountainy.
 Toneduff: Ton Dubh; a mountainy tract on the south end of this townland would give rise to the name.

Derivation of Townland Names

Ardground: written Ardgrowe on Thomas Phillips'

Parish of Cumber

map. It is Ardgriffin in the Book of Survey and Distribution, and Ardgrown by Sampson. The meaning of the latter part is uncertain. It might be *Ard Creamh Fhiadhain* "or of wild garlic hill." [Insert addition: Skinners' lands].

Ballynamore: called in the charter Ballenemoyre one balliboe of land, and Ballinamore by Sampson. It is called *Baile-na-maor* i.e. "the townland of the stewards or overseers" by the natives. *Maor*, which is evidently of the same origin with the English word mayor, and which anciently meant the steward who collected the chieftain's rents, is now applied by the natives of the mountains of Derry and Tyrone to a herdsman or shepherd, which is a great debasement of the word. The Scotch family of Stewart are called by this name in the Irish Annals and genealogical tracts. For the meaning of *maor*, see O'Flaherty's *Ogygia*.

[Insert addition: Ballynemoyre (James I), Ballinemoire (Cromwell), Ballinemoyre (Charles II), [all] Charter of Derry; Ballene Moyre, Sir Thomas Phillips' map (Goldsmiths' Company); Ballenemore, Book of Survey and Distribution (Goldsmiths)].

Ballygroll: the signification is obscure. It is better not to explain such names as are obscure than to disgrace the *science* of etymology by giving a visionary explanation. O'Reilly thought it might signify *Baile Grothail* "gravel town."

[Insert addition: Bollegroll, Sir Thomas Phillips (Grocers' Company); Ballegroll, Book of Survey and Distribution (Grocers)].

Brackfield: called in the charters by the more correct name of Brackmoy. Here is an instance of an Irish name being half translated, the Irish moy "a plain" being translated to "field." The Irish natives of the valley of Glencankeine in Ballynascreen remember that the original name of this place was *Breac Mhagh*, which means "spotted or mottled plain," a name which is truly descriptive of its surface. The appearance of the moor of Brackfield is described by Mr Sampson thus: "Entering on Brackfield moor, in order to trace back the passage of the slack which opens at Muff glen to the north west, you pass, in the first place, over the barren moor of Brackfield. The stony substances occasionally coming above the surface of the bog are all schist <shist> and stratified, except in the instances of those detached fragments, which are bleached on the surface like bones whitened by the weather. There are traces of ancient timber." (*Memoir of the chart and survey of Londonderry*).

[Insert addition: The small proportion of Brackmoy (James I and Charles II), Brockmoy (Cromwell), [both] Charters of Derry; Brackmoy, being one balliboe of land, Charters of Derry; the small proportion of Brackmoy, Charters of Derry; Brackmoy, Sir Thomas Phillips' map (Skinners' lands); Brockway, Book of Survey and Distribution (Skinners)].

Brockagh: called in the charters Brackagh one balliboe of land. For the signification of this name see Ardnabrocky in Clondermot parish. [Insert addition: Brackagh (James I and Charles II), Brackhah (Cromwell), [both] Charters of Derry; Brackah, Sir Thomas Phillips' map (Grocers' Company); Broaka, Book of Survey and Distribution (Grocers)].

Derivation of Townland Names

Clonmakane: does not occur in any of the ancient documents. It is called Clunmakane by Sampson. The meaning is evidently *Cluain-mhic-Chathain*, "the clon of the son of Cahan or Kane." For the meaning of the word *cluain*, see townland of Clooney in the parish of Clondermot. It is found variously anglicised clon, claon, cloane, clone, cloyne and even clen in the old English documents relating to Ireland, but on the Ordnance maps it has been attempted to make clon the standard, unless where custom has too firmly established the contrary. *Cathan*, which was the name of the progenitor of the O'Kanes (i.e. nepotes Cahani or Cahanides), was common in Ireland as the proper name of a man, and signifies a warrior (bellator), it being formed from *cath* "a battle," similar to *Cathal, Cathmhaol*, and *Cathaoir*, and similiar to the Welsh Cadell, which is formed from the British cad "a battle."

[Insert addition: Carlongford occurs in Sir Thomas Phillips' map, see Mullaboy townland; Clonmakam, Sir Thomas Phillips' map (Grocers' Company); Clanvokaine, Book of Survey and Distribution (Grocers)].

Crossballycormick: does not occur in any of the old authorities. The meaning is unquestionably *Cros Bhaile Chormaic* "Cormac's cross town." Cormac is still very common in Ireland as the name of a man and now generally, but incorrectly, anglicised Charles. It is explained in *Cormac's Glossary* thus: "Cormac rectius Corbmac. Corbmac then means 'the son of the chariot.' Cormac Gelta Gaeth, one of the Lagenians, was the first so called because he was born in a chariot. The correct orthography of this name is Corbmac with a 'b' in the first syllable; non Cormac sine b scribitur." This name, like many others, was originally a soubriquet of distinguished men which afterwards became proper names among their descendants. See Verstegan's explanation of the Saxon name William.

[Insert addition: Crosballe Cormak, Sir Thomas Phillips' map (Goldsmiths' Company); Crostallcormick, Book of Survey and Distribution (Goldsmiths)].

[Insert note: Doongillen occurs in the charter, see Monnehanegan, townland in Faughanvale parish].

Ervey: seems to be the balliboe of land called Irremach in the charters. If it were at all allowable to conjecture, one would be inclined to dispose that this is a corruption of *An Dhair Mhagh*, a name which exists in other parts of Ireland, and which was translated Campus roborum by Bede and Roboretum campi by Adamnam. *Ar Mhagh* means "arable land," but the former is much more probable and more borne out by the existence of native oak timber in the townland. The meaning of the greater part of these townlands is evident and unquestionable, but some are sometimes so shortened and anglicised that etymology can do no more than offer a feeble conjecture. Throughout this Memoir, however, it has been thought better to offer no conjecture on obscure names than to indulge in anything like visionary etymologies, which have brought the writings of the Irish authors of the last century into so much disrepute. [Insert addition: Irreniegh (James I), Irremeigh (Cromwell), Irremegh (Charles II), [all] Charters of Derry; Enie, Sir Thomas Phillips' map (Grocers' Company); Ervey, Book of Survey and Distribution (Grocers)].

Fawney: called in the charter Nefawney one balliboe of land. The meaning is *Fanadh* "a declivity." The name in the charter has the plural article *na* "they" prefixed and means *Na Fanaidhe* "the declivities." [Insert addition: Nefawnat, Sir Thomas Phillips' map (Goldsmiths' Company); Nefawney (James I and Cromwell), Nefawny (Charles II), [last 3] Charters of Derry; Ffawnin, Book of Survey and Distribution (Goldsmiths)].

Derivation of Townland Names

Gortinreid: called in the ancient authorities Gortindrohid, which unquestionably means Gort-an-droichid "gort or field of the bridge." Droichid, "a bridge," is now generally pronounced draid in Ulster. The correct orthography of this would be Gortindraid. [Insert addition: Gortendrohid (James I), Gortindronhide (Cromwell), Gortendrohide (Charles II), [all] Charters of Derry, in the small proportion of Kildonan; Gortnarede (Grocers) in Cumber parish, Book of Survey and Distribution.

It would appear that this is the townland called Gortnare on Sir Thomas Phillips' map of the Grocers' lands, yet it is possible to identify the name on Sir Thomas Petty's map with the situation of Monnaboy in Faughanvale (qv), particularly as we find mention of a Gortinary in the charter, in the same proportion of Kildonan; see Monnaboy in Faughanvale]. [Insert marginal note: This may be Monnaboy in Faughanvale, though placed by the Book of Survey in Cumber; see also Monnehanegan in Faughanvale)].

Gosheden: called Gouseden in the Down Survey and Gaussidon in Sir William Kelly's Tracts. It is called *Geosadan* by the few who speak Irish in the parish and Goshedon by Mr Sampson. *Geosadan* generally signifies "a stalk," but is used in some parts of Munster to signify the "sow thistle." It is probable that gort, bally, moy or some other word was originally prefixed to this name and that it meant "field, plain or townland of the stalks or thistles."

[Insert addition: Neither this name Gosheden nor Legachory occurs on Sir Thomas Phillips' map (plantations of lands belonging to the Skinners), but on that part of the map on which they would appear are marked the names Tully, Letrimkenat, Formoyle and Moy Coshell. Tullie, Book of Survey and Distribution (Skinners); Tullie, (James I), Tulla, (Cromwell and Charles II), [both] being one balliboe of land, Charters of Derry, identified by situation with the Tully on Sir Thomas Phillips' map. Gousidone half towneland, forfeited by Gilaglass McGory O'Chan, leased to Allexander Thomkins and Edward Carey Esquires, [both] Book of Survey and Distribution].

Highmoor: this must be a translation of Currach Ard.

Killennan: called in the charters Kildonan one balliboe of land, and Kileenan by Sampson. The meaning is probably *Coill Dhonain* "Donan's woods," or *Cill Donain* "Donan's church." There was a celebrated saint of this name who lived early in the 7th century. [Insert addition: Kilonell, Sir Thomas Phillips' map (Goldsmiths' Company); Killonan, Book of Survey and Distribution (Goldsmiths); the small proportion of Killdonan (James I), Kildonan (Cromwell), Kildenan (Charles II), [last 3] Charters of Derry, being one balliboe of land, the small proportion of Kildonan lying in the barony or precinct of Armagh (Charters of Derry)].

Derivation of Townland Names

Killaloo: does not occur in any of the ancient

Parish of Cumber

authorities. It seems to be the same name as Killaloe in Munster. If so it must signify Cill Dalua "the church of St Dalua," the deanery of St Bernard. [Insert addition: Liskillaleigh (James I), Lisskillaleigh (Cromwell); Liskellaleigh (Charles II), being one balliboe of land, occurs in the Charters of Derry, mentioned between Kilkattin and Laghtmanus; Killeloy, Sir Thomas Phillips' map (Skinners' lands).

The portion of Killaloe townland marked on Sampson's map as belonging to the bishop, i.e. coloured with purple, and in which the church is situated, is called Cumber on Thomas Phillips' map; yet the townland called Cumber on Sir Thomas Phillips' map may be Cumber in the parish of Upper Cumber. The map is so incorrectly drawn that there is some difficulty in deciding: the latter opinion is more likely; see Cumber townland in Upper Cumber. Tristram Thorneton, Protestant, Killaloy, Book of Survey and Distribution].

Kildoag: called in the charter Cooledoogie one balliboe of land, and pronounced *Cul Dhubhoige* by those who speak Irish. Dabhog was a man's name in ancient Ireland. *Cul* means "the back part of a hill or mountain." [Insert addition: Cooladogh, Sir Thomas Phillips' map (Skinners' lands); Killdoge, Book of Survey and Distribution (Skinners)].

Lackagh: called in the charter Lackah [insert superscript: Lackagh] one balliboe of land. *Leacach* and *leacain* are topographically used in Ireland and in the Highlands of Scotland to signify the side of a hill or mountain, steep shelvy ground, a name which is very applicable to this townland. [Insert addition: Lackah, Sir Thomas Phillips' map (Skinners' lands); Laccogh, Book of Survey and Distribution (Skinners)].

Legaghory: called in the Down Survey by the more correct name of Legecory, and Legachory by Sampson. It is called *Lag-a-choire*, i.e. "hollow of the cauldron" by the natives, who preserve a foolish legend touching the origin of the name, about Finn MacCooil and the enchantress Mave of Croghan. There is a very remarkable hollow in this townland which is the feature called *Lag-a-choire* where, according to tradition, Mave used to boil in a cauldron the venison stolen from the Fingallian hunters by the power of magic; but as this legend can have no foundation in truth, it may be rationally supposed that this very remarkable hollow was called *Lag-a-choire* from its resemblance to a cauldron.

There are many townlands of the same name, and containing similiar hollows, to be found in the province of Ulster. As it is impracticable to represent the guttural sound of [c aspirated] in every instance, it would be better, as in the Down Survey, to write this with a c hard, thus Lega *c*urry, than to disguise the latter part of this compound by throwing in gh.

Derivation of Townland Names

Lettermire: called in the Down Survey Lettermoyre, and Lettermoyer by Mr Sampson. *Litir* forms the first of countless of places in Ireland, but still no Irish authority has been discovered for the exact meaning of it. O'Reilly has translated it "a retreat" in a manuscript explanation of the names of this parish, but no authority has been found to bear him out in that explanation, and he has committed so many blunders that his bare word cannot be received in deciding upon the meaning of so important a topographical word.

Some think it means *Leth Tir*, i.e. "half a tir or territory," and others will have it a corruption of *Leth Triocha*, i.e. "half-cantred or barony;" but as letter is found in the names of townlands only, it cannot be assumed that it ever meant so large a tract. Colgan mentions this word frequently throughout his works, as Letter Othrain, Letter Chatuise, but he does not translate it in any part of his printed works. The word is explained in *Cormac's Glossary* as if it meant "half moory or marshy land," thus "*Letir, .i. tirm a leth agus flich an leth naile*, "letir, i.e. dry its half and wet the other half." Whether this last explanation is or is not the true meaning of this word, or whether it refers to this word at all, must now be decided from the localities of the townlands called Letter.

[Insert marginal note: Peter Connell in his dictionary explains leitir as signifying "hillside, a steep ascent or descent, a cliff," and states that the word has the same meaning in Welsh; and his explanation seems to be borne out by the Dinnseanchus account of Tara in which the word occurs twice, thus: *Lecht Con agus Cethen isin leitir i comharddus ratha righ siar* "the monument of Con and Cethenn are situated in the leitir in the neighbourhood of Rathree to the west." The hill of Tara slopes almost immediately to the west of Rathree].

Moyer or mire: the latter part of this compound is an anglicising of *maoir* i.e. "of the steward or overseer;" see Ballynamore townland.

[Insert addition: Littermoyr, Sir Thomas Phillips' map (Skinners' lands); Lettremoore, Book of Survey and Distribution (Skinners)].

Lettershendony: does not occur in any of the ancient documents. In Sampson's Memoir this name is explained Litter Sion Danach "the solemnity of the valiant leagues," but as there is not a word in the compound that signifies either solemnity, valiant or leagues, that explanation must be rejected. It is called in the country *Litir Seanduine*, i.e. "the old man's letter" (see Lettermire), but is now impossible to trace out the cause of the original imposition of such a name. [Insert addition: Littershandeny, Sir Thomas Phillips' map (Grocers' Company); John Gifford, Protestant, Letteshanne, Book of Survey and Distribution].

Listress: called in the charter Lisdrasse one balliboe of land. The meaning is unquestionably *Lios Dreasach* "the fort of brambles." Such names are very common in Irish topographical nomenclature, as Lisnaskeagh "fort of thorns," Rath-na-ndealg idem. It has been found that whenever the ancient names of forts are preserved, they are commonly formed from rath, lios or dun, and the name of some Pagan or early Christian proprietor. [Insert addition: Lissdrass, Charter of Derry; Lisdras, Sir Thomas Phillips' map (Grocers' Company); Lisstrass, Book of Survey and Distribution (Grocers)].

Derivation of Townland Names

Mullaboy: called in the charter Mullahboy one balliboe of land, and Malaboy by Sampson. The meaning of this name is *Mullach Buidhe* "yellow summit." The name given by Sampson means *Mala Buidhe* "yellow brow or brae," but as the summit of Slieve Buck (height 822 feet) is in this townland, the first part of the compound must be *mullach*, "summit;" and as it is supported by the authority of the charter, it has been adopted on the Ordnance map. The termination *buidhe* "yellow," which so frequently forms the last syllables of names of places in Ireland, is pronounced in the original language bwee, but as it has been so invariably anglicised boy in the names of men and places in all the old English records relating to Ireland, it has been thought the best spelling to make general on the Ordnance maps.

[Insert addition: Malloboy, Book of Survey and Distribution (Grocers); Mullaboy being one balliboe of land, Charters of Derry; Mallaboy, Sir Thomas Phillips' map (Grocers' Company). On the same map between Lettershendony, Malaboy, Ervey and the site of Ballinamore (see map of Goldsmiths' Company), Sir Thomas Phillips places a townland called Carlongford (cannot be identified). Carralafort, Book of Survey and Distribution (Grocers), immediately after Mallaboy and before Listress].

Oughtagh: called Nahautowhy on Sir Thomas Phillips' map and Ultagh in the Book of Survey and Distribution. It is an anglicising of the Irish *Ochtach* which is an adjective dervived from *ocht* "the breast" and signifying having breasts or hills resembling the breast. The word *ocht* "a breast," frequently enters into the names of townlands and alludes to a peculiar feature of a hill or mountain situated in them. It will be shown in the course of this Memoir that places have received names from a similiarity of some striking feature in them with every member of the human frame; see Oughtymoyle in Magilligan. [Insert addition: Nahautowhy, Sir Thomas Phillips' map (Grocers' Company); Ultagh, Book of Survey and Distribution (Grocers)].

Oghill: written in the charter and called Oghill one balliboe of land, and Oehill by Sampson. Called in Irish *Eochaill*, which is also the name of countless places in Ireland, of which the best known and most celebrated is *Eochaill*, now Youghall, in the county of Cork. No authority has been yet discovered for the meaning of this very general name, but is more probable that these places were called Eo Chaill which (si vocis etymon spectes) signifies "a yew wood," from an abundance of that ancient tree now nearly extinct in Ireland.

That the word *eo*, which is evidently of the same origin with the English "yew," was anciently used in Ireland as well as, or perhaps previously to *iur* or *iubhar*, the present name of that tree, can be directly proved: *Eo Rosa* i.e. "the yew of Ross" was a celebrated yew tree which stood to the east of Drumbar; is recorded to have been prostrated by a storm in the year 665; see *Ogygia*; and the word *eo* is explained by O'Clery and other glossographists by *iubhar*, the present Irish name for that tree. [Insert addition: Ouill, Sir Thomas Phillips' map (Grocers' Company); Edward Lewise, Protestant, Oghill, Book of Survey and Distribution].

Slaghtmanus: called in the charter by the more correct name of Laghtmannus one balliboe of land, and Slaughtmanus, Slahtmanus and Slaghmanus by Sampson, who translates it "the place of the death of Manus." The meaning is unquestionably *Sleacht* (more correctly *Leacht*)-*Mhaghnuis*, i.e. "Manus' monument," a name derived from a very remarkable monument in the townland. It is strange that *leacht* (which is used throughout Munster, Leinster and Connaght to

Parish of Cumber

signify an honorary monument of any kind, a pile of stones or an ancient token with a heap of stones around its foot, erected or planted in memory of any person), is in this and the adjoining counties called *sleacht*, a form of the word which does not appear in any Irish writings except *Cormac's Glossary*, in which *tamhlachta* is explained *tamhsleachta* "a cutting off by the plague."

The tradition in every part of Ireland is that the *leacht Ultonice sleacht* was erected on the spot where some person met a violent or unexpected death. *Sleacht* means "cutting down or felling" when it is applied to timber, and "cutting or slaying" when applied to men, and may be the most original form of this word. *Leacht*, however, is the form which prevails in Irish books and manuscripts, and it is curious that this townland of Slaghtmanus, as also those of Slaghtaverty and Slaghtneill, are called Laghtmanus, Laghtaverty and Leaghtneill in the charter or in the Down Survey; see townlands of the parishes of Errigal and Maghera.

Maghnus was a man's name borrowed by the Irish from their intermarriage with the Danes about the beginning of the 10th century. It first appears in the Irish Annals at the year 973 as a name of a Dane, but henceforward it occurs frequently as a name of Danes and of Milesians descended from Danish mothers. It is probable that this name was derived from the Latin and adopted as a cognomen by the Scandinavian rovers after they had pushed their conquests into France and other countries where that language was known. This name was anciently and is at present very common in the families of the O'Kanes and the O'Donnells. If Slaghtmanus be the original name of this cromlech, it cannot be of pagan origin as the name Manus was not in use in Ireland before the 9th century.

[Insert addition: Laghtmanus (James I and Charles II), Laghmanus (Cromwell), [both] Charters of Derry; Slatmanus, Sir Thomas Phillips' map (Grocers' Company); Matthew Babbington, Protestant, Slaghtmanus, Book of Survey and Distribution. [Insert query: Is the cromlech in this townland the object which is called *leacht* or *sleacht*? Perhaps there is another in the form of a thorn, with a heap of stones around its foot?]

Derivation of Townland Names

Strathall: does not appear in any of the ancient authorities. It is called Strathail by Sampson. For the meaning of strath, see Stradreagh in the townland of Clondermot. Hall, the latter part, is obscure. *Srath Chathail* "Cahal's strath or holme" would approach the name given by Sir Thomas Phillips. [Insert addition: Shrahekall, Sir Thomas Phillips' map (Goldsmiths' Company); Straitall alias half of Golissidan, Book of Survey and Distribution (James O'Quin, Protestant)].

Tamnaherin: does not appear in any of the old documents. It is called Tamneyeerin by Mr Sampson. The meaning is *Tamhnach-a-chaorthainn* "flat of the rowans or wild mountain ash;" see Tamnymore in Clondermot. [Insert addition: Tawnyherrin, Sir Thomas Phillips' map (Grocers' Company); Tawnarine, Book of Survey and Distribution (Grocers)].

Tamnamore: called in the charter Tawnamore one balliboe of land, and Tamnymore by Sampson. For the meaning of this name see Tamnymore in Clondermot parish. The Irish word *tamhnach* "a flat" is pronounced taunagh (the au like the German au), but as custom has, in many instances, restored the original sound of the m in the anglicised form of the term, it has been thought advisable to make tamny the general standard of the word on the Ordnance map, unless in very Irish places where the aspirate sound of the [m aspirated] is too well established, in which case it has been made tawny or tawnagh, with every deference, however, to the pronunciation and established orthography in each district. Indeed the only change that has been made on the Ordnance map is that a standard anglicised form has been established for each important word or termination such as moy, drum, ard; and the terminations rae, duff, bane, reagh have been reduced to as fixed a standard as custom would lawfully permit.

[Insert addition: Tawnaghmor, Sir Thomas Phillips' map (Goldsmiths' Company); Tawnimore, Book of Survey and Distribution (Tristram Thorneton, Protestant)].

Tamnyreagh: does not occur in any of the ancient documents. It is called *Tamhnach Riach* or "greyish flat" by the Irish. For the meaning of *riach*, see Edenreagh in the parish of Clondermot. [Insert addition: Tawnyreagh, Sir Thomas Phillips' map (Grocers' Company); Sarah Goodwine, Protestant, Tawnereagh, Book of Survey and Distribution].

Toneduff: called in the charter Tonduffe one balliboe of land, and Toneduf by Sampson. This townland is called by the Irish *Toin Dubh*, which means "black bottom." The Irish word *toin* is the common word for the podex, but when applied to land it has two different meanings, namely the bottom or lower part of a place, and a round hill. In the latter sense is to be understood *Toin Re*

Gaoith, i.e. "hill to the wind," now Tanderagee in the county of Armagh, and *Toin Re Go* "hill to the sea," now Tanrego in the county of Sligo.

Dubh, the latter part of the compound, has been most generally anglicised duff in the names of men and places in all the old English records relating to Ireland, but the [b aspirated] is pronounced very soft in some parts of Ulster, so that it was found impracticable to make duff the standard; therefore duff and doo have been adopted on the Ordnance map, duff being used where the pronunciation is hard and doo where it is soft. Dhu is rejected as altogether foreign to English and Irish orthography. In pronouncing the names of places in Ireland when they are anglicised, they must be pronounced according to the powers of English consonants. In the original Irish the consonants are either thick or liquid, and it is impracticable and even incorrect to attempt to represent their sounds by any combination of English ones.

[Insert addition: Tonduff (James I), Clonduffe (Cromwell), Tonduffe (Charles II), [all] Charters of Derry; Tonduff, Sir Thomas Phillips' map (Skinners' lands); Tonduffe, Book of Survey and Distribution (Skinners).

Minor Place-Names

Minor place-names in the parish not being townlands.

Craigastuke: called by the Irish *Creag-a-tseabhaic* "the hawk's rock." This should be spelled Craigatoke; see Cregnashoke in Ballynascreen parish.

Faughan river: this river is called Fochmhuin in the *Tripartite life of St Patrick*; thus speaking of 7 churches erected by that saint in its neighbourhood: "venit inde ad Dagart in agro de Magh-dula et per septem hebdomadas circa flumen Fochmuine regionesque adjacentes moram contraxit." Colgan in a note upon this clearly shows the Fochmhuin to be the present Faughan. "Flumen Fochmuine est in regione de Oireacht-y-Chathain et diocesis Derensis ab ipsa civitate Derensi duobus circiter millibus passuum distans;" *Triad. Thau.*

Meenyarnet burn: *Sruth Mine Ui Artniada*, i.e. "the stream of Meenyarnet" or "Arnet's misk." For the meaning of meeny, see Minegallagher Glebe in Faughanvale; and for arnet, see Ballyarnet in Templemore parish.

Burntollet river: this is a hybrid compound of the Teutonic word bourn which Verstigan explains "a water springing out of the earth also the brook issuing thereof," and its original Irish name of *tuille* "a flood."

Slieve Buck: called by the Irish *Sliabh Boc* i.e. "the mountain of the bucks or roes."

Slieve Kirk: called by Sampson Sliave Kark, by the Irish *Sliabh Circe* "the mountain of the hen," so called from the *cearca fraoigh*, i.e. "heath hens or grouse."

The Ness: is a corruption of the Irish word *eas* "a waterfall or cataract;" the n prefixed in the English is the n of the Irish article *an*.

Notes on Name: Cumber

[Insert addition by G. Petrie: The word cumber, the ancient name of the 2 parishes now distinguished as Upper and Lower, has been explained by Mr O'Reilly as signifying "a valley," but this interpretation appears to be too indefinite, the more literal signification of the word being simply "a meeting of rivers;" and consequently that it is only applicable to valleys in which one or more glens or rivers meet].

[Insert addition: The church of Cumber (James I and Charles II), Cumber (Cromwell), [both] Charters of Derry. [Insert query: This or Upper Cumber)].

Notes on Townland Names in Upper Cumber by John O'Donovan

Notes on Townland Names

All [Alla] Upper and Lower: woody.

Altaghony: Alt-a-dhonaidhe, Alt-a-conaigh, conach.

Ballyartan: Baile-Ui-Artain.

Ballycallaghan: Ballycallaghan.

Ballyholly: Buaile Salach.

Ballymaclanigan: [blank].

Ballyrory: [blank].

Barr Cregg: barr also means "a piece of land running into a bog or moor."

Binn: Beann.

Carnanbane: "white hill."

Carnanreagh: brackish, "grey hills."

Claudy <Clady>: Cladach.

Coolnacolpach: [blank].

Cregg: Craig.

Cumber: a remarkable meeting of rivers here.

Dunady: has no dun.

Dungorkin: has a fine dun.

Glenlough: has no lough.

Gortilea: Gort-an-fleadha.

Gortnaskey: Gortnasceach.

Parish of Cumber

Gortnaran: "of the spades."
Gortsgreachan: "screeching."
Kilgort: Caolghort is a narrow townland.
Killcaltan: Cill Chatain.
Killy-corr: Coill-Ui-Chorr.
Kinculbrack: terminates in a remarkable brack, cuil to the north east.
Kilculmagrandall: [blank].
Letterlougher: Letir Luachra.
Lear: Laghar; the laghar or fork is formed by Glen Doalt and another nameless glen.
Lettermuck: "a litter of pigs."
Ling: Laidheng "the border of the sea;" this townland is skirted by a river on the west.
Lios Bunny, a dirty name.
Mulderg: Mullach Dearg, "red top hill."
Raspberry Hill: [blank].
Sallawilly: is high ground, *Sal-a-mhullaigh* "heel of the hill."
Stranagalwilly: Srath-na-Gallbhuaile.
Teenacht: [blank].
Tiriechter: Tiriochtar.
Tullintrain: "hill of the brave."

Minor Place-Names

Craigartake: townland of Slaughtmanus.
Burntollet: falls into the Faughan in the townland of Brackfield, Lower Cumber.
Sliabh Buck: townland of Ballygroll.
Sliabh Kirk: townland of Gosheden.
Ness waterfall: on the Burntollet, between the townlands of Ouchtach and Listress.
Doalt glen: townland of Lear.
Glenrandall river: falls into the Faughan in the townland of Cumber.

Derivation of Townland Names

Alla Upper and Lower: called in the Down Survey Alla, arable pasture and mountain. Called by the Irish *Allaidh*, a word which according to the best Irish authority signifies "a forest or wilderness." Colgan translates the word by the Latin "saltus" (*Triad. Thau.*) and O'Cleary says that the wolf was called *madra allaidh*, from his being an inhabitant of the woods. [Insert addition: George Corke, Alla, Book of Survey and Distribution].

Altaghoney: does not occur in any of the ancient documents. It is called Altahoney and Altnahoney by Sampson and *Alt-a-chonaidh* by the Irish natives, who understand it to mean "glen of firewood." For the correct meaning of alt, see townlands of Clondermot, no.1 Altnagelvin. *Conadh* is used in every part of Ireland to signify "firewood" or "decayed timber." [Insert addition: Altchoney, Sir Thomas Phillips' map (Skinners' lands); Lieutenant-Colonel Michael Beresford, Protestant, Aldecunne, Book of Survey and Distribution].

Ballyartan: called in the charter "Balliartan one balliboe of land, Ballyarten by Sampson, Ballyarton in most modern authorities and *Baile-Ui-Artain* by the Irish natives. The meaning is "O'Hartan's town," but no such family name exists at present in the county. 2 ancient families of the name existed in Ireland, one in Thomond and the other in Leinster (*Book of Lecan*), and the MacArtans of Kinelarty in the county of Down have derived their name from a progenitor of the name Artan, which is a diminutive of the proper name *Art*, now generally anglicised Arthur. As none of these families, however, have been recorded to have existed here, it is probable that the name was given in comparatively modern times when many Irish families fled from the south to the northern chiefs.
[Insert addition: Ballyartan (James I and Cromwell), Balliartan (Charles II), [both] Charters of Derry; Ballyarton, Sir Thomas Phillips' map (Skinners' lands); Lieutenant-Colonel Michael Beresford, Protestant, Balleharton, Book of Survey and Distribution].

Ballycallaghan: not in the charter (Ballyfallaghan?). It is called by the Irish natives *Baile-Ui-Cheallachain*, i.e. "O'Callaghan's town." It might be O'Keileachan of Oriel. This is another instance of a southern name entering into the name of a townland in the north. It can be proved historically that many families emigrated from the south to the northern province in the beginning of the reign of Elizabeth. [Insert addition: Ballikellaghan (James I), Ballikilligan (Cromwell), Ballykillaggan being one balliboe of land (Charles II), [all] Charters of Derry; Ballykillohan, Sir Thomas Phillips' map (Skinners' lands)].

Ballyholly: called in the charter Boylisallagh one balliboe of land. Called *Baile Shaliagh* by the natives, who understand it means "townland of the dirty man," but as the charter makes it Boylisallagh, it is more than probable that the ancient name was *Buaile Salach*, i.e. "dirty bolie or cow shed;" see "bolie" in Clondermot. [Insert addition: Boylysallagh (James I and Charles II), Boylesallagh (Cromwell), [both] Charters of Derry; Ballehally, Book of Survey and Distribution (Fishmongers)].

Ballymaclanigan: does not appear in the ancient records. It is called by Irish natives *Baile-MhicLannagain*, i.e. "MacLanigan's town." Of the origin of this family, see MacFirbis' *Pedi-*

grees. [Insert addition: Mrs Elizabeth Holland, Protestant, BallemcClainegan, Book of Survey and Distribution; Balleclannigan, Book of Survey and Distribution (Skinners)].

Ballyrory: does not appear in the old documents. It is called by the Irish natives *Baile Ruaidhri* i.e. "Rory's town," a name which it certainly derived from some ancient proprietor. *Ruaidhri*, a man's name, anciently and at the present day very common in Ireland, and the same as the Scandinavian Rutheric, is now variously anglicised Roderic, Rory and Roger, but now most generally the last. It is probable that the Irish borrowed this name from the Danes, as it does not occur in their annals previously to the year 780, when the Danes were certainly among them. The following names were also borrowed from the Northmen: Randal, Ranulph, Roolo, Amlaff or Olaff, Sitric, Ivor, Blacker, Hammond, Harold, Otter, Broder, Magnus, Godfrey, Goffrey or Gorry. [Insert addition: Lieutenant Thomas Skipton, Protestant, Ballrory, Book of Survey and Distribution].

Barr Cregg or Barr of Cregg: by the barr of a townland the inhabitants of this and the surrounding counties meaning the mountain land belonging to it. The Irish word *barr* signifies a "top" or "summit;" see *Acta Sanctorum*, where it is translated "vertex." See Cregg townland, of which this [is] the mountainous part.

Derivation of Townland Names

Binn: called in the Down Survey Binhenry and represented [as] arable pasture mountain, with a lough of 4 acres leased to George Corke gentleman, and by Sampson Byn Upper and Lower. The Irish word *beann*, always pronounced *binn* in the province of Ulster, is now understood to mean "the steep face of a hill, the apex of a mountain" and "the gable end of a house;" but the most general meaning of the word in Ulster has been ascertained from the places into whose names it enters as "the steep face of a hill or mountain." It looks to the same origin as the Welsh pin and the Latin pinna, and has been translated pinna by O'Sullevan Beare; thus in *Historia Catholicum*. fol 147, Beaun Boruib, now Benburb in Tyrone, he translates Pinna Superba, by which he understands "proud or superb pinnacle," a name which is truly descriptive of the situation of that famous castle. Dr O'Connor in his *Annals of Tigernach* translates it "vertex." On the Ordnance maps of Ulster this has been anglicised either Bin or Ben accordingly as custom favoured either, but most generally Bin when in compounds and Binn when simple. Henry, the adjunct in the Down Survey, must have been the name of some ancient proprietor, it being a family name of the Kinel Owen located in this neighbourhood. [Insert addition: George Corke, Binhenry, Book of Survey and Distribution].

Carnanbane: does not occur in the ancient documents. It is called *Carnan Ban* by the Irish natives, who understand it to mean "white heap." *Carnan* is a diminutive of *carn*, a heap of anything, but generally applied to a sepulchral heap of stones in this and the other northern counties (see Carn in Clondermot parish). In the Irish language diminutives are formed by adding the terminations *an*, *og* and *in*, but still there are some words in the language with these terminations that are not *now* taken in a diminutive sense, as *cainneog*, a churn, which is a diminutive of *cann*, a can, and yet the sense is diametrically opposite; see Ardnaguinnog townland in Faughanvale. [Insert query: Could this be the Carravan of the said Thomas Phillips' map (Skinners' land)? Does not agree in situation. Carnanbane, Book of Survey and Distribution (Skinners)].

Carnanreagh: called Carne-reagh one balliboe of land in the charter, and Carnan by Sampson. [Insert note: Not this Carnanreagh, but Carrowreagh in Tamlaght Finlagan parish; see charter]. It is called by the natives *Carnan Riach*, i.e. "greyish carn." The adjectives *ban* "white" and *riach* "brownish" were added to the names of these 2 last townlands for the sake of distinction, and it is probable that carnan is the name of 2 hills in these townlands and not of any sepulchral monuments. [Insert addition: Lieutenant Thomas Skipton, Protestant, Carrnanreagh, Book of Survey and Distribution].

Claudy: called Cladogh on the Down Survey, Clady by Beaufort, Seward and Carlisle, and Clady and Claudy by Sampson. Called by the Irish natives *Claidighe*. (The Irish word *cladach* or *claideach*, which seems to look to the same origin with the British word cluith, now clyde (see shwyd), is now understood in Ireland to signify "the strand of the sea, lake or river," and this townland must have received its name from its situation on the bank of the River Faughan. This place is generally called Cumber Clady to distinguish it from Clady in the River Finn in the county of Tyrone. [Insert addition: George Corke, Cregg and Cladogh, Book of Survey and Distribution].

Derivation of Townland Names

Coolnacolpagh: does not appear in the ancient

Parish of Cumber

documents. It is called Cuilnagolpah by Sampson, but *Cul-na-gcupach* by the natives, who understand this name to signify "back place of the slothful persons." *Cupach*, the latter part of this compound, is a local word, but certainly the same as *cobuch*, which in the south of Ireland means "a churl." This interpretation of name will appear strange to several, but to those who are acquainted with the names bestowed by the ancient Irish on men and places, it will by no means appear etymological speculation. Mr Sampson has certainly misnamed this townland, and his mistake has been perpetuated on the Ordnance map. The name should be anglicised Coolnagoopagh, which is the only form and pronunciation understood in the country. It is probable that Mr Sampson was induced to alter the latter part of the name from the odd interpretation given of it by the natives, but no such liberty should be taken with a name which custom had so long and so firmly established.

Cregg: in the Down Survey Cregg and Cladogh are laid down as one denomination and represented as "arable pasture and mountaine." It is called by the natives *Creag*, a name which is always applied to craggy land. [Insert addition: George Corke, Cregg and Cladogh, Book of Survey and Distribution].

Cumber: called Coomer in an inquisition taken at Cloghtel, called in the Down Survey Cumber alias Ballintemple and represented as arable pasture and mountain. For the meaning of Cumber, see the name of the parish. [Insert addition: The church of Cumber (James I and Charles II), Cumber (Cromwell), [both] Charters of Derry; Cumber, Sir Thomas Phillips' map (Skinners' lands), see Killaloo townland in Lower Cumber; George Corke, Cumber alias Ballintemple, Book of Survey and Distribution].

Ballintemple: in Irish *Baile-an-teampuill*; the alias name in the Down Survey signifies "church town," so called from the situation of the ancient parish church in it.

Derivation of Townland Names

Dunady: called in the charter Downedie one balliboe of land, and by Sampson Duneddy. [Insert addition: Downedye, James I, Downedy, Charles II and Cromwell, [both] Charters of Derry]. It is called by the native Irish *Dun Eidigh*, i.e. "the dun or fort of Edech [insert corrected spelling: Eideach] or Eteach." Edeach or Eiteach was the proper name of a man in ancient Ireland and the ancestor of the MacEtighs (Macedys), a family of the Kinel Owen who were located in the barony of Keenaght. See Annals of Derry at the year 11 [blank: absence of last 2 figures queried], where it is recorded of this family to have robbed the altar of the cathedral church of Derry. [Insert addition: Doneydy, Sir Thomas Phillips' map (Skinners' lands); Downedee, Book of Survey and Distribution (Skinners)].

Dungorkin: called in the charter Drumkarkan or Dromkarkan one balliboe of land, and by the natives *Dun Goircin*, which is probably a corruption of Dun-mhic-Orcain, "the fortress of the son of Orcan." The Magorkans, a family of the Kinel Owen, must have given name to this place. [Insert addition: Mrs Elizabeth Holland, Protestant, Dongorcan, Book of Survey and Distribution].

Glenlough: called in the charter Clonelogh one balliboe of land, and *Gleann-a-locha* by the native Irish, who understand it to mean "glen of the lake." It is probable, however, that Cluain-a-locha, "the clon or pasturage of lake," otherwise Clonelagh, would hardly have been adapted in the charter. [Insert addition: Clonelogh (James I and Charles II), Clonelagh (Cromwell), [both] Charters of Derry; Clonlogth, Sir Thomas Phillips' map (Skinners' lands); Clonlogh, Book of Survey and Distribution (Skinners)].

Gortilea: called in the charter Gortebegh one balliboe of land, and *Gort-a-fhleadha* by the native Irish, who understand it, and correctly, to mean "gort of the chicken weed;" see Fallowlea in the parishes of Faughanvale and Maghera. [Insert addition: Mrs Elizabeth Holland, Protestant (identified), Gortnally *Gort-an-fhleadha*, Book of Survey and Distribution].

Gortnaskey: not in the ancient documents. It is called *Gort-na-sceach* "the gort of the thorns." [Insert addition: Gortskeah, Sir Thomas Phillips' map (Skinners' lands); Gortneske, Book of Survey and Distribution (Skinners)].

Derivation of Townland Names

Gortnaran: called in the Down Survey Gortinera, Gortrarane by Sampson and *Gort-na-ran* by the native Irish, which means "gort of the spades." [Insert addition: Gorbierat, Sir Thomas Phillips' map (Skinners' lands); Gurteneraine, Book of Survey and Distribution (Skinners)].

Gortscreagan: called in the charter Gorescreghan [insert queried spelling: Gortscreghan?] one balliboe of land, Gortscreighan in most modern documents and *Gort Sgreachain* by the Irish natives, who understand it to mean "gort of the screeching;" see Lisnascreaghog in Errigal parish. The correct spelling of this name is Gortnascreaghan. [Insert addition: Goresecreghan (James I and Charles II), Goresecreighan (Cromwell), [both] Charters of Derry; Gortsmahan, Sir Thomas Phillips' map (Skinners' lands), see Ling; Lieutenant Thomas Skipton, Protestant, Gortskraghan, Book of Survey and Distribution].

Kilgort: does not appear in the ancient authorities. It is called more correctly Keelgort by Sampson and *Caol-ghort* by the Irish natives. It means "narrow gort or field" and should be anglicised Keelgort as Sampson has it. [Insert addition: Kildunecory [insert query: identified ?], Sir Thomas Phillips' map (Skinners' lands); Lieutenant Thomas Skipton, Protestant, Cullgort, Book of Survey and Distribution].

Kilcaltan: called in the charter Kilkaltyn one balliboe of land, Kilcattan by Sampson and *Cill Chatain* by the native Irish. It means "the church of St Catan or Catanus," who was one of the disciples of St Patrick, according to Tirechan's lists, and who is also the patron saint of Tamlaght and also of Magilligan. This name has been by mistake made Kilcaltan on the Ordnance map. [Insert addition: Kilkattin (James I and Charles II), Killattin (Cromwell), [both] Charters of Derry; Cilkallan, Sir Thomas Phillips' map (Skinners' lands); Killcatton, Book of Survey and Distribution (Skinners)].

Killycor: does not appear in the ancient documents. It is called Killycorr by Sampson and *Coill-Ui-Corra* by the native Irish. It evidently signifies "O'Corr's wood." O'Corr is the name of a family of the Clanna Rury, still in existence in the county. [Insert addition: Killecorra (James I and Charles II), Killecora (Cromwell), [both] Charters of Derry; Killcorr, Book of Survey and Distribution (Fishmongers)].

Kinculbrack: does not appear in any of the ancient authorities. It is called Kincuilbrack by Sampson. [Insert addition: Kemkeile (James I), Kemkoyle (Cromwell), Kimcoyle (Charles II), [all] being one balliboe of land, Charters of Derry; Killcull Brack, Book of Survey and Distribution (Fishmongers)].

Derivation of Townland Names

Kilculmagrandal: does not appear in any of the ancient authorities. It is incorrectly written Kilcuilbrack on Sampson's map, and in consequence of too much reliance being placed on his authority, as well as on that of Barre Beresford and the Revd Francis Gouldsberry, the same error has been perpetuated on the Ordnance map. These 2 last townlands are called by the Irish natives *Ceann Coill Ban* and *Ceann Coill Dubh*, which would be anglicised Kinguilbane and Kinguilduff, and meaning "white and black Kincuil" or "head of the wood." They were originally one townland and should now be both be spelled Kincuil or Kinguill; Magrandal, added to the latter, is a family name. [Insert addition: Kincullmcrannold, Book of Survey and Distribution (Fishmongers)].

Letterlougher: does not appear in the ancient records. It is called Letterlogher by Sampson and *Litir Luachra* by the Irish natives, which means "letter or wet land of the rushes." For the meaning of *litir*, generally anglicised letter, see Lettershendony in Lower Cumber.

Lear: called in the charter by the more correct name of Loyer one balliboe of land, and by the native Irish *Ladhair* "a fork." This name must have allusion to the meeting of the 2 streams or glens: *ladhair* signfies "a fork" or the space between 2 fingers when opened out. The best anglicised spelling is Loyer, as in the charter. [Insert addition: The middle proportion of Loyer (James I and Charles II), the middle proportion of Loyre (Cromwell), [both] Charter of Derry (in Armagh); Loyer being one balliboe of land, Charter of Derry (James I and Charles II); Loyre being one balliboe of land, Charter of Derry (Cromwell); Lieutenant Thomas Skipton, Protestant, Leyre, Book of Survey and Distribution].

Derivation of Townland Names

Lettermuck: called in the charter Lettermuicke one balliboe of land, and *Litir Muc* by the aborigines. Peter Connell explains leitir as meaning "hillside," muc "of the swine;" see Lettershendony in Lower Cumber. [Insert addition: Lettermuck (James I and Cromwell), Lettermucke (Charles II), [both] Charter of Derry; Littermack, Sir Thomas Phillips' map (Skinners' lands); Littermuck, Book of Survey and Distribution (Lieutenant-Colonel Michael Beresford, Protestant)].

Ling: called in all the charters Loonge one balliboe of land, by Sampson Lyng and by the aborigines *Laoidheang* [crossed out: a name which they do not understand], which means "of a ship," but unde nomen ignoratur. [Insert addition: Longe and Gortsmahan, Sir Thomas Phillips' map (Skinners' lands); Longe, Book of Survey and Distribution (Skinners)].

Lisbunny: does not appear in any of the ancient documents. It is called Lisbunea by Sampson and *Lios Buinnighe* by the native Irish, a name which

Parish of Cumber

is not now easily understood. *Buine* was a name of a woman celebrated in ancient Irish romances. [Insert addition: Lisboy (James I) being one balliboe of land, with middle proportion of Loyer, Lisbore (Charles II and Cromwell), [both] Charter of Derry; Lisbuney, Sir Thomas Phillips' map (Skinners' lands); Lisaboyne, Book of Survey and Distribution (Skinners)].

Mulderg: called in the charter Moyledirge or Moylederge one balliboe of land, Mulderrig by Sampson and *Maol Dearg* by the Irish natives. It signifies "red hill." The most analogical anglicised spelling would be Moylederg [insert note: right]. [Insert addition: Mullderrig, Book of Survey and Distribution (Fishmongers)].

Raspberry Hill: this name was given by the present proprietor. It is a subdivision of [insert query].

Sallowilly: called in the charter Sallaboley one balliboe of land, Sallaghwilly by Sampson and *Salach Bhaile* by the native Irish, who understand it to mean "dirty or miry townland," which is doubtlessly the correct interpretation. [Insert addition: Sallaboly (James I and Charles II), Salaboly (Cromwell), [both] Charter of Derry; Sallah Boyle, Sir Thomas Phillips' map (Skinners' lands); Salloghwelle, Book of Survey and Distribution (Skinners)].

Derivation of Townland Names

Stranagalwilly: does not occur in any of the ancient authorities. It is called Stranagalwilly in Sampson's memoir, where he translates it "the loame or grazing flat for foreign cows." It is called *Srath-na-Gallbhuaile* by the aborigines, which unquestionably means "the holm of the English bolie or cowsheds." By the word gall the Irish anciently meant "the Danes" or any foreigners, but in latter ages the English or Scotch Protestants. *Gallbhaile* or Englishtown is also the name of several places in Ireland.

Teenagh: called in the charter Tinagh one balliboe of land, Tenaght, arable pasture mountain, Teenagh by Sampson and *Taomhnach* by the native Irish. This name has been translated "swampy or watery land" by O'Reilly, but it has not been discovered upon what authority. This name should not have a "t" at the end, but should be anglicised Teenagh as Sampson has it. [Insert addition: Tynagh (James I and Charles II), Tinagh (Cromwell), [both] Charters of Derry; Tenagh, Sir Thomas Phillips' map (Skinners' lands); glebe <glcabe> land, Tenaght, Book of Survey and Distribution].

Tireighter: called in the charter [crossed out: Tireighter] one balliboe of land, Tirreighter by Sampson and *Tir Iachtair* by the native Irish, who understand it to mean "lower land," "terra inferioris partis." Trieneighter of the charter signifies "lower third." [Insert addition: Trieneighter (James I and Charles II), Trineighter (Cromwell), [both] being one balliboe of land, Charter of Derry; Lieutenant Thomas Skipton, Protestant, Terreoughter, Book of Survey and Distribution].

Tullintrain: called in the Down Survey Tulletraine "arable pasture mountain," Tullantrean by Sampson and *Tulaigh-an-trein* by the Irish natives, who understand it to mean "hill of the mighty man." [Insert addition: Tubbaru [insert query], Sir Thomas Phillips' map (Skinners' land), situation agrees; glebe land, Tulletraine, Book of Survey and Distribution].

Minor Place-Names in Upper Cumber

Boltabracken: called by the Irish *Buailte Bhreacain* "St Bracken's bolies or dairie places." There is another mountainous spot near Lough Patrick in the parish of Ballynascreen called *Buaile Coluim Chille* or "Columbkille's bolie." St Bracken or Brecan is the patron of Armagh church.

Crookdooish: called in Irish *Cnoc Dubhrais*, which certainly means "Dourish's hill." Dourish, anciently O'Doorish (of which family there are several interred in the old church of Maghera), was a family of the Kinel Owen, located in this and the county of Tyrone. This name is now generally shortened to Crockdooish, which is most certainly a corruption. *Cnoc*, which is made knock in other parts of Ireland, is here most generally pronounced and anglicised crock or cruck.

Dooalt glen: understood in the country to mean *Gleann-a-dubhaltaigh*, i.e. "Duald's, Dwalto's or Dudley's glen," which is most probably the correct explanation, and corresponding with Glenrandal. Doailt, however, was the name of a river in the rectory of Ross, which seems very like this name. *Dubh alt* means "black banks or precipices;" see Altnagelvin in Clondermot parish.

Glenrandal

Glenrandal river: called now by the natives *Abhainn Ghleanna Raghnaill*, i.e. "the river of Randall's glen or valley." Randall is a man's name borrowed by the Irish from the Danes. It is sometimes latinised Reginaldus and sometimes Ranelphus; see *Usher Primordia* and Colgan,

Triad. Thau. This river, which now takes the name of the glen through which it glides [insert superscript: flows], was anciently called the Bangibon river, as appears from Norden's map of Ulster, on which the Bangibon [insert correction: Bangibbon] is shown as running in a north eastern direction from the very verge of Tyrone until it met the Faughan. Donnogh O'Kane of Lamevadde, in his surrender to Queen Elizabeth, 18th September 1602, calls this river by the name Bangybbon.

"I, Donogh O'Cane of Lamevadde, do by these presents give and grante to my sovereign Ladye Queene Elizabeth my castle or mansion house called Aynough, together with all landes to the saide castell or mansyon house belonging, and also all other lands, tenements to me at any tyme before the date of thes presents belonginge, sett lying and beinge betweene the river of Foghan and Lough Foyle, so farr as to one other ryver called Bangybbon which runneth into the said ryver of Foghan, and from thence between the same ryver of Bangibbon and Lough Foyle, so farr as any of my lands and possessions do reache." This name is now totally [insert query] forgotten in the country, where indeed the names of rivers are sooner forgotten than those of any other topographical features.

Minor Place-Names

Cloghoge river: this name signifies "stony river."

Inver river: the Irish word *inbhear* is now understood to mean "the mouth of a river," but the word is used by Keating to mean simply "river" or "stream," thus *Inbhear Slainge a shnigheas tre lar Laighean go Loch Garmann* "Inver Slainge (now the River Slany) which glides through the middle of Leinster (and falls) into Lough Garmlan (Wexford harbour). *Bear* or *bior* is an original Irish word for "water," and is analogous with burn, river, aber.

Meeny mountain: called by the native Irish *Min Fheadha* "mist of the rushes," a name which has allusion to the rushy smooth spots in this mountain. *Min or mine*, is always understood in Ulster to signify "a smooth grassy spot on a mountain," in contradistinction from the rough stony or leathery parts.

Slieve Dornog: in Irish *Sliabh Dornog*, i.e. "the mountain of the round stones." The Irish word *dornog*, which is derived from *dorn* "the fist," is in most parts of Ireland applied to a round stone which may be thrown from the hand. This mountain is so called from the number of such stones that appear on its surface.

School Statistics

SOCIAL ECONOMY

Schools in 1824

[Table contains the following headings: name of townland where situated, name and religion of master or mistress, free or pay school, annual income, description and cost of schoolhouse, number of pupils subdivided by religion, sex and the Protestant and Roman Catholic returns, societies with which connected].

Killycore, master Thomas Ross, Roman Catholic; pay school, annual income about 14 pounds; accommodation in a farmhouse; number of pupils by the Protestant return: 16 Established Church, 21 Presbyterians, 23 Roman Catholics, 40 males, 20 females; by the Roman Catholic return: 16 Established Church, 24 Presbyterians, 20 Roman Catholics, 36 males, 24 females; connected with London Hibernian Society.

Killcalton, master Pat McCloskey, Roman Catholic; pay school, annual income about 16 pounds; schoolhouse a slated barn, cost 20 pounds; number of pupils by the Protestant return: 2 Established Church, 15 Presbyterians, 3 other denominations, 15 Roman Catholics, 18 males, 17 females; by the Roman Catholic return: 5 Established Church, 15 Presbyterians, 15 Roman Catholics, 20 males, 15 females; societies with which connected: none.

Gortilea, master Bryan McCloskey, Roman Catholic; pay school, annual income 12 pounds from the Fishmongers' Company and 10d per quarter from scholars; a temporary schoolroom, a schoolhouse is about to be built; number of pupils by the Protestant return: 19 Presbyterians, 6 Roman Catholics, 10 males, 15 females; societies with which connected: London Hibernian Society and Fishmongers' Company.

Crage, master John McLoughlin, Roman Catholic; pay school, annual income about 13 pounds; schoolhouse a poor thatched cabin; number of pupils by the Protestant return: 14 Established Church, 19 Presbyterians, 21 Roman Catholics, 40 males, 17 females; by the Roman Catholic return: 5 Established Church, 34 Presbyterians, 27 Roman Catholics, 39 males, 27 females; connected with London Hibernian Society.

Gortscreaghan, master Bernard O'Friel <O'Freel>, Roman Catholic; pay school, annual income about 8 pounds; schoolhouse [in] Roman Catholic chapel; number of pupils by the Protestant return: 20 Roman Catholics, 14 males, 6 females; by the Roman Catholic return: 20 Roman

Parish of Cumber

Catholics, 13 males, 7 females; societies with which connected: none.

Tireighter <Tyreighter>, master James McCloskey, Roman Catholic; pay school, annual income 1s 8d to 2s 6d per quarter from pupils; a new schoolhouse is building; number of pupils by the Protestant return: 1 Established Church, 1 Presbyterian, 18 Roman Catholics, 15 males, 5 females; by the Roman Catholic return: 2 Established Church, 20 Roman Catholics, 17 males, 5 females; societies with which connected: none.

Lisbunney, mistress Mary McCormick, Presbyterian; pay school, annual income 1s 8d per quarter from pupils; schoolhouse a poor cabin; number of pupils by the Protestant return: 13 Established Church, 2 Presbyterians, 5 Roman Catholics, 12 males, 8 females; by the Roman Catholic return: 3 Established Church, 23 Presbyterians, 4 Roman Catholics, 13 males, 17 females; societies with which connected: none.

Tullentrain, master Hugh McCloskey, Protestant; pay school, annual income about 4 pounds; schoolhouse a small cabin; number of pupils by the Protestant return: 2 Established Church, 10 Presbyterians, 8 males, 4 females; by the Roman Catholic return: 10 Established Church, 5 Presbyterians, 7 males, 8 females; societies with which connected: none.

Gortneskea, master Dennis McElwell, Roman Catholic; pay school, annual income about 8 pounds; schoolhouse dry stone walls, cost 5 pounds; number of pupils by the Protestant return: 6 Established Church, 18 Presbyterians, 6 Roman Catholics, 12 males, 13 females; by the Roman Catholic return: 6 Established Church, 18 Presbyterians, 6 Roman Catholics, 12 males, 18 females; societies with which connected: none.

Gortilea, master James O'Neil, Roman Catholic; pay school, annual income about 8 pounds; schoolhouse stone and mortar, cost 4 pounds; number of pupils by the Protestant return: 2 Established Church, 8 Presbyterians, 12 Roman Catholics, 20 males, 10 females; by the Roman Catholic return: 2 Established Church, 8 Presbyterians, 25 Roman Catholics, 18 males, 17 females; societies with which connected: none.

Alla Lower, master Francis Griffith, Protestant; free school, annual income 35 pounds, plus 4 acres of land; schoolhouse stone, lime and slated, in good repair, cost 322 pounds, of which sum the board of Erasmus Smith's fund contributed 300 pounds; number of pupils by the Protestant return: 14 Established Church, 18 Presbyterians, 18 Roman Catholics, 30 males, 20 females; by the Roman Catholic return: 14 Established Church, 18 Presbyterians, 18 Roman Catholics, 30 males, 20 females; societies with which connected: the board of Erasmus Smith's fund; parish school, the incumbent gave 21 pounds towards building schoolhouse, besides 3 acres of land and 5 pounds per annum to the master.

[Insert rough total of pupils: 354].

Schools in 1834

[The number of pupils is recorded through the Protestant return only].

Kilcaltan, master James Simpson, Presbyterian; free and pay school, annual income 15 pounds; schoolhouse thatched, built by subscription, cost 16 pounds; number of pupils: 10 Established Church, 38 Presbyterians, 18 Roman Catholics, 40 males, 26 females; under London Hibernian Society.

Killycor, master Patrick McCloskey, Roman Catholic; free and pay school, annual income 40 pounds; schoolhouse slated, built by Fishmongers' Company, cost 300 pounds; number of pupils: 24 Established Church, 62 Roman Catholics, 43 males, 43 females; under the Fishmongers' Company.

Gortilea, master Cormac Feeney, Roman Catholic; free school, annual income 50 pounds; schoolhouse slated, built by the Fishmongers' Company, cost 320 pounds; number of pupils: 30 Presbyterians, 60 Roman Catholics, 50 males, 40 females; connected with Fishmongers' Company.

Cregg, master John McLoughlin, Roman Catholic; free and pay school, annual income 10 pounds; schoolhouse thatched, cost 13 pounds; number of pupils: 6 Established Church, 44 Presbyterians, 70 Roman Catholics, 80 males, 40 females; connected with London Hibernian Society.

Claudy <Clady>, mistress Eliza Montgomery, Protestant; free and pay school, annual income 10 pounds; schoolhouse thatched, built by Mr Brown; number of pupils: 14 Established Church, 6 Presbyterians, 20 Roman Catholics, 6 males, 34 females; connected with the family of J. Brown Esquire.

Ballyartan, master John Young, Presbyterian; free and pay school, annual income 20 pounds; schoolhouse thatched, cost 30 pounds; number of pupils: 14 Established Church, 40 Presbyterians, 30 Roman Catholics, 30 males, 54 females; connected with London Hibernian Society.

Lower Alla,(parish school), master Francis Griffith, Protestant; free school, annual income 30 pounds; schoolhouse slated, cost 322 pounds; number of pupils: 20 Established Church, 8 Presbyterians, 12 Roman Catholics, 25 males, 15 females; connected with board of Erasmus Smith.

Stranagalwilly [insert note: county Tyrone], master James McDermott, Roman Catholic; free and pay school, annual income 16 pounds; schoolhouse thatched, cost 30 pounds; number of pupils: 80 Roman Catholics, 55 males, 25 females; connected with National Board of Education.

Tireighter, master Hugh McLoughlin, Roman Catholic; pay school, annual income 12 pounds; schoolhouse slated, cost 240 pounds; number of pupils: 5 Established Church, 6 Presbyterians, 35 Roman Catholics, 34 males, 12 females; connected with Kildare Street Society.

Upper Alla, master Andrew Porter, Presbyterian; pay school, annual income 5 pounds; schoolhouse thatched, cost 2 pounds; number of pupils: 10 Established Church, 14 Presbyterians, 2 Roman Catholics, 12 males, 14 females; societies with which connected: none.

[Insert rough total of pupils: 678].

[Insert query: By whom are numbers 4, 6, 7, 8, 9, 10 built: [Claudy, Gortilea, Kilcaltan, Killycor, Stranagalwilly, Tireighter]?.

School Statistics

Table of Schools

[Table contains the following headings: name of townland where held, name and religion of master or mistress, free or pay school, annual income of master or mistress, description and cost of schoolhouse, number of pupils subdivided by religion, sex and the Protestant and Roman Catholic returns, societies with which connected].

1834: Tamnymore, master James McDavid, Roman Catholic; free and pay school, annual income 16 pounds; schoolhouse slated, cost 300 pounds; number of pupils by the Protestant return: 3 Established Church, 20 Presbyterians, 7 other denominations, 20 Roman Catholics, 22 males, 28 females; parish school, under the National Board.

Tamnymore female school, mistress Racheal McDavid, Roman Catholic; free school, annual income 4 pounds; schoolhouse slated, cost 300 pounds; number of pupils by the Protestant return: 13 Presbyterians, 3 other denominations, 12 Roman Catholics, total 28; [under the] National Board, the female school is mixed with the male school at certain hours, the individuals composing the number 28 are identical.

Ervey, master Robert Davis, Presbyterian; free and pay school, annual income 13 pounds 12s 6d; schoolhouse slated, cost 700 pounds; number of pupils by the Protestant return: 20 Established Church, 45 Presbyterians, 2 other denominations, 5 Roman Catholics, 34 males, 38 females; under the support and patronage of the Grocers' Company, not connected with any society.

Tamnaherin, master Michael McClane, Roman Catholic; pay school, annual income 8 pounds; schoolhouse thatched, cost 14 pounds; number of pupils by the Protestant return: 3 Established Church, 27 Presbyterians, 30 Roman Catholics, 30 males, 30 females; no associations; the Grocers' Company pays 2 pounds annually.

Tamnyreagh, master William Jamieson, Presbyterian; pay school, annual income 10 pounds; schoolhouse slated, cost 500 pounds; number of pupils by the Protestant return: 2 Established Church, 22 Presbyterians, 22 Roman Catholics, 23 males, 23 females; no associations; formerly connected with the Kildare Street Society, partly supported by the rector.

Ballinamore, master Robert Rogers, Presbyterian; pay school, annual income of master 8 pounds; schoolhouse slated, cost 46 pounds; number of pupils by the Protestant return: 1 Established Church, 33 Presbyterians, 6 Roman Catholics, 26 males, 14 females; no associations; formerly connected with the Kildare Street Society.

Lackagh, master Joshua Wells, Protestant; pay school, schoolhouse thatched, cost 10 pounds; number of pupils by the Protestant return: 12 Established Church, 8 Presbyterians, 3 Roman Catholics, 10 males, 13 females; associations none.

1824: [In a different hand] Kildoag, master John Young, Presbyterian; pay school, annual income 17 pounds 4s 10d; schoolhouse a slated barn, cost 30 pounds; number of pupils by the Protestant return: 19 Established Church, 58 Presbyterians, 7 Roman Catholics, 48 males, 36 females; by the Roman Catholic return: 24 Established Church, 60 Presbyterians, 10 Roman Catholics, 55 males, 39 females; connected with London Hibernian Society, incumbent pays 2 guineas per annum.

Ballinamore, master William Dougherty, Presbyterian; pay school, annual income 22 pounds 10s; schoolhouse stone and lime, cost 7 pounds 10s; number of pupils by the Protestant return: 4 Established Church, 40 Presbyterians, 1 Roman Catholic, 32 males, 13 females; by the Roman Catholic return: 4 Established Church, 39 Presbyterians, 2 Roman Catholics, 30 males, 15 females; associations none.

Parish of Cumber

Tamnyerin, master Michael <Michle> McClean, Roman Catholic; pay school, annual income 6 pounds 14s 4d; schoolhouse stone and lime, rented by master; number of pupils by the Protestant return: 3 Established Church, 21 Presbyterians, 7 Roman Catholics, 22 males, 9 females; by the Roman Catholic return: 22 Presbyterians, 9 Roman Catholics, 23 males, 8 females; associations none.

Brockagh, mistress Eliza Johnston, Protestant; pay school, annual income 3 pounds 5s; schoolhouse a poor cabin; number of pupils by the Protestant return: 3 Presbyterians, 12 Roman Catholics, 7 males, 8 females; by the Roman Catholic return: 3 Presbyterians, 12 Roman Catholics, 7 males, 8 females; associations none.

Ervey, master Patrick Brawley, Roman Catholic; pay school, annual income 18 pounds; schoolhouse stone and lime, cost 10 pounds; number of pupils by the Protestant return: 3 Established Church, 21 Presbyterians, 12 Roman Catholics, 14 males, 22 females; by the Roman Catholic return: 3 Established Church, 21 Presbyterians, 12 Roman Catholics, 34 males, 2 females; associations none.

Tonduff, master James McDavid, Roman Catholic; pay school, annual income 17 pounds 5s; schoolhouse stone and lime, cost 5 pounds 10s; number of pupils by the Protestant return: 3 Established Church, 18 Presbyterians, 2 Roman Catholics, 13 males, 10 females; by the Roman Catholic return: 3 Established Church, 18 Presbyterians, 2 Roman Catholics, 13 males, 10 females; associations none.

Oakes, master or mistress none, [superintended by] ladies of the parish, Presbyterians; free school, annual income none, school held 2 days in the week and on Sundays; schoolhouse a cottage, cost 8 pounds; number of pupils by the Protestant return: 4 Established Church, 5 Presbyterians, 6 Roman Catholics, all females; by the Roman Catholic return: 3 Established Church, 5 Presbyterians, 2 Protestants, 5 Roman Catholics, all female; under the patronage of several ladies.

Table of Schools

[Table contains the following headings: name, situation and description, when established, income and expenditure, physical, intellectual and moral education, number of pupils subdivided by age, sex and religion, name and religion of master and mistress].

Bond's glen, public school, a small thatched house, established 1826; income: supported by Kildare Street Society, from Revd Mr Brownlow 2 pounds, from Revd Mr Hayden 1 pound, [?] 1s 1d to 1s 2d ha'penny from pupils; expenditure: salaries none, repairs 3 pounds; physical education none; intellectual education: books from Kildare Street Society, Dublin, sundry books, Scripture lessons; moral education: Revd Mr Burrop, curate, [visited] by Mr Mills and Mr Fitzgerald, inspectors, and Revd J. Allison; Scriptures read, no catechism; number of pupils: males, 29 under 10 years of age, 14 from 10 to 15, 2 above 15, total 45; females, 22 under 10 years of age, 9 from 10 to 15, total 31; total number of pupils 76, 42 Protestants, 33 Presbyterians, 1 Roman Catholic; master Joshua Wilson, Protestant.

Ballynamore, public school, built by the Kildare Street Society; a small slated house, established 1827; income: no society pays any; 3 pounds from the Revd John Hayden, 6 pounds from pupils; expenditure: salaries 9 pounds, no support for other expenses; physical education none; intellectual education: all books brought into school by the scholars; moral education: Revd Hayden 12 times yearly, catechism by master, Authorised Version; number of pupils: males, 8 under 10 years of age, 12 from 10 to 15, total 20; females, 10 under 10 years of age, total 10; total number of pupils 30, 4 Protestants, 23 Presbyterians, 3 Roman Catholics; master Robert Rogers, Presbyterian, no mistress.

Tamnyreagh, a public school, a large slated house 2-storeys high, established 1825, under Kildare Street Society; income: no income from any society, rector Hayden 3 pounds, from pupils 15 pounds; expenditure none; physical education none; intellectual education: from Kildare Street Society, *Dublin Reading book*, Rector Hayden gave 12 testaments; moral education: Rector Hayden 12 times a year, Authorised Version, catechism by master; number of pupils: males, 36 under 10 years of age, 6 from 10 to 15, total 42; females, 45 under 10 years of age, 1 from 10 to 15, total 46; total number of pupils 88, 8 Protestants, 40 Presbyterians, 40 Roman Catholics; master William Jamieson, Protestant, no mistress.

Tamnymore, Lower Cumber national school, a large slated house, established 1825; income: from National Board 12 pounds, from master 8 pounds, from mistress 4 pounds, from pupils 8 pounds; expenditure on salaries: master 8 pounds, mistress 4 pounds; school requisites about 8 pounds; physical education: after the model school plan; intellectual instruction: National Board; moral instruction: no visits from clergy, catechisms taught by teacher; number of pupils: males, 18 under 10 years of age, 9 from 10 to 15, total 27; females, 22 under 10 years of age, 11 from 10 to 15, total 33; total number of pupils 60, average for the year, 6 Protestants, 34 Presbyterians, 20 Roman Catholics; master James McDavid, Roman Catholic.

Ervey, public school, under the Grocers' Company, a large slated house, established 1832; income: from Grocers' Company 10 pounds, 2 pounds 10s from pupils; expenditure: salaries 10 pounds, materials 23 pounds 6s 8d; physical education: Lancasterian system; intellectual education: from Grocers' Company; moral education: Revd J. Hayden, Revd J. Alison, the Authorised Version read, catechism by master; number of pupils: males, 29 under 10 years of age, 21 from 10 to 15, total 50; females, 36 under 10 years of age, 6 from 10 to 15, total 42; total number of pupils 92, 17 Protestants, 46 Presbyterians, 29 Roman Catholics; master Robert Davis, Presbyterian.

School Statistics

Table of Schools

[Table contains the following headings: name, situation and description, when established, income and expenditure, physical, intellectual and moral education, number of pupils subdivided by age, sex and religion, name and religion of master and mistress].

Alla Lower, a large slated house, cost 322 pounds, a public school, established 1813; income: supported by the Erasmus Smith's [trustees], Dublin, 30 pounds, from Revd Mr Brownlow 10 pounds, from pupils 1 pound 10s; only 6d per quarter, half of them go free; expenditure: repairs 2 pounds; physical education none; intellectual education: books from the Kildare Place Society, *Dublin Reading book*, Scripture lessons; moral education Revd Mr Brownlow weekly, Lady C. Brownlow weekly, Authorised Version not read, catechisms not read; number of pupils: males, 52 under 10 years of age, 20 from 10 to 15, total 72; females, 29 under 10 years of age, 9 from 10 to 15, total 38; total number of pupils 110, 30 Protestants, 58 Presbyterians, 22 Roman Catholics; master Francis Griffith, Protestant.

Alla Upper, [insert addition: thatched, cost 2 pounds, income from pupils 5 pounds; number of pupils: 12 males, 14 females, total 26, 10 Protestants, 14 Presbyterians, 2 Roman Catholics; master: Andrew Porter, Presbyterian]; withdrawn 1st May 1835, none in his place.

Ballyarton, a small thatched house, cost 30 pounds, a public school, established 1823; income: from the London Hibernian Society 12 pounds, from the Revd F. Brownlow 2 pounds, from pupils 8 pounds; expenditure none; physical education none; intellectual education: *English reader's dictionary*; moral education: visited by Mr Allison 12 times a year, Mr Brownlow occasionally, Authorised Version read, catechism not read; number of pupils: males, 16 under 10 years of age, 12 from 10 to 15, 12 over 15, total 40; females, 26 under 10 years of age, 12 from 10 to 15, 5 over 15, total 43; total number of pupils 83, 14 Protestants, 39 Presbyterians, 30 Roman Catholics; master John Young, Presbyterian.

Claudy, [insert addition: thatched, built by Mr Browne; income: patrons, family of J. Browne Esquire, from pupils 10 pounds; number of pupils: males 6, females 34, total 40, 14 Protestants, 6 Presbyterians, 20 Roman Catholics; mistress Eliza Montgomery, Presbyterian]; schoolmistress deceased, none at present: it is contemplated to fill her place shortly. September 18th 1835.

Cregg, a small thatched cabin, cost 13 pounds, a public school, established 1824; income: from the London Hibernian Society 8 pounds, from pupils 2 pounds; expenditure: salaries 2 pounds, rent 1 pound; physical education none; intellectual education: Authorised Version, small spelling books; moral education: Revd Mr S. Burrows, curate, 8 times a year, Authorised Version, catechism not read; number of pupils: males, 30 under 10 years of age, 29 from 10 to 15, total 59; females, 26 under 10 years of age, 22 from 10 to 15, total 48; total number of pupils 107, 11 Protestants, 35 Presbyterians, 61 Roman Catholics; master John McLaughlin, Roman Catholic, mistress Mary McLaughlin, Roman Catholic.

Gortilea, a large slated house, built by the Fishmongers' Company, cost 320 pounds, a public school, established 1829; income: from the Fishmongers' Company 50 pounds, from pupils 5 pounds; better than [blank] per cent of the scholars goes free; expenditure and salaries none, other expenses none; physical education none; intellectual education: Scripture lessons, *Dublin Reading books, Murray's Reader*, Bible and Testament read; moral education: visited by committee quarterly, Mr Craig 12 times a year, Authorised Version and Douay Bible, catechism not read; number of pupils: males, 39 under 10 years of age, 2 from 10 to 15, total 41; females, 46 under 10 years of age, total 46; total number of pupils

Parish of Cumber

87, 28 Presbyterians, 59 Roman Catholics; master Cormac Feeney, Roman Catholic.

Kilcaltan, thatched, built by subscription, cost 16 pounds; income: from London Hibernian Society [blank], from pupils 15 pounds; expenditure: no report; number of pupils: 40 males, 26 females, total 66, 10 Protestants, 38 Presbyterians, 18 Roman Catholics; master James Simpson, Presbyterian.

Killycorr, a large slated house, built by the Fishmongers' Company, cost 300 pounds, a public school, established 1833; income: from the Fishmongers' Company 40 pounds, from pupils 4 pounds; the company pays for the most part of the pupils; expenditure: none; physical education none; intellectual education: *Dublin Spelling books, Dublin Reading books*, Bible not read; moral education: Revd Mr Sampson every half-year, Revd Mr Brownlow occasionally, by a committee the school is visited quarterly, Authorised Version and catechisms on Sunday; number of pupils: males, 28 under 10 years of age, 20 from 10 to 15, 2 over 15, total 50; females, 28 under 10 years of age, 12 from 10 to 15, total 40; total number of pupils 90, 8 Protestants, 22 Presbyterians, 60 Roman Catholics; master Pat McCloskey, Roman Catholic.

Stranagalwilly [insert addition: county Tyrone], a public school, built by James Sinclair Esquire, [insert addition: cost 30 pounds], a large thatched house, established 1828; income: from the National Board of Education 8 pounds, from Mr Sinclair Esquire 2 pounds, from Revd Mr Brownlow 2 pounds, from pupils 6 pounds; expenditure on salaries none; repairs for house 30 pounds yearly [insert addition: 1 pound 10s yearly]; physical education none; intellectual education: books selected from the Scriptures; moral education: Revd Mr Brownlow twice a year, Revd Mr Hunter quarterly, Revd M. Henry, priest, yearly, Authorised Version not read, catechisms not read; number of pupils: males, 40 under 10 years of age, 7 from 10 to 15, total 47; females, 22 under 10 years of age, 1 from 10 to 15, total 23; total number of pupils 70, 3 Protestants, 67 Roman Catholics; master James McDermott, Roman Catholic.

Tireighter, a public school, built by Mr Beresford, cost 240 pounds, a large slated house, established 1824; income: from Mr Beresford 5 pounds, from pupils 12 pounds; expenditure none; physical education: play; intellectual education: *Dublin Reading book*; moral education: [visited] by Mr Beresford monthly, Revd Mr Henry occasionally, Testaments read, catechisms not read; number of pupils: males, 26 under 10 years of age, 6 from 10 to 15, 8 over 15, total 40; females, 17 under 10 years of age, 6 from 10 to 15, total 23; total number of pupils 63, 6 Protestants, 6 Presbyterians, 51 Roman Catholics; master Hugh McLoughlin, Roman Catholic.

Tireighter, this is a large slated house in good repair, established 2nd September 1827; income: from Mr Beresford 5 pounds, from pupils 10 pounds; expenditure on salaries: 10 plus 5 [equals] 15 pounds; intellectual education: *Dublin Reading books*, Scripture lessons; moral education: catechisms once a week, Bible and Testament, [visited] by the Revd Henry, Mr N. Hunter; number of pupils: males, 30 under 10 years of age, 10 from 10 to 15, 9 over 15, total 49; females, 20 under 10 years of age, 10 from 10 to 15, 9 over 15, total 39; [total number of pupils 88], 19 Presbyterians, 9 Protestants, 60 Roman Catholics; master Hugh McLaughlin <McGlaughlin>, Roman Catholic. [Insert query: Should not "Scripture lessons" be transferred to moral [education].

School Statistics

Table of Schools

[Table contains the following headings: name, number of scholars subdivided by religion and sex, remarks as to how supported].

Alla, 88 Protestants, 42 Catholics, 94 males, 36 females, total 130; the parish school, Upper Cumber, on the foundation of the late Erasmus Smith Esquire; total annual support of this establishment is estimated to be worth about 60 pounds, derived from various sources.

Ballyarton, 68 Protestants, 38 Catholics, 63 males, 43 females, total 106; supported by the London Hibernian Society, from which it receives the annual stipend of 10 pounds; a small contribution of 1s per quarter is paid by such of the pupils as are able to pay, this amounts to about 8 pounds.

Ballycallaghan, 53 Protestants, 30 Catholics, 50 males, 33 females, total 83; formerly received a grant from the Kildare Street Society; none held out as likely this year; receives no other support but what is paid by the scholars, which averages about 7 pounds per annum.

Cregg <Craig>, 60 Protestants, 60 Catholics, 70 males, 50 females, total 120; supported by the London Hibernian Society, annual stipend 10 pounds; a small contribution of 1s per quarter from the parents of such as are able to pay, amounting to about 4 pounds.

Gortilea, 45 Protestants, 54 Catholics, 65 males, 34 females, total 99; supported by the Fishmongers' Company, annual stipend averages 45 pounds per annum.

Kilkaltin, 34 Protestants, 17 Catholics, 23 males, 28 females, total 51; receives no support whatever but from the parents of the children, who pay about 1s 6d per quarter; this amounts to about 14 pounds 6s per annum.

Killycor, 40 Protestants, 45 Catholics, 47 males, 38 females, total 85; supported by the Fishmongers' Company; the annual stipend averages nearly 40 pounds per annum.

Park, [blank].

Tirieghter <Tyrreeghter>, 8 Protestants, 78 Catholics, 72 males, 14 females, total 86; receives no support but what is paid by the scholars, which averages about 4 pounds per quarter.

Stranaganwilly [insert alternative: Stranagalwilly], 6 Protestants, 50 Catholics, 35 males, 21 females, total 56; receives 4 pounds annually from James Sinclair Esquire; a small contribution of 1s per quarter from such of the pupils as are able to pay.

Total number of scholars: 402 Protestants, 414 Catholics, 519 males, 297 females, total 816.

Queries by R.K. Dawson, with Answers by C.W. Ligar and J. Stokes, December 1834

MEMOIR WRITING

Queries and Answers

Forwarded to Lieutenant Larcom, 26th December 1834 [signed] R.K. Dawson, Lieutenant Royal Engineers.

"The road to Strabane passes through Bond's glen;" query, from whence, what road? Is it the road from Dungiven to Strabane? [Answer] The best road from Newtown and Dungiven to Strabane passes through Bond's glen. There is, however, another road through Glenrandal which some persons travel.

It is stated that "the deposits of the Faughan, which are of fine sand, enrich the ground it overflows." In Williams' Memoir of Upper Cumber it is stated that the soil deposited by the Faughan consists of sand and fine gravel "and is almost always injurious. It has in general to be taken away off the land." How is this apparent contradiction to be reconciled? [Answer] My first information was obtained from the Revd Mr

Grocers' coat of arms from Ervey

Parish of Cumber

Allison <Ellison>, the Presbyterian minister of the parish, and on applying to Alexander Ogilby Esquire I find that the sand and fine gravel which the Faughan deposits does injure the land upon which it is thrown, in most cases.

The fall of the Ness is stated to be about 30 feet. In the extract from Mr Sampson is is said to be about 60 feet. Which of these is to be taken as the correct height, or I should rather ask what is the actual height, for both the above statements are given as approximations? [Answer] The exact fall is 30 feet, which the water descends in 2 leaps. The first leap is 8 feet and the other 22 feet. From the appearance of the rocks, it is evident that the water did formerly fall a distance of 60 feet, but it has worn a deep channel for itself.

The dispensary and schoolhouse in Tamnymore, as also the schoolhouses in Tamnyreagh and Ballynamore, stated to have been built "by private subscriptions and a grant from the Kildare Street Society:" the exact sums contributed in each case would be desirable. [Answer] See document interleaved and marked no.1 for the dispensary and schoolhouse opened in Tamnymore. The persons who managed the building of the other schoolhouses are dead; the cost cannot be ascertained.

The schoolhouse built by the Grocers' Company in Ervey and a similar one in the parish of Clondermot cost 1,100 pounds. What was the separate cost of each? [Answer] Mr Cuthbert, agent for the Grocers' Company, [remainder illegible].

Queries and Answers on Natural Features

In General Appearance and Scenery 2 views are described, one looking down the valley of the Faughan, the other up Bond's glen "from the same part of the parish." Query, what part of the parish are these views to be seen from? [Answer] From the eastern extremity of the parish, near the road from Londonderry to Dungiven.

A detached portion of Lower Cumber appears on the index between the parishes of Upper Cumber and Banagher. Should not some allusion be made to it, and some particulars given relative to its natural features and modern topography, which may possibly differ in some respects from those of the bulk of the parish, which is several miles distant? It will be valuable at all events to mention it should the circumstances continue the same in character. [Answer] [See earlier account].

Stokes' account of the bog in Lower Cumber appears to have been rejected by Mr Ligar; query the reason [signed] Robert K. Dawson, Lieutenant Royal Engineers, 3rd December 1834. [Answer] Mr Stokes' account of the bogs in the parish described each townland separately; mine is a more general description, such as is required from us, [signed] C.W. Ligar Esquire.

Bond's glen: "through it the road passes to Strabane;" from what place? [Answer] Dungiven and Claudy and its neighbourhood.

Is the stream in Bond's glen usually called the Bond's glen stream? [Answer] It is usually called Bond's glen stream or Bond's glen burn.

The bog in the mountains is seldom more than 8 feet deep and varies from that to 2. Mr Stokes says 1 and a half; query? [Answer] None is cut which is less than 2 feet in depth; 8 to 2 may be taken, although it is in some places less than 1 foot in depth.

400 feet is given as the minimum height of the bog above the sea. Mr Stokes gives "in general 250 feet above the sea;" query? [Answer] The 400 feet given as a minimum relates to the mountains; the 250 feet relates to detached portions in the lower ground not yet cut away or reclaimed.

Approach to the Ness: "beyond the green the small pathway (query hitherto pursued?) leads through a deep shade of trees." [Answer] Yes, hitherto pursued.

Queries and Answers on Modern Topography

Public buildings: are there still no means of ascertaining the cost of building the parish church? [Answer] There are not.

And did the meeting house really cost 3,200 pounds; and how was the money obtained? [Answer] The cost was 1,000 pounds and it was erected about 85 years ago; see Revd James Allison's note to me, which is interleaved in the list of queries, [signed] Charles W. Ligar, 14th May 1835.

Gentlemen's seats: "Oaks Lodge, the residence of Hugh Lyle." [Answer by Stokes] Oaks Lodge is a joint residence of Mrs Lyle and her son Hugh Lyle Esquire.

Mr Lyle has erected a bridge to connect his grounds with those of Oaks Lodge, Mr Hugh Lyle's bridge. [Answer] This should be Mr Acheson Lyle's bridge.

Would not these statements be reconciled by erasing "lodge" from the first? But is not Oaks properly the residence of Mrs Lyle, but inhabited also by Mr Hugh Lyle? [Answer] Oaks is the joint residence of Mrs Acheson and her nephew Acheson Lyle Esquire. [Crossed out: Hugh Lyle

Esquire resides at Carnegarve near Moville, county Donegal, at his house in Castle Lane, Derry, at Oaks Lodge and occasionally at Tamnagh Lodge in the parish of Banagher. [Insert note by Dawson: Not called for].

Bleach greens: who is the owner of the bleach green at Oaks Lodge (query Mr Acheson or Mr Acheson Lyle). [Answer] The owner is Samuel Lyle Esquire.

Who is the owner of the bleach green in Ardground? [Answer by Ligar] William Dunn, tenant, Robert Ogilby Esquire, landlord.

Who is the owner of the corn mill and flax mill in Listress? [Answer] Widow of Alexander Galagher, tenant, the Grocers' Company proprietor.

Note from James Allison to Ligar

Sir,

The question you ask regarding Cumber meeting house: what was the cost of erecting it? I reply: from all the information I could procure, the cost of the house amounted to nearly 1,000 pounds. It was erected 85 years ago. I have the honour [signed] James Allison [to] Mr Ligar.

Queries and Answers on Social Economy

Dispensaries: could reports or even totals be procured for the years ending in April 1832 or 1833? What salary has the dispensary physician? [Answer] Shall be sent if the information can be procured, [signed] Charles W. Ligar.

What are the names of the Covenanting clergymen? [Answer] The Covenanting minister of Clondermot acts for Lower and Upper Cumber.

What are the names of the Catholic clergymen (parish priest, curate no.1, curate no.2)? [Answer] The parish priests of Clondermot and Upper Cumber divide Lower Cumber between them. The parish priest of Clondermot officiates at the chapel on Sliaboy. Therefore there are no curates or priests for this parish.

What is the emolument of the rector and of the curate? [Answer] There is no curate. Mr Hayden peforms all the duty himself. The rector's emolument is as follows: tithes under the Composition Act amount to 560 pounds, Glebe House and glebe lands worth about 130 pounds per annum, total 690 pounds.

What is the present number of the Catholics? Are there 607 individual Covenanters, or is that the number of families? [Answer] The following is copied from the abstract of the census as amended in 1834, for the purpose of ascertaining the religious denominations: Established Church 625, Presbyterians 2,334, Roman Catholics 1,618, Methodists 7, total 4,584. There is but 1 family of Covenanters, which were included under the head of Presbyterians.

Emigration: to what parts of America do the parishioners usually emigrate? [Answer] Most of the emigrants from this parish go to New York and Philadelphia, [J. Stokes] the poorest to Canada.

The income of the Revd James Allison, Presbyterian minister, amounts to 205 pounds per annum, which is made up from the following items: Fishmongers' Company 10 pounds, Grocers' Company 10 pounds, Skinners' Company 10 pounds, stipend 75 pounds, regium donum 100 pounds, total 205 pounds.

Queries and Answers on Natural Features

Bogs: the Killaloo bog is 250 feet above the Faughan: query, above the nearest part of the Faughan? [Answer] The nearest part of the Faughan.

How many Toneduff bogs are there? Is the "large bog of Toneduff" the same as the "main mountain bog?" [Answer] 5.

Which of the Lower Cumber bogs are flow bogs? NB Should any other river be nearer the above bogs, it may be substituted for Faughan. [Answer] The Faughan is the only river properly so called.

[Insert note on remaining queries: Answers are on their way from the north; see Ordnance map].

Queries and Answers on Memoir Writing

Is John Acheson Esquire, who improved the parish by erecting houses and bleach greens, still living? [Answer] He is dead.

"Slamsmen [slanesmen]:" meaning? [Answer] Turf assistants to turf-cutters.

Lewis removed the crucifix at Gortycross with "other large stones." Were these stones sacred or merely accidental? [Answer] They were sacred.

"From 80 to 100 persons have migrated within the last year;" query 1834? [Answer] 1834.

Memoir Writing by George Downes and J. Stokes, with Notes by R.K. Dawson

Query and Answer about Proprietor

[J. Stokes] Why was Captain Sinclair left out? The townland of Stranagalwilly is represented on the plans as belonging to the parish and he is its proprietor. [Insert answer initialled by R.K. Dawson

The name of Captain Sinclair is omitted in the list of proprietors as his property (the townland of Stranagalwilly) is not in the county of Derry, though it belongs to the parish of Upper Cumber; and it is presumed that this is the reason of his exclusion from the first of the 3 attached slips.

Query and Answer on Productive Economy

[G. Downes] Mr Stokes will please to recast the opening of his article on Productive Economy (Rural). Some differences appear between his statements and those contained in 2 of the 3 slips wafered to the enclosed portion of his report. The information in pencil also was not well understood. The interlineations were intended to reconcile the differences alluded to.

[J. Stokes] I wish to defend (if it is allowed me to do so) the wording of that opening, as far as it has excluded the smaller proprietors. I would recast it thus: "The proprietors (excluding the word "great") are the Fishmongers' and Skinners' Companies, the Church, H. Barre Beresford Esquire, the Bishop of Meath, the Revd R. Alexander." If the word "great" was included, people would ask why we make Mr Alexander (who only has a townland and a half) as *great* a proprietor as the Skinners' Company, who have nearly half the parish? It appears to me that the word is only applicable to the 2 companies and the hurch, for this reason. The remainder have but a small fraction of the parish. [Insert note by R.K. Dawson: It appears to me that the word "great" had better be omitted, as the above are the *only* proprietors].

I have ranked them above according to their *importance*, as well as the size of their estates. Thus, I hold the Fishmongers to be more important than the Skinners because they hold it themselves, and the Bishop of Meath more important than Mr Alexander. The Bishop of Meath's property is *not* churchland. The quantity of ground *cultivated* is much smaller than the quantity *held*. The holdings considered as the quantity *cultivated* are from 5 to 15 acres, but that which is included in the lease is from 10 to 20.

Working Papers on Ancient Topography

Queries and Answers on Stokes' Memoir

Forwarded to Mr Stokes, to be by him forwarded to Lieutenant Larcom, 9th December 1834 [signed] Robert K. Dawson, Lieutenant Royal Engineers.

The mutilated stone cross: this is the first I ever heard of a cross. There should be a slight sketch, ever so slight, to show its form. The crosses have various forms.

In a field a short way off a square stone of peculiar form: this is so indefinite as to make the whole useless. A short distance off the foundations of a building, same remarks. [Answer by Stokes]: The above [2 drawings] was probably its form. It is in the centre of a hedge. The above is its present form (nearly). The country people do not recollect anything more. It may have been the foot of the cross. The country people found what they conceived to be fair dealing.

Bell Stones: there ought to be more dimensions; the height of the supporting stones is not given, nor the thickness of the cove in [feet ?]. Conjecture ingenious, but [if] it be meant as a mode of bringing the stones up the hill, not very probable; easier to slide them on, and if they were turned over, it certainly would not be endways, as the drawing represents, when it was so much easier to roll them by their sides; but certainly the holes are very curious.

Tamnareagh very satisfactory, but be cautious of those carvings: if real they are of the highest interest. The carving on monuments of that date is commonly lozenge shaped, zig-zag, spiral or volutes differently combined.

No runic descriptions have been found yet in Ireland: I would not be greatly surprised if there were some at Slaght[manus ?]. They are something like this [drawing], sometimes like points of fingers, or fancied so.

Ancient fences: "made by huge blocks of stones laid in covering stone." The drawing is good, but I would rather have dimensions than height. It is a great pity there are no dimensions. I take the stone to be about 3 or 4 feet high by the drawing: is it so? The account of Thomson's farmhouse very good. I should have liked a plan or view of the fort, house and fences. [Answer] Fences in oblongs and parallelograms, like other fields. I would rather [like?] dimensions than height.

Sketch of a fence of small vertical stones in Ballygroll: sad pity not a single dimension.

The ancient houses should be looked at carefully. How were they roofed? Do none remain buried which have roofs yet perfect? [Answer] None of them have roofs; the foundations only are now to be seen. There are no buried houses.

Pray make better drawing and plan of the Slaghtmanus itself: you give an outline of the doorway and omit its height, though you give its breadth. [Answer] Larger.

Ancient wall in Highmoor: if the shed is large

Bell Stones in Tamnyreagh

Parish of Cumber

enough for the broom-maker to sit in, the wall must be 10 or 12 feet high. How high is it? How large the stones? This is very curious; take the Etruscan walls. Pray give dimensions everywhere, sad pity; sometimes introduce a figure to afford a scale if you have not time to measure. [Answer] See Lieutenant Dawson's drawings.

Some of those "slaughts" are perhaps the ancient houses of which the roofs remain. Scroby's House must be one; is it circular or oval? [Answer] Scoby's House is merely a circular foundation; the walls do not rise more than 18 inches above the surface.

If the Slaghtmanus houses were arched and covered with earth, would they be like Scroby's house? [Answer] No.

All these "houses" appear similar [or ought?] to have a very careful section and drawing, with dimensions of one of the most perfect. [Answer] When I came on the ground a second time with Lieutenant Dawson, I could not succeed in finding these houses of Sliabhgore.

Giant's grave in Brown's farm in Slaghtmanus: 25 feet long 9 feet broad, enclosed by stones of prodigious size (no dimension) and on the top a flag weighing 4 tons. Is there not some mistake in the dimensions: 1 flag 25 feet by 9? [Answer] This I have found, on enquiring from Mr Ross of Banagher, to have been that drawn in Sampson's survey as "the cromlech of Slaghtmanus;" I send a tracing. These dimensions are from the words of the people.

Was not this the real Slaghtmanus (tomb of Manus)? Weapons were found. There is no use in calling them altars. Popular tradition is right there: they were graves. [Answer] Probably it was.

Is Tirkeeran Fort earth or stone? You say in the midst of a pond: is it on piles? There is nothing impossible in its giving name to the barony, or rather their having a common origin. [Answer] I went to look for this fort but I could not find it. Thomas Fagan says it was of earth, but was not on piles.

Annagh Fort: no scale nor dimensions were in the description; it is said to be a hill rising [blank] feet from its base. [Answer] The scale is 1 inch to a chain, the blank has been filled up.

Working Papers on Natural Features and Modern Topography

Suggestions and Queries about Upper Cumber

[Crossed out queries mostly on Social Economy, with answers by Stokes].

How many acres are cultivated, including Gilky Hill and excluding Stranagalwilly? NB Gilky Hill is a new townland cut off from Teenaght, the insulated portion of Lower Cumber. [Answer] 521 acres subtracted from the quantity of cultivated ground which I have already sent will include Gilky Hill and exclude Stranagalwilly.

Information wanted about bogs. [Answer] I believe there is nothing more to ascertain. They are all grazing bogs, except those I mentioned.

Information wanted about climate. [Answer] No parishioners can give any distinct information about the climate. I concluded that Captain Portlock had made some inquiries into that subject.

In which Alla are these old trees? [Answer] In Lower Alla.

Is Learmount church for the convenience of any particular townlands? How is the clergyman supported; his Christian name? [Answer] It is. He is paid by Mr Ross, Mr Haydn and Mr Brownlow. From these 3 he receives altogether about 90 pounds a year. These 3 are the rectors of Banagher, Lower Cumber and Upper Cumber respectively. The clergyman's name is James Hunter.

Does Brown or Browne reside at Cumber House? [Answer] Browne.

What rector resides at the Glebe House? [Answer] The Revd Charles Brownlow.

Beaufort belongs to J. Browne, but who resides at it? [Answer] A cottier and his children.

"A bridge in Kilcaltan." Should not this be "between Gortnaran and Ballyartan?" [Answer] It should.

Fishmongers' dispensary: in the engineer's report it is stated that candidates for the situation of medical officer to the Fishmongers dispensary must belong to the "army or *navy*;" but in the additions the 9th rule states that the surgeons must be "qualified as full surgeons in the *army*," without mention of the navy; which is correct? [Answer] It is evidently intended that the 9th rule should include the navy, as well as the army, the surgeon at the Ballykelly dispensary being a navy surgeon.

"4,542 cases from the [insert addition: 1st] March 1831 to 14th May 1834:" fill blank before March. [Answer] Filled.

Furnish list table of diseases at Fishmongers' dispensary. [Answer] They cannot give a sufficiently accurate account.

In enumerating the rules of the Fishmongers' schools they run thus: 1, 2, 3, 4, 12. Why are the rules between 4 and 12 omitted? Is their substance condensed in the paragraph headed "of the government of the institution?" [Answer] Yes, from 4 to 12 the rules for the schools are word for word the same as those from 4 to 12 for the dispensaries. They relate to the peculiar construction of the boards.

Rule 18 runs this: "No payment will be allowed by the company for those children who shall have attained the instruction as specified in the first rules; and therefore they direct that, if any scholars continue longer at the schools, the parents shall be required to pay the full amount of the stipend to the master or mistress." The sentence is imperfect. [Answer] I have not got the book, having been obliged to return it, but I have completed it to the best of my remembrance.

Christian names of Revd Brownlow, rector: [answer] Charles; Revd Henry, parish priest: [answer] M.

Revd Conloge, Revd McPheely, Catholic curates: are these names correctly spelt? [Answer] I don't know the Christian names of these two; are they of much consequence? [Insert addition: Revd Michael Henry, PP, Revd Patrick McFeely, Revd Bernard McConilogue, curates].

Revd Brown or Browne, Presbyterian minister? [Answer] Brown.

Do not the Fishmongers pay 10 pounds a year to the Presbyterian minister, and the same to the parish priest? [Answer] They do.

Do they pay a stipend to any other clergymen? [Answer] No, and they give this reason: "that the Established Church was sufficient to pay its own ministers."

In what townland is the tannery? Add some particulars about its products. [Answer] It is in the townland of Clagan, parish of Banagher; see plans. Therefore I concluded that I might omit it at present.

To whom is Mr Browne agent? [Answer] I did not call Mr Browne an agent: I said "that none of the agents reside within the parish but Mr Browne's, adding the "s," which you have overlooked. Mr Handcock is his agent and lives in Cregg.

Are not Claudy and Cumber-Claudy only different names for the same village? [Answer] They are: Cumber is added for a distinction from some other village of the same name.

In which Alla is the parish school, Mr Griffith master? [Answer] Lower Alla.

Is Claudy school thatched or slated? [Answer] Thatched.

Queries and Answers

[Crossed out queries, with answers by J.B. Williams].

Forwarded to Lieutenant Larcom, 26th December 1834, signed Robert K. Dawson, Lieutenant Royal Engineers.

The banks of the Faughan are said to be "perculiarly beautiful" at Learmount, at Cumber and at Kilcaltan, and a picturesque old bridge is spoken of at the latter place. I think it would be very desirable to accompany the description with landscape sketches of such views in all cases, where it can be done without a great loss of time or inconvenience. [Answer] I have made one landscape view of the banks of the Faughan near Kilcaltan, which I shall forward as soon as penned in. When my inquiries in the parish of Banagher take me towards Learmount, I shall make some sketches there also. As to Cumber, perhaps the expression "perculiarly beautiful" may be too strong, although there certainly is much beauty there also, but it is owing to the banks of the Glenrandal, to the church, as well as to the banks of the Faughan.

Boveva should be spelt Bovevagh. [Answer] Altered.

Timber is said to occur "in every part of the bogs, but has not been found so abundant in the elevated mountainous district." Query, the fact of any timber being found in the bogs on the top of the mountains? [Answer] Timber has not infrequently been found on the tops of the mountains, for instance a great deal was found on the top of Crookdooish.

Dungorkin Fort: the plan might with advantage have been a little more special. The section is described as being "from west to east:" it should have been south to north, if the letters on the line itself be correct. [Answer] Should have been described from south to north.

Killicor bog: section not special; it does not appear to be a correct representation of any one particular portion of the bog, but a sort of random representation (drawn from memory perhaps). [Answer] The former section of Killycor bog was drawn on the spot during misty weather. I now send another section from nearly the same point of view, and on a larger scale.

Claudy is said to consist of "a few houses." When the number of houses is so small, it would be very desirable to count them and then to specify the exact amount. [Answer] 25 houses, besides a police barrack and a session house, both being one building.

Query, the hours at which the mail car passes, to and fro, through Claudy? [Answer] 8.30 morning to Derry, 4.00 afternoon to Dungiven, during the winter, and 3.00 afternoon to Dungiven during the summer.

Park is said to be a group of about half a dozen well-built slated houses." It is a pity the exact number has not been specified. [Answer] Park is a group of 6 houses.

What are the "skutches" of the flax mills? [Answer] The "skutches" of flax mills are those wheels which, revolving with great rapidity, serve to beat and soften the flax, which is held by a man at a particular part of the wheel.

What is meant by the word "geared" as applied to mills, for instance a single-geared mill? [Answer] A corn mill with a single pair of stones is said to be "single geared;" with a double pair or more it is called "double geared."

Killycor school, built by the Fishmongers' Company, is said to have cost more than 300 pounds. Memorandum: inquire of Mr Sampson the exact amount. [Answer] The memorandum taken and inquiry to be made from Mr Sampson.

Also the amount required for its annual support, stated to be "about 40 pounds." [Answer] The average sum given for its support is 40 pounds. The master being paid according to the merit of the pupils causes this sum to fluctuate.

Communications: it is stated that the direction of the road from Derry to Dungiven "might be changed with advantage and trying hills avoided." A more particular discription of the part of the road and the hills alluded to would be desirable, as well as of the course of the better line which is here suggested. Something of a section too would be very valuable, if it could be easily made (even in a general way), but the more special the better. [Answer] The road from Derry to Dungiven, when in the townland of Kilcaltan about 1 and a half miles west of Claudy, instead of being carried on in a straight line over the hill, to a height of about 510 feet, ought to have been made more to the south, nearer the River Faughan, and certainly not have ascended to a greater elevation than 350 feet. It then should join the present line of road about 200 yards west of the bridge over Fore Glen river.

Again, in the townland of Killycor east of this bridge, instead of being carried up the hill to the height of upward of 460 feet, it ought to have again been made more to the south nearer to the River Faughan, and not to have risen more than 350 feet above the sea.

Mr Brownlow's suspension bridge: sketch very pretty, but not special. It appears to owe its beauty to the care taken in penning it in, rather than to the accuracy of the sketch made on the ground, whereas that alone is what would make it valuable. I should very much like to give a good elevation or working plan of it on a larger scale, showing the nature of its construction, the dimensions of the several parts and the mode of putting them together, so that any person might be enabled from it to construct a similiar work, [signed] R.K. Dawson, Lieutenant Royal Engineers, 3rd December 1834. [Answer] North elevation and horizontal plan furnished, [signed] J.B. Williams, Dungiven, 23rd December 1834.

Queries, with Answers by C.W. Ligar, J. Stokes and Others

Queries and Answers

Meenie or Menie hill? Is it identical with Main mountain? [Answer] It is not identical; it should be Menie.

Main mountain appears to be important. To which range does it belong, the Stranaganwilly, that in which Menie hill (if not identical with Main mountain) occurs, or that in which Crookdouish (?) occurs? [Answer] The Stranaganwilly range [insert query: Stranagalwilly?].

"To the east of Crookdouish or Crookdooish, and separated by Glenrandal, rises Slaboy." Query, the River Glenrandal? [Answer] Both the glen and the river are called Glenrandal. Mr Sampson spells it Crookdoish.

"At Kilcalten it (natural oak) again makes its appearance." Is this Kilcalten the gentleman's seat so called, or is the townland at large intended? [Answer] It is the townland at large which is intended.

"The eastern arm of the transverse" in Claudy chapel. Is transverse preferable to transept, and why? [Answer] Transept is the best.

Do not modern chapels always lie east and west? [Ground plan of chapel] If it be so here, the sacristy must be in the southern arm of the transverse? [Answer] It is in the eastern arm: modern chapels are not always east and west. [Insert note: Query this].

The discrepancy between the statement in the population abstract for 1831 and that in the Ordnance report is very great respecting the houses in Park, the former giving 21, the latter only 6. Are there 15 cabins in addition to 6 slated houses? [Answer] There are 6 houses in Park. The discrepancy may be explained by a confusion between Park and Tireighter. There are 15 houses in the townland of Tereighter, in addition to 6 houses, not all slated, in that part called Park.

"The chapel of ease was built for the accommodation of . . . Banagher." Query: The neighbouring parts of Banagher, or that part of Banagher which is in Tirkeeran barony? [Answer] The neighbouring parts of Banagher.

Is Mr H.B. Beresford's place ever called Learmount House? Is it not simply Learmount, similiarly to Kilcalten, Mr A. Ogilby's? [Answer] It is called simply Learmount.

There are 2 Sir Robert Batesons. Was it not the proprietor of Belvoir Park near Belfast [insert note: M.P. for the county] that contributed towards the building of the meeting house? [Answer] It was the proprietor of Belvoir Park near Belfast.

Is the name of John McCleery Esquire contributor to the meeting house (once of Beaufort), spelled correctly? [Answer] It should be McCleery.

Was it not H.B. Beresford Esquire that subscribed towards building the chapel? [Answer] It was.

Who is the medical officer of the dispensary? [Answer] Dr Matthew Robinson.

Could a table of cases in the dispensary be procured for the last year, with totals for 2 or 3 years preceding? [Answer] See table interleaved and marked no.1.

Queries and Answers

Are the following mills single geared: the paper mill in Lettermuck? [Answer] Double geared; is on the old system and has wooden works.

Corn mills in Killycor and Ling? [Answer] Single geared.

Are flax mills throughout the parish? [Answer] There are 5 flax mills in the parish, 1 in each of the following townlands: Learmount, Cregg, Killycor, Dungorkin and Ballycartin. [Insert note by R.K. Dawson: Not answered as to the flax mills being single geared or otherwise].

"About 3 miles higher up the river at Stranagalwilly, there is a corn mill and a tuck mill." In what townland? [Answer] Stranagalwilly. Are they single geared and what are the diameter and breadth of the wheels? [Answer] The corn mill has a water wheel 12 feet in diameter and 1 foot 4 inches in breadth. The tuck mill water wheel is of exactly the same diameter and breadth. [Insert note by R.K. Dawson: Not answered as to being single geared or otherwise].

"On the Fore Glen river, near to where it falls into the Faughan, is a small flax mill." In what townland? Is it single geared? [Answer] Dungorkin, single geared.

For how many miles does the "main road from Newtownlimavady to Strabane" lie through the parish? [Answer] From Strabane to Newtownlimavady through Claudy 8 miles. [Insert query: Statute miles?].

The Revd Charles or Francis Brownlow? [Answer] Francis Brownlow.

Rivers: the Fore Glen river and the Burntollet stream rise in Bovevagh and run several miles before they join the Faughan. How many miles? [Answer] The Fore Glen river 7 and a half miles; the Burntollet, the extreme source of which appears to be in Tamlaght Finlagan parish, is 11 and one-third miles.

Towns: "Claudy ... about 9 miles from Londonderry." Another report gives 7; what is the fact in statute miles? [Answer] Will be ascertained from the maps.

Public buildings: at what expense did Mr Browne erect the building which contains, combined, the petty sessions house and police barracks? [Answer] Mr Browne does not know the sum which it cost.

What was the cost of the building of the chapel of ease? The report gives a list of items amounting to 747 pounds 5s, but another report states 640 pounds. Did it cost only 640 pounds; and if so, how was the surplus of the sum subscribed disposed of? [Answer] The sum sent in the Memoir giving a list of items was correct, as it was obtained from the Revd James Hunter, curate.

Revd Francis Gooldsbury, query Goldsbury? [Answer] Should be Gouldsbury.

Gentlemen's seats: Cumber House, "the plantations which were put down about 25 years are extensive and very judiciously laid out." Does this mean that the planting was conducted during a period of 25 years, or is ago (or since) omitted after 25? [Answer] "Since" has been omitted.

Glebe House, Dean Edward Ledwidge, query Ledwich? [Answer] Ledwich.

Bleach greens, manufactories and mills: who are the proprietors of the paper mill of Lettermuck? [Answer] The proprietor of this paper mill is Robert Mathews, who holds it in perpetuity.

Who are the proprietors of the corn mill and flax mill in Ballyartan? [Answer] The present Bishop of Meath is the head proprietor and the occupying tenant is John Irwin.

Who are the proprietors of the corn and flax mills in Cregg? [Answer] John Browne Esquire, Cumber, is the head proprietor and Thomas McCandlas the occupying tenant.

Who are the proprietors of the corn mill and flax mill in Killycor? [Answer] Fishmongers' Company are the proprietors and John Miller the occupying tenant.

Queries and Answers

[List of schools]: There appears to be a school at

Park; is it identical with any of the above? [Answer] It is identical with Tireighter.

"The McLoughlins are the prevailing family of the Menie Ballymullins." Does this mean that part of the Ballymullins district contained by the Menie mountain? [Answer] It means that part of the Ballymullins district contained in the valley between the Menie hill and that of Kilgort.

Should the following be placed between inverted commas, as being the actual words prefixed to their rules? "The following are the rules for the government of the schools on the Fishmongers estate, adopted 1828, revised 1832?" [Answer] They should not, but they are the actual sense of the title page prefixed.

"A particular report of each school within their respective division is furnished annually." Query divisions? [Answer] It should be divisions.

Does the 18th of the rules of the Fishmongers' schools run thus, word for word? "No payment will be allowed by the company for those children who shall have attained the instruction specified in the first rules; and therefore they direct that, if any scholars continue longer at the schools, the parents shall be required to pay the full amount of stipend to the masters or mistresses?" [Answer] It does.

The Roman Catholics are to the Protestants as (about) 3 to 2. What is the proportion of the Presbyterians? [Answer] The proportion included Presbyterians also; by Protestants all those who were not Catholics were meant. The Presbyterians are to those of the Established Church as 2 to nine-tenths nearly, or as 20 to 9 nearly.

"In Bond's glen the cattle are brought home from the hills at the hour of 11 o'clock in the forenoon." At what hour in the morning are they first sent out? [Answer] About sunrise.

"The farmer gives him (the cottier) ground gratuitously." Does he not pay for it in labour or some other way? [Answer] He does. [Insert query: How? [Answer] I do not know].

Have any tidings yet been heard of Lampen (query orthography), the excise man who disappeared from Lettermuck in 1833, or can particulars of his disappearance be furnished? [Answer] No tidings have yet been heard of him (*Lampan*). The last time he was seen was when in the vicinity of the paper mill in Lettermuck, against which he was about to strike a heavy fine. The owners were arrested on suspicion, but no proof could be obtained against them. Every search was made for his body but without success.

What may be said about fuel? [Answer] It is chiefly consumed within the parish. It is used as charcoal by the smiths and varies in quality.

Account of a runaway (marriage): "They are *entertained* there by the owner of the house until they are married. Every friend is also *entertained* by offering a glass of whiskey. After marriage a *second entertainment* takes place." Now "entertain" when it first occurs seems to mean "lodged and dieted;" "entertain" when it next occurs seems to mean "complimented;" "entertainment" seems to mean "feast." Why then is "second" prefixed, as there appears to have been no set feast before? [Answer] For "second entertainment" read a "set feast;" second is wrong. There was no set feast before. Drinking, however, is always partly considered in the light of an "entertainment."

Obstructions to improvement: "Many of the farms are still disposed in rundales;" what are these? [Answer] Scattered fields disposed in such a manner that to reach a field those of other farmers must be crossed.

Religion: the Revd James Hunter receives from the rectors of the Cumbers and Banagher stipend amounting to *about 90 pounds* a year. What is the exact amount received from each? Upper Cumber, Lower Cumber, Banagher? [Answer] Will be forwarded immediately, [signed] C.W. Ligar, Newtown, 13th May 1835.

Working Papers

Query on Petty Sessions

At what expense was the petty sessions house built by John Browne Esquire? [Answer] Mr Browne himself does not know.

Queries and Answers on Religious Administration

The names and denominations of the parishes constituting each benifice or union. [Answer] Cumber Upper.

Whether with or without cure of souls, and of any chapelry belonging thereto not having a separate incumbent, and whether subject to episcopal or to what peculiar or exempt jurisdiction. [Answer] A rectory with cure; subject to episcopal jurisdiction.

The extent of the respective parishes. [Answer] 10 miles 1 perch 32 feet length, 6 miles 5 perches 20 feet the greatest breadth at right angles.

The reputed acreable contents in statute measure in each parish respectively. [Answer] 26,328 acres 2 roods 5 perches statute measure per Ordnance Survey.

And in what county or counties each is locally situated, with an account of the general quality of the land in each. [Answer] Londonderry, except 1 townland in county Tyrone. The general quality of the land in this parish has not been reported.

The population of the respective parishes, according to the census taken in 1831. [Answer] 5,430.

The names of the respective incumbents and the dates of their admission, with the names of the curates employed and for what parishes. [Answer] Francis Brownlow, clerk, admitted 23rd December 1830, incumbent; 1 stipendiary curate employed.

And the amount of stipend or allowance paid to each and every curate. [Answer] At a yearly stipend of 75 pounds British.

Gross amounts of the annual income of the respective parishes and benefices, on an average of 3 years ending with December 1831, or to the latest period to which the returns have been made. [Answer] 1,410 pounds.

The sources from whence the said yearly incomes arise, specifying how much from tithe or tithe composition and how much from glebe or any source. [Answer] From tithe composition 740 pounds, 1,123 acres 18 perches statute measure of profitable glebe let for 610 pounds, 80 flat acres of glebe in incumbent's use, valued at 60 pounds, total 1,410 pounds.

With the acreable contents, profitable or not, of the glebe in statute measure, and its average value per acre; whether subject to any rent and whether let or in occupation of the incumbent. [Answer] NB Exclusive of the aforesaid glebes, there are 246 acres 3 roods 22 perches statute measure of unprofitable mountain glebe; the profitable glebe is reported to be worth 18s per acre.

The amount of any yearly payments or temporary charges, each under its proper title, made out of the gross incomes of the respective benefices, on an average of 3 years ending as before, *excepting rates and taxes for the Glebe House and offices, repairs and curates' stipends*; and if only temporary, the time at which the same will terminate. [Answer] To collector's salary 60 pounds; to visitation fees 1 pound 13s 4d; to support of schools 15 pounds; to interest, at the rate of 10 pounds per cent, on 543 pounds 9s 10d sunk in Glebe House, 54 pounds 7d; interest, at 5 pounds per cent, on 827 pounds 10s 2d expended on same and recoverable from successor, 41 pounds 7s 6d; to perpetual curate of Learmount 40 pounds; total 212 pounds 7s 10d.

The net amounts of the annual incomes of the benefices respectively, after deducting such benefits (except as aforesaid); and whether such incomes may be fairly considered as the average amounts of net income for the future or otherwise. [Answer] 1,197 pounds 12s 2d.

The time and expense at which the respective glebe houses were built, from what funds. [Answer] Cumber Upper Glebe House, built in the year 1772, under the old acts, at the cost of 1,070 pounds 12s 4d British, and improved in 1818 at the cost under certificate of about 1,103 pounds 6s 11d British. Whether under the old or new acts. [Answer] Under the old acts.

With the amounts of the sums certified to have been paid by the present incumbents, as well as the amounts of those payable to him, by their successors, or those remaining a charge on the benefice. [Answer] The present incumbent, being fourth in succession from the builder and next in succession to the improver, was chargeable to his predecessor with the sum of 1,371 pounds on account of the building and improvement charges, and will be entitled to receive from his successor 327 pounds 10s 2d on account of the improvement charge.

And whether the incumbent or his curate usually reside in the Glebe House. If there be no glebe house or none fit for residence, the amount of rent paid by the incumbent for a house or lodging for himself. [Answer] Incumbent is constantly resident in the Glebe House.

The number of churches and chapels in each benefice, the accommodation which each is capable of affording, the duties performed in each, their distance from one another, if more than one, when each was built, at what expense and from what funds. [Answer] One parochial church capable of accommodating 200 persons. Divine service is performed twice on Sundays from March to November, and once during the rest of the year and on holidays. The sacrament is administered quarterly. The parochial church is distant 5 miles from the chapel of ease in the district cure of Learmount, for the particulars of which see [below]. So extremely old that the date and expense of its erection are unknown. Some years since the church was repaired by private subscriptions, but at what expense is not stated.

How much of the cost of building remains charged on the benefice, and when the same will be paid off. The average annual amounts of the sums assessed upon the respective benefices, at vestries in the 3 years ending as aforesaid, distinguishing as far as the same appears by the returns, the sums raised at the exclusive vestries from

Parish of Cumber

those raised at the open or general vestries. [Answer] Exclusive vestries: to clerk's salary 9 pounds 3s 4d; to sexton's salary 2 pounds 8d; to comm. elements 10s; to churchwardens' expenses 2 pounds 2s; to applotter's fees 1 pound; to repairs of church 1 pound; total 15 pounds 16s. General vestries: to support of foundlings 4 pounds 15s 4d. NB The foregoing are the average amounts of the sums voted at vestries for the 3 years ending 1832.

The name of the person or body to whom the advowson of each benefice belongs, or is reputed to belong. [Answer] The diocesan.

If the benefice be not a rectory, the name of the person to whom the rectory is reputed to belong, its reputed value, how paid, and if from portions of tithes, distinguishing the amount payable to the rector from that payable to the vicar. [Answer] The benefice is a rectory.

Whether incumbents are, in right of their benefices, patrons of any, and what, ecclesiastical benefices, perpetual curacies or chapelries; and if so, the diocese in which they are situate. [Answer] An alternate right of presentation to the district perpetual cure of Learmount, in the county of Londonderry and diocese of Derry, belongs to the incumbent of this benefice.

The names and proper titles of every dignity, prebend or other ecclesiastical preferment or office whatever, now held by any incumbent and in what county or diocese situate; and whether with or without cure of souls. [Answer] None, besides the benefice of Cumber, with cure, forming the corps of Cumber prebend, founded in the cathedral church of Derry.

Queries and Answers on Religious Administration

Learmount chapel of ease.

The names and denominations of the parishes constituting each benefice or union. [Answer] Learmount, a district perpetual cure.

Whether with or without cure of souls? [Answer] With spiritual duties annexed.

And of any chapelry belonging thereto, not having a separate incumbent; and whether subject to episcopal or to what peculiar or exempt jurisdiction. [Answer] Subject to episcopal jurisdiction. NB This district cure, which contains 18 townlands, formed from portions of the contiguous parishes of Banagher, Cumber Upper and Cumber Lower, viz. 8 townlands from each of the 2 former and 1 from the last-mentioned parishes.

The extent of the respective parishes, and the reputed acreable contents, in statute measure, of each parish respectively. [Answer] Length 7 Irish miles, breadth 3 Irish miles; the acreable contents of this cure are included in those of the parishes out of which the same has been erected.

And in what county or counties each is locally situate, with an account of the general quality of the land in each. [Answer] County Londonderry; the land in this cure consists of arable and bog, but the relative proportions of each are not specified.

The population of the respective parishes according to the census taken in 1831. [Answer] 4,411.

The names of the respective incumbents and the dates of their admission, with the names of the curates employed and for what parishes, and the amount of stipend or allowance paid to each and every curate. [Answer] James S. Hunter, clerk, lic. [licentiate?] in December 1831, perpetual curate, no assistant curate employed.

Gross amounts of the annual income of the respective parishes and benefices, on an average of 3 years ending with December 1831 or to the latest period to which the returns have been made. [Answer] 85 pounds.

The sources from whence the said yearly incomes arise, specifying how much from tithes or tithe composition, and how much from glebe or any other source, with acreable contents, profitable or not, of the glebe in statute measure, and its average value per acre; whether subject to any rent and whether let or in occupation of the incumbent. [Answer] From salary payable by the rector of Banagher benefice 40 pounds, from salary payable by the rector of Upper Cumber benefice 40 pounds, from salary payable by the rector of Lower Cumber benefice 5 pounds, total 85 pounds.

The amount of any yearly payments or temporary charges, each under its proper title, made out of the gross incomes of the respective benefices, on an average of 3 years ending as before, excepting rates and taxes for the Glebe House and offices, repairs and curates' stipends; and if only temporary, the time at which the same will terminate. [Answer] To house rent 30 pounds.

The net amounts of the annual incomes of the benefices respectively, after deducting such payments (except as aforesaid); and whether such incomes may be fairly considered as the average amounts of net income for the future or otherwise. [Answer] 55 pounds.

The time and expense at which the respective glebe houses were built, from what funds; whether under the old or new acts, with the amounts of the sum certified to have been paid by the present incumbents, as well as the amounts of those payable to them by their successors, or those remaining a charge on the benefice; and whether the incumbent or his curate usually resides in the Glebe House, or if not, for what reason and where resident, with the name of the person by whom the Glebe House is occupied; or if there be no glebe house or none fit for residence, the amount of rent paid by the incumbent for a house or lodging for himself. [Answer] No glebe house; incumbent resides within the benefice and pays an annual rent of 30 pounds per annum for his residence.

The number of churches and chapels in each benefice, the accommodation which each is capable of affording, the duties performed in each, their distance from one another if more than one, when each was built, at what expense and from what funds. [Answer] Learmount church, capable of accommodating 200 persons; divine service is performed once on Sundays; the sacrament is administered 4 times in the year. Built in the year 1831, at the probable expense of 700 pounds British, by means of a gift to the amount of 400 pounds granted by the late Board of First Fruits, and private subscriptions to the amount of 300 pounds.

How much of the cost of building remains charged on the benefice, and when the same will be paid off? [Answer] No charge on the parish in 1832, on account of the church.

The average annual amounts of the sums assessed upon the respective benefices at the vestries in the 3 years ending as aforesaid, distinguishing, as far as the same appears by the returns, the sums raised at the exclusive vestries from those raised at the open or general vestries. [Answer] Exclusive vestry: to clerk's salary 5 pounds; to sexton's salary 2 pounds; total 7 pounds. General vestry: to support of a foundling 4 pounds. There was only 1 vestry holden within the 3 years, viz. in 1832, as the church was not erected till 1831.

The name of the person or body to whom the advowson of each benefice belongs, or is reputed to belong. [Answer] The right of nomination to this perpetual cure belongs alternately to the incumbents of Banagher and Cumber Upper benefices.

If the benefice be not a rectory, the name of the person to whom the rectory is reputed to belong, its reputed value, how paid; and if from portions of tithes, distinguishing the amount payable to the rector from that payable to the vicar. [Answer] The benefices from portions of which this district cure has been formed are rectories.

Whether the incumbents are, in right of their benfices, patrons of any, and what, ecclesiastical beneices, perpetual curacies or chapelries; and if so, the diocese in which they are situated. [Answer] None.

The names or proper titles of every dignity, prebend or other ecclesiastical preferment or office whatever now held by any incumbent, and in what county and diocese situate, and whether with or without cure of souls. [Answer] None.

PRODUCTIVE ECONOMY

Tithe Composition

Volume 12, 1836; Upper Cumber, including 169 pounds 1s in Tyrone: annual value of land 5,477 pounds 5s; annual value of land exempt from tithe composition 401 pounds 18s; annual value of titheable land 5,075 pounds 7s; tithe 740 pounds; proportion of tithe to 1 pound in the value of titheable land 2s 11d. Volume 43 (tithe composition), 309, 1833; Upper Cumber, 1834: amount of tithe 740 pounds; tithe owners Francis Brownlow; capacity of owner, rector.

SOCIAL ECONOMY

Visit to Cumber School

Report of Deputation of Irish Society, 1836.

We also visited the school kept at Cumber which is patronised by Mr Brown[e] of Cumber and the Revd Frank Barlow, and superintended by the ladies of their families; it is in a most thriving state. Both Mr Brown[e] and Mr Frank Barlow are actively employed here in promoting the comfort of those around them.

Transition Papers by George Downes, May 1838

MEMOIR WRITING

Queries and Answers on Religion

The names and denominations of the parishes constituting each benefice or union? [Answer] Cumber Lower.

Whether with or without cure of souls? [Answer] A rectory with cure.

And of any chapelry belonging thereto, not having a separate incumbent; and whether subject to episcopal or to what peculiar or exempt jurisdiction? [Answer] Subject to episcopal jurisdiction.

Parish of Cumber

The extent of the respective parishes, the reputed acreable contents in statute measure of each parish respectively. [Answer] Length 8, breadth 4 English miles, 14,782 acres 3 roods 21 perches statute measure, per Ordnance Survey.

And in what county or counties each is locally situate? [Answer] County Londonderry.

With an account of the general quality of land in each. [Answer] The arable land in this parish is reported to be of a good quality, but a large portion of it to consist of uncultivated mountain and bog.

The population of the respective parishes according to the census taken in 1831. [Answer] 4,584.

The names of the respective incumbents and the dates of their admission, with the names of the curates employed and for what parishes. [Answer] John Heyden [insert alternative: Hayden], clerk, admitted 17th February 1831, incumbent; no curate employed.

And the amount of stipend or allowance paid to each and every curate. [No answer].

Gross amounts of the annual income of the respective parishes and benefices on an average of 3 years ending with December 1831, or to the latest period to which the returns have been made. [Answer] 641 pounds 14s 2d.

The sources from whence the said yearly incomes arise, specifying how much from tithes or tithe compositions and how much from glebe or any other source. [Answer] From tithe composition 560 pounds, 106 acres Cunningham or 148 acres 7 and three-quarter perches statute measure of glebe, valued at 15s 5d per Cunningham acre, 81 pounds 14s 2d, [total] 641 pounds 14s 2d.

With the acreable contents, profitable or not, of the glebe in statute measure and its average value per acre. [Answer] NB Of the glebe lands, about 15 acres consist of bog, 15 acres of inferior land, 12 acres of plantation, 13 acres of arable and 51 acres of meadow and pasture-land.

Whether subject to any rent and whether let or in occupation of the incumbent? [Answer] The Glebe, with the exception of land to the value of 12 pounds per annum, is occupied by the incumbent.

The amount of any yearly payments or temporary charges, each under its proper title, made out of the gross incomes of the respective benefices, on an average of 3 years ending as before, excepting rates and taxes for the Glebe House and offices, repairs and curate's stipends; and if only temporary, the time at which the same will terminate. [Answer] Glebe rent 10s, county cess 4 pounds, subscriptions to schools 15 pounds, agent's salary 40 pounds, visitation fees 19s 6d, perpetual curate of Learmount 5 pounds, interest at 10 pounds per cent on 255 pounds 11s 3d 3 farthings sunk on Glebe House, 25 pounds 11s 1d ha'penny, interest at 5 pounds per cent on 470 pounds 17s 11d expended on same and recoverable from successor, 23 pounds 10s 10d 3 farthings, [total] 114 pounds 11s 6d farthing.

The net amounts of the annual incomes of the benefices respectively, after deducting such payments (except as aforesaid); whether such incomes may be fairly considered as the average amounts of net incomes for the future or otherwise. [Answer] 527 pounds 2s 7d 3 farthings.

The time and expense at which the respective glebe houses were built; from what funds; whether under the old or new acts? [Answer] Cumber Lower Glebe House built in 1797 at an expenditure of 600 pounds British, of which sum 92 pounds 6s 1d 3 farthings was granted in way of gift by the late Board of First Fruits and the residue of 507 pounds 13s 10d farthing was supplied out of the private funds of the builder; under the old acts. In 1807 an additional sum of 162 pounds 9s 2d 3 farthings and in 1814 a further sum of 520 pounds 4s 3d were expended on improvements by the incumbents of the day.

With the amounts of the sums certified to have been paid by the present incumbents, as well as the amounts of those payable to them by their successors, or those remaining a charge on the benefices. [Answer] The present incumbent is third in succession from the builder and, having paid his predecessor 726 pounds 9s 2d 3 farthings, he will be entitled to receive 470 pounds 17s 11d from his successor.

And whether the incumbent or his curate usually resides in the Glebe House; or if not, for what reason and where resident, with the name of the person by whom the Glebe House is occupied; or if there be no glebe house or none fit for residence, the amount of rent paid by the incumbent for a house or lodging for himself. [Answer] Incumbent is constantly resident in the Glebe House.

The number of churches and chapels in each benefice, the accommodation which each is capable of affording, the duties performed in each, their distances from one another if more than one, when each was built, at what expense and from what funds; how much of the cost of building remains charged on the benefice and when the same will be paid off. [Answer] One church, capable of containing 250 persons. Divine service is performed twice on Sunday during the summer months and once during the rest of the year, and on the principal holidays. The sacrament is administered 4 times in the year. Built in 1796 by means, as far as incumbent can ascertain, of a gift of 464 pounds 10s 9d farthing British, granted by the late Board of First Fruits. There was not any charge on the parish in 1832, on account of the church.

The average annual amounts of the sums assessed upon the respective benefices at vestries in the 3 years ending as before said, distinguishing, as far as the same appear by the returns, the sums raised at the exclusive vestries from those raised at the open or general vestries. [Answer] Church purposes: clerk's salary 7 pounds 10s, sexton's salary 2 pounds 13s 4d, [comm. elements ?] 10s, churchwardens 2 pounds 8d, applotter's fees 10s, repairs of church 5 pounds 4s, a chalice 10s 8d, [total] 18 pounds 18s 8d. General purposes: care of a foundling 3s 4d. NB The foregoing are the average amounts of the sums voted at exclusive vestries for 3 years ending 1832; no general vestries have been held in this parish.

The name of the person or body to whom the advowson of each benefice belongs or is reputed to belong. [Answer] The diocesan.

If the benefice be not a rectory, the name of the person to whom the rectory is reputed to belong, its reputed value, how paid; and if from portions of tithes, distinguishing the amount payable to the rector from that payable to the vicar. [Answer] The benefice is a rectory.

Whether the incumbents are, in right of their benefices, patrons of any and what ecclesiastical benefices, perpetual curacies or chapelries; and if so, the diocese in which they are situated. [Answer] None.

The names and proper titles of every dignity, prebend or other ecclesiastical preferment or office whatever now held by any incumbent, and in what county or diocese situate, and whether with or without cure of souls. [Answer] None.

PRODUCTIVE AND SOCIAL ECONOMY

Tithe Composition

Lower Cumber, 1836 (volume 12): annual value of land 3,812 pounds 10s, annual value of land exempt from tithe composition 127 pounds 17s, annual value of titheable land 3,684 pounds 13s, tithe 560 pounds, proportion of tithe to 1 pound in the value of titheable land 3s ha'penny.

Tithe composition, 1834 (volume 42): amount of tithe 560 pounds, tithe owners John Hayden, capacity of owner rector.

Fawney Cross School

Report of the Deputation of the Irish Society, 1836: A memorial was presented us from the inhabitants of Fawney Cross, Usmdeanot, Ballinamore, Tawnamore and others, praying for aid to build and furnish a Sunday schoolhouse there for the purpose of educating the now neglected children. We recommend that 20 pounds be granted them in aid of building and furnishing the same, with school requisites, to be paid when the whole shall be completed, and 5 pounds per annum towards maintaining the school.

Memoir Section on Productive Economy by Captain J.E. Portlock, April 1838

PRODUCTIVE ECONOMY

Remarks on Land and Farms

Of this parish, more than one-half is bog waste or mountain; and though some part of this large proportion is profitably employed as summer grazing for cattle, it is still a matter of regret that more exertion is not made to improve the character of the mountain pasturage by draining, irrigation and other modes of reclaiming, as it is manifest, from its moderate elevation, that a large tract of the upper land might be rendered fit for the support of sheep and cattle, whilst the lower lands could be made subservient to the same purposes by turnips and other green crops. The smaller farms under 10 acres are only one-fifth of the whole, but the farms under 35 acres are to those above as 241 to 79.

In respect to natural position, most of the townlands are only a short distance from deposits of lime, but the features of the country and the want of roads oppose difficulties of access to many and force the use of lime from more distant localities. This is a serious evil, and is much complained of in the north eastern and central parts of the parish, but it is hoped that the limestone discovered in the Burntollet (see Geology) may in part supply the defect and facilitate the use of this most valuable manure, more particularly as a new road has been projected which, keeping at a short distance from the Burntollet, will open a much more ready channel of communication, both to manure deposits and markets, than the central portions of the parish at present possess.

Suggestions for Improvement

The quantity of manure in some instances is high,

and this is especially the case in regard to composts, the actual cost of which, when put on the land, is often very great, the augmentation in quantity rendering the carriage expensive. The rotations exhibit the same want of system which has been already commented on, 2 or 3 exhausting crops occurring either between the pasture and the potato crop, or between the potato crop and the grass. How easily might landlords introduce better systems by giving a profitable motive for their adoption, such, for instance, as that suggested in subsection 1, namely contracts with the tenants to furnish a given quantity of turnip or other food during winter, for either sheep or cattle, the property of the landlord, which might for the time be billeted, as it were, on the several farms.

The produce is variable, being small in some townlands, though generally equal or above the Scotch average.

In respect to planting, much of the parish is totally bare, but on the Burntollet and Faughan there is a considerable quantity of wood, some of which is applied to profitable use; planting might, however, be extended with advantage.

In stock the horses are as 1 for each 30 acres on the whole parish, or as 1 to 13 on the cultivated land; cattle as 1 to 8 or 1 to 3 and one-third; sheep as 1 to 26 or as 1 to 10 and three-fifths; hogs as 1 to 111 or as 1 to 46.

Besides a small number of asses, goats and beehives and a large quantity of poultry, nearly one to each cultivated acre referring to those proportions, it appears that on the cultivated land the number of cattle exceeds that maintained on an equal quantity of the cultivated land in the south of Scotland, in nearly a duplicate ratio; but here it must be remembered that the mountain land either does, or ought to, contribute to the support of the cattle, and taking into consideration the proportion, would fall below that of Scotland.

The quantity of sheep is, on the contrary, below the proportion of Scotland, whether referred to the cultivated land alone or to the cultivated and mountain conjointly. Mr Low estimates the sheep stock of a farm of 500 acres, on the 15th May of each year, at 302 sheep and 180 lambs. Taking therefore account only of the stock sheep, the proportion becomes 1 to 1 and three-fifth acres, being 16 times greater than that of the whole parish, or 6 times greater than that of the cultivated land. The number of horses on the whole parish is about the same as that of Scotch farming, though more than double if taken on the cultivated land.

These remarks combined together are suffi-cient to show that were the present wastelands turned to better account, a great extension might be given to the stock maintained in this parish; and as one of the simplest modes of extension would be by the increase of the sheep, and that in the way suggested, it may be added as useful information that Mr Low estimates for the winter food of the ewe and wether hogs at the rate of three-quarters of an acre of turnips to every 10 sheep, and allows one and a half acres for the ewes in the lambing season, making altogether 15 acres of turnips for a stock of 302 sheep, or 1 acre to 20 sheep; but as this supposes the sheep to be fed on young grass, a different proportion would hold in reference to mountain land, the deficiency of winter feeding being greater. Let therefore the proportion be taken as 1 acre to every 15 sheep, and it is evident that every farm with 20 acres and a 5-shift rotation, including a turnip crop, might supply the winter food of 60 sheep.

As such farms could easily be arranged along the base of the highlands, would it not be worthy of the attention of the proprietors to investigate the facilities and advantages of such a system, by which the small farmer would be made to co-operate with the grazier, his land being enriched by the droppings of the sheep whilst feeding on the turnips, and employment as shepherd's boys afforded to his children.

The value of the live and other stock of this parish, or the amount of auxiliary capital, is about 3 pounds per acre, estimated on the cultivated land alone, a reduction of one-fourth being made for depreciated value by use; the actual cost value therefore would be about 4 pounds per acre.

Family Labour and Cottiers

The family aid rarely falls below 2 and as rarely exceeds 4. The average days labour on the whole parish seems small, namely 35 per acre, the quantity of waste being great; but on the cultivated land it is high, namely 76 per acre. The simple labour in quarries is very small, not exceeding the constant employment of 9 persons and the gain by machinery in mills is also very inconsiderable. The mills employ for only a very short time and, having little to do, the total gained does not exceed the constant employment of 11 men. The number of cottiers, 404, is great, being more than sufficient by at least 100 for the cultivation of the land independently of the farmers' aid.

As regards their condition, it is variable: in some townlands they have only 1 apartment, a cow occasionally sharing it with the family, and the beds being stuck into recesses of the walls. In others they have 2 apartments, but there is generally a want of minor comforts, and damp floors, bad beds and clothing are far too common. The farmers are possessed of more comforts, sometimes even possessing luxuries such as sofas and clocks, though it is probable that in few instances the first impression on looking at a mountain town (village) would be favourable, the irregular walls built without regard to system or neatness and the coarse <course> thatch being the very reverse of the picturesque in village or cottage.

Industry: Weaving

Although the return of the farming product must be considered in this instance somewhat below the truth, the increased value, including labour, not being above 1s 8d of the original cost price, whereas in preceding cases it was about one-fifth, the example only adds another proof that farming under the disadvantage of high priced bark can only be supported by the gain of the retail trade.

The number of looms is considerable and the quantity of linen manufactured rises to 183,292 yards, of cotton to 10,824 yards and of woollen to 2,900 yards. The gain on the whole, or the increased value arising out of the manufacture of linens, cottons and woollens, amounts to 1,776 pounds, equivalent to 5s 9d per acre on the cultivated land in the parish, or to more than one-quarter of the farmer's profit, a consideration which powerfully proves the importance of these manufactures, even in their present state. The bleaching greens exhibit nearly the usual amount of profit, whilst the quantity operated upon is nearly double that manufactured in the parish.

Trades

The trades of distribution are to the manufacturing trades as 1 to 8 and one-third, and it is remarkable that neither baker or butcher appears amongst them, although there are 6 spirit sellers and 4 grocers. Signed J.E. Portlock, Captain Royal Engineers, 30th April 1838.

Productive Economy Tables for Lower Cumber by Captain J.E. Portlock, April 1838

Distribution of Land

[Table contains the following headings: name of townland, proprietor, chief tenure, acreage, aspect, ground levels, surface, soil, subsoil, proportions of land, supply of water, size of farms, manures: lime and shells, distances estimated in miles from the quarry or other locality to the centre of the townland, communications, markets. Bog is not used as manure in any townland].

1, Ardground, proprietor Skinners' Company, tenure [blank] lives and [blank] years and at will; 430 acres 2 roods 30 perches; winds: southerly, exposed to the same, sheltered from northerly; ground levels: highest 940 feet, lowest 195 feet, average 550 feet; surface: hilly and mountainous; soil: depth from 6 inches to 1 foot 2 inches, red clay; subsoil: blue clay and rock; land: 48.1% tillage, 20.4% bog waste and mountain pasture, 1.2% meadow, 26.7% pasture, 1% plantation, 2.6% roads; 1 river, 4 brooks, 6 springs; farms: 2 under 20 acres, 7 under 50 acres, 1 over 50 acres; manures: lime, half a mile from quarry, half a mile from locality used; communications: branch road to Strabane and Derry, branch road to Dungiven, good; markets: Londonderry, 7 and a half miles.

2, Ballygroll, proprietor Grocers' Company, tenure [blank] lives and [blank] years and at will; 334 acres 22 perches; winds: north easterly, exposed to the same, sheltered from south westerly; ground levels: highest 794 feet, lowest 400 feet, average 570 feet; surface: mountainous and sloping; soil: depth from 4 inches to 1 foot 2 inches, clay and loam; subsoil: hard gravel till and slate; land: 23.9% tillage, 65.6% bog waste and mountain pasture, 9% plantation, 1.5% roads; 4 brooks and 2 springs; farms: 1 under 20 acres, 6 under 50 acres, 1 over 50 acres; manures: lime, 1 and three-quarter miles from quarry, 2 and a half miles from locality used; shells, nearest source 6 and a quarter miles; communications: branch to the Dungiven and to the Newtownlimavady road, middling; markets: Londonderry, 6 miles.

3, Ballynamore, proprietor Leslie Alexander Esquire, tenure 3 lives, 72 years and at will; 493 acres 1 rood 25 perches; winds: westerly, exposed to the same, sheltered from easterly; ground levels: highest 500 feet, lowest 250 feet, average 360 feet; surface: hilly, mountainous and sloping; soil: depth from 4 inches to 1 foot 4 inches, clay, loam and bog; subsoil: blue clay and rock; land: 35.2% tillage, 44.2% bog waste and mountain pasture, 0.4% meadow, 18.2% pasture, 2% roads; 2 brooks and 4 springs; farms: 12 under 10 acres, 1 under 20 acres; manures: lime, 1 and a quarter miles from quarry, 3 and three-quarter miles from locality used; shells, nearest source 5 miles; communications: 2 branches to the Derry and Dungiven road, bad; markets: Londonderry, 5 miles.

4, Brackfield, proprietor Skinners' Company,

Parish of Cumber

tenure [blank] lives and [blank] years and at will; 438 acres 8 perches; winds: north westerly, exposed to the same, sheltered from north easterly; ground levels: highest 400 feet, lowest 128 feet, average 320 feet; surface: hilly and undulating; soil: depth from 3 inches to 1 foot 4 inches, gravelly clay; subsoil: blue clay and gravel; land: 32.5% tillage, 41.7% bog waste and mountain pasture, 0.9% meadow, 16.4% pasture, 6.8% plantation, 1.7% roads; 2 rivers, 4 brooks and 2 springs; farms: 4 under 20 acres, 4 under 50 acres, 4 over 50 acres; manures: lime, quarter of a mile from quarry, 2 and a half miles from locality used; communications: road from Derry to Dungiven and branch from Dungiven road, good; markets: Londonderry, 6 miles.

5, Brockagh, proprietor Grocers' Company, tenure [blank] lives and [blank] years and at will; 564 acres 27 perches; winds: north westerly, exposed to northerly, sheltered from south easterly; ground levels: highest 684 feet, lowest 140 feet, average 400 feet; surface: hilly, mountainous and sloping; soil: depth from 3 to 10 inches, loam; subsoil: hard gravel till and rock; land: 15.6% tillage, 72.2% bog waste and mountain pasture, 0.4% meadow, 9.4% pasture, 1.2% plantation, 1.2% roads; 4 brooks and 4 springs; farms: 7 under 10 acres, 3 under 20 acres, 3 under 50 acres; manures: lime, 1 mile from quarry; shells, nearest source 4 and a half miles; communications: 2 branches to the Dungiven and 1 to the Newtownlimavady roads, good; markets: Londonderry, 8 miles.

6, Clonmakane, proprietor Grocers' Company, tenure [blank] lives and [blank] years and at will; 387 acres 24 perches; winds: north westerly, exposed to the same, sheltered from south easterly; ground levels: highest 678 feet, lowest 228 feet, average 450 feet; surface: hilly, mountainous and sloping; soil: depth from 4 inches to 1 foot, clay and loam; subsoil: hard gravel till and rock; land: 11.6% tillage, 84% bog waste and mountain pasture, 2.8% pasture, 1.6% roads; 2 brooks and 1 spring; farms: 1 under 50 acres, 2 over 50 acres; manures: lime, 1 and a quarter miles from quarry; shells, nearest source 4 and a quarter miles; communications: 1 branch to the Dungiven and 1 to the Newtownlimavady roads, good; markets: Londonderry, 9 miles.

7, Crossballycormick, proprietor Leslie Alexander Esquire, tenure 3 lives and 72 years; 327 acres 7 perches; winds: south westerly, exposed to the same, sheltered from westerly; ground levels: highest 250 feet, lowest 100 feet, average 200 feet; surface: hilly; soil: depth from 4 inches to 1 foot 3 inches, gravelly clay; subsoil: clay and sand; land: 47.4% tillage, 14.4% bog waste and mountain pasture, 2.4% meadow, 30.3% pasture, 2.4% plantation, 3.1% roads; 1 river, 3 brooks and 4 springs; farms: 1 under 10 acres, 2 under 20 acres, 3 under 50 acres, 3 over 50 acres; manures: lime, 1 and three-quarter miles from quarry, 5 miles away from locality used; communications: road from Derry to Dungiven and branch to Newtownlimavady, good; markets: Londonderry, 4 and a half miles.

8, Ervey, proprietor Grocers' Company, tenure at will; 520 acres 2 roods 17 perches; winds: southerly, exposed to the same, sheltered from north west and north easterly; ground levels: highest 510 feet, lowest 157 feet, average 360 feet; surface: mountainous and sloping; soil: depth from 6 inches to 1 foot 2 inches, clay and bog; subsoil: red till and rock; land: 17.9% tillage, 62.3% bog waste and mountain pasture, 6.7% pasture, 11% plantation, 2.1% roads; 1 river, 2 brooks and 3 springs; farms: 2 under 10 acres, 1 under 20 acres, 5 under 50 acres, 2 over 50 acres; manures: lime, 1 mile from quarry, 5 miles from locality used; shells, nearest source 7 and a half miles; communications: branches to the Dungiven and to the Newtownlimavady roads, good; markets: Londonderry, 6 and a half miles.

9, Fawney, proprietor Leslie Alexander Esquire, tenure 3 lives and 72 years; 297 acres 2 roods 10 perches; winds: north westerly, exposed to the same, sheltered from easterly; ground levels: highest 400 feet, lowest 182 feet, average 300 feet; surface: sloping; soil: depth from 3 inches to 1 foot 2 inches, red clay; subsoil: red gravel and slate; land: 47.7% tillage, 24.5% bog waste and mountain pasture, 1% meadow, 23.5% pasture, 3.3% roads; 2 brooks, 1 lake and 3 springs; farms: 12 under 20 acres, 4 under 50 acres; manures: lime, 1 and a half miles from quarry, 5 and three-quarter miles from locality used; shells, nearest source 5 miles; communications: 2 branches to the Dungiven and 1 to the Newtownlimavady roads, good; markets: Londonderry, 4 and a half miles.

10, Gortinreid, proprietor Grocers' Company, tenure at will; 136 acres 3 roods 36 perches; winds: westerly, exposed to the same, sheltered from south easterly; ground levels: highest 346 feet, lowest 126 feet, average 230 feet; surface: sloping; soil: depth from 8 inches to 1 foot 3 inches, loam; subsoil: clay and till; land: 42.3% tillage, 6.6% bog waste and mountain pasture, 38.7% pasture, 9.5% plantation, 2.9% roads; 3 brooks and 2 springs; farms: 1 under 10 acres, 1 under 20 acres, 3 under 50 acres; manures: lime, three-quarters of a mile from quarry; shells, nearest source 3 and three-quarter miles; communications: 2 branches to the Dungiven and 1 to the Newtownlimavady roads, good; markets: Londonderry, 7 and a half miles.

11, Gosheden, proprietor Lord De Blacquiere, tenure 3 lives and 31 years; 572 acres 2 roods 34 perches; winds: northerly, exposed to the same, sheltered from south westerly; ground levels: highest 1,074 feet, lowest 125 feet, average 740 feet; surface: hilly and mountainous; soil: depth from 4 inches to 1 foot 3 inches, clay and loam; subsoil: blue clay and rock; land: 17.9% tillage, 65.9% bog waste and mountain pasture, 0.7% meadow, 9.6% pasture, 4.7% plantation, 1.2% roads; 1 river, 4 brooks and 4 springs; farms: 5 over 50 acres; manures: lime, 1 and a half miles from quarry, 2 and a half miles from locality used; communications: branch to the Dungiven road and branch road to Strabane, good; markets: Londonderry, 5 miles.

12, Highmoor, proprietor W.H. Ash Esquire, tenure at will; 618 acres, 3 roods 16 perches; winds: northerly and southerly, exposed to the same, sheltered from southerly and northerly; ground levels: highest 605 feet, lowest 400 feet, average 500 feet; surface: mountainous and sloping; soil: depth from 6 inches to 1 foot 3 inches, loam; subsoil: red clay and rock; land: 14.3% tillage, 71.4% bog waste and mountain pasture, 1.3% meadow, 11.8% pasture, 0.7% plantation, 1.1% roads; 4 brooks and 7 springs; farms: 3 under 20 acres, 2 under 50 acres, 1 over 50 acres; manures: lime, 1 and a quarter miles from quarry; shells, nearest source 5 and three-quarter miles; communications: branch to the Dungiven and branch to the Newtownlimavady roads, good; markets: Londonderry, 6 miles.

13, Kildoag, proprietor Skinners' Company, tenure [blank] lives and [blank] years and at will; 705 acres 1 rood 17 perches; winds: south easterly, exposed to the same, sheltered from north westerly; ground levels: highest 1,074 feet, lowest 226 feet, average 500 feet; surface: hilly and mountainous; soil: depth from 4 inches to 1 foot 4 inches, gravelly clay and loam; subsoil: blue clay, till and rock; land: 24.4% tillage, 64.6% bog waste and mountain pasture, 1.1% meadow, 6.4% pasture, 1.8% plantation, 1.7% roads; 5 brooks, 2 lakes and 14 springs; farms: 10 under 20 acres, 8 over 50 acres; manures: lime, half a mile from quarry, three-quarters of a mile from locality used; communications: branch road to Strabane and Derry, good; markets: Londonderry, 8 miles.

14, Killaloo, proprietors Rector Hayden and Richard Hunter Esquires, tenure 3 lives and 31 years and perpetuity; 270 acres 2 roods 10 perches; winds: south westerly, exposed to the same, sheltered from westerly; ground levels: highest 400 feet, lowest 152 feet, average 350 feet; surface: sloping; soil: depth from 4 inches to 1 foot, loam; subsoil: red clay, gravelly clay and rock; land: 38.2% tillage, 21% bog waste and mountain pasture, 11.9% meadow, 22.9% pasture, 3.4% plantation, 2.6% roads; 1 river, 1 brook and 2 springs; farms: 1 under 10 acres, 4 under 20 acres, 1 over 50 acres; manures: lime, 1 and a quarter miles from quarry, 3 and three-quarter miles from locality used; communications: road from Derry to Dungiven, good; markets: Londonderry, 7 miles.

15, Killenan, proprietor Leslie Alexander Esquire, tenure 3 lives and 72 years; 360 acres 2 roods 37 perches; winds: north westerly, exposed to the same, sheltered from north easterly; ground levels: highest 409 feet, lowest 220 feet, average 300 feet; surface: sloping; soil: depth from 5 inches to 1 foot 1 inch, loam and boggy clay; subsoil: red gravel and slate; land: 50.6% tillage, 17.8% bog waste and mountain pasture, 1.7% meadow, 26.9% pasture, 3% roads; 2 brooks and 4 springs; farms: 1 under 20 acres, 5 under 50 acres, 2 over 50 acres; manures: lime, 2 miles from quarry, 5 and three-quarter miles from locality used; shells, nearest source 6 and a quarter miles; communications: 2 branches to the Dungiven and 1 to the Newtownlimavady roads, good; markets: Londonderry, 5 miles.

16, Lackagh, proprietor Skinners' Company, tenure [blank] lives and [blank] years and at will; 622 acres 3 roods 24 perches; winds: south easterly, exposed to southerly, sheltered from northerly; ground levels: highest 1,073 feet, lowest 272 feet, average 480 feet; surface: hilly and mountainous; soil: depth from 1 inch to 1 foot 2 inches, clay and loam; subsoil: clay, rock and till; land: 16.9% tillage, 71.5% bog waste and mountain pasture, 1.4% meadow, 4.9% pasture, 4.8% plantation, 0.5% roads; 4 brooks and 4 springs; farms: 4 under 50 acres, 4 over 50 acres; manures: lime, 1 mile from quarry, 1 and a quarter miles from locality used; communications: branch road to Strabane and Derry, good; markets: Londonderry 9 miles, Strabane 9 miles.

17, Legahory, proprietor Skinners' Company, tenure [blank] lives and [blank] years and at will; 579 acres 3 roods 18 perches; winds: north easterly, exposed to the same, sheltered from south westerly; ground levels: highest 986 feet, lowest 130 feet,

Parish of Cumber

average 550 feet; surface: mountainous, sloping and undulating; soil: depth from 3 inches to 1 foot 2 inches, clay; subsoil: red clay, gravel and rock; land: 31.9% tillage, 32.6% bog waste and mountain pasture, 8.9% meadow, 16.2% pasture, 7.6% plantation, 2.8% roads; 1 river, 5 brooks and 5 springs; farms: 2 under 10 acres, 3 under 20 acres, 3 under 50 acres, 2 over 50 acres; manures: lime, 1 and three-quarter miles from quarry, 2 miles from locality used; communications: branch road to Strabane and Derry, good; markets: Londonderry, 5 and a half miles.

18, Lettermire, proprietor Skinners' Company, tenure [blank] lives and [blank] years and at will; 399 acres 2 roods 39 perches; winds: westerly, exposed to the same, sheltered from easterly; ground levels: highest 815 feet, lowest 400 feet, average 600 feet; surface: hilly, mountainous and sloping; soil: depth from 4 inches to 1 foot 3 inches, blue clay and loam; subsoil: blue clay and till; land: 18% tillage, 72% bog waste and mountain pasture, 1.5% meadow, 7% pasture, 1.5% roads; 4 brooks and 4 springs; farms: 3 under 10 acres, 3 under 20 acres, 5 under 50 acres; manures: lime, 1 and a quarter miles from quarry, 2 miles from locality used; communications: branch to Dungiven road, good; Newtownlimavady road in progress; markets: Londonderry, 8 miles.

19, Lettershendony, proprietor William H. Ash Esquire, tenure at will; 299 acres 1 rood 16 perches; winds: north westerly, exposed to the same, sheltered from north easterly; ground levels: highest 368 feet, lowest 260 feet, average 300 feet; surface: hilly and sloping; soil: depth from 6 inches to 1 foot 4 inches, clay and gravel; subsoil: clay and sand; land: 26.7% tillage, 54.7% bog waste and mountain pasture, 0.9% meadow, 15% pasture, 2.7% roads; 3 brooks and 4 springs; farms: 3 under 20 acres, 3 under 50 acres, 1 over 50 acres; manures: lime, 2 miles from quarry; shells, nearest source 7 and a half miles; communications: 2 branches to the Dungiven road, 1 to Newtownlimavady, good; markets: Londonderry, 5 miles, Newtownlimavady 13 and a half miles.

20, Listress, proprietor Grocers' Company, tenure at will; 314 acres 3 roods 30 perches; winds: south easterly, exposed to the same, sheltered from north westerly; ground levels: highest 500 feet, lowest 225 feet, average 300 feet; surface: hilly and convex; soil: depth from 4 inches to 1 foot 3 inches, red clay; subsoil: red gravel and rock; land: 18.1% tillage, 62.9% bog waste and mountain pasture, 11.4% pasture, 6.3% plantation, 1.8% roads; 1 river, 3 brooks and 2 springs; farms: 2 under 20 acres, 6 under 50 acres; manures: lime, 1 and a quarter miles from quarry, 5 miles from locality used; shells, nearest source 7 miles; communications: 1 branch to the Dungiven road, 1 to Newtownlimavady, good; markets: Londonderry 7 miles.

21, Mullaboy, proprietor Grocers' Company, tenure at will; 640 acres 10 perches; winds: southerly, exposed to the same, sheltered from northerly; ground levels: highest 823 feet, lowest 340 feet, average 700 feet; surface: hilly and mountainous; soil: depth from 4 inches to 1 foot, gravelly clay and loam; subsoil: till and rock; land: 15% tillage, 78.6% bog waste and mountain pasture, 0.5% meadow, 3.6% pasture, 2.3% roads; 4 brooks and 7 springs; farms: 2 under 10 acres, 8 under 20 acres, 7 under 50 acres; manures: lime, 2 and a half miles from quarry; shells, nearest source 6 and a quarter miles; communications: branch to the Dungiven and to the Newtownlimavady roads, good; markets: Londonderry, 5 and a half miles.

22, Oghill, proprietor Acheson Lyle Esquire and others, tenure 3 lives and at will; 271 acres 3 roods 10 perches; winds: north westerly, exposed to the same, sheltered from south easterly; ground levels: average 360 feet; surface: sloping; soil: depth from 8 inches to 1 foot 2 inches, loam; subsoil: blue clay and till; land: 42.6% tillage, 26.4% bog waste and mountain pasture, 0.5% meadow, 27.9% pasture, 2.6% roads; 4 brooks and 5 springs; farms: 4 under 10 acres, 7 under 20 acres, 3 under 50 acres; manures: lime, 1 and a half miles from quarry, 5 miles from locality used; shells, nearest quarry 6 and a quarter miles; communications: 3 branches to the Dungiven and 1 to the Newtownlimavady roads, good; markets: Londonderry 5 miles.

23, Oughtagh, proprietor Grocers' Company, tenure at will; 668 acres 2 roods 25 perches; winds: northerly, exposed to the same, sheltered from southerly; ground levels: highest 623 feet, lowest 225 feet, average 490 feet; surface: mountainous and sloping; soil: depth from 3 inches to 1 foot 3 inches, red clay; subsoil: red gravel and rock; land: 10% tillage, 74.7% bog waste and mountain pasture, 0.1% meadow, 9.7% pasture, 5.1% plantation, 0.4% roads; 1 river, 2 brooks and 2 springs; farms: 3 under 10 acres, 2 under 20 acres, 1 under 50 acres; manures: lime, 1 mile from quarry, 4 and a half miles from locality used; communications: by-roads to the Dungiven and to the Newtownlimavady roads, good; markets: Londonderry 7 miles.

24, Slaghtmanus, proprietor Revd Henry Gamble, tenure at will; 2,115 acres 1 rood 17 perches;

winds: southerly, exposed to the same, sheltered from north easterly; ground levels: highest 978 feet, lowest 379 feet, average 600 feet; surface: mountainous; soil: depth from 3 inches to 1 foot 3 inches, red clay and bog; subsoil: red gravel and slate; land: 6.6% tillage, 90.9% bog waste and mountain pasture, 2.2% pasture, 0.3% roads; 1 river, 8 brooks and 10 springs; farms: 6 under 10 acres, 13 under 20 acres, 6 under 50 acres, 1 over 50 acres; manures: lime, 3 miles from quarry, 7 and a half miles from locality used; shells, nearest source 7 and a half miles; communications: branch road to the Dungiven and to the Newtownlimavady roads, middling; markets: Londonderry, 9 and a half miles.

25, Strathall, proprietor Acheson Lyle Esquire, tenure in perpetuity; 205 acres 2 roods 37 perches; winds: southerly, exposed to the same, sheltered from north westerly; ground levels: highest 300 feet, lowest 123 feet, average 250 feet; surface: hilly and level; soil: depth from 3 inches to 1 foot 4 inches, bog, clay and sand; subsoil: blue clay and till; land: 19% tillage, 26.9% bog waste and mountain pasture, 19% meadow, 13.2% pasture, 19% plantation, 2.9% roads; 1 river, 1 brook and 1 spring; farms: 1 over 50 acres; manures: lime, 1 and a half miles from quarry, 3 and a quarter miles from locality used; communications: road from Derry to Dungiven, good; markets: Londonderry 5 miles.

26, Tamnaherin, proprietor Grocers' Company, tenure at will; 790 acres 3 roods 37 perches; winds: north westerly, exposed to the same, sheltered from south easterly; ground levels: highest 655 feet, lowest 200 feet, average 400 feet; surface: hilly, mountainous and sloping; soil: depth from 5 inches to 1 foot 1 inch, loam and clay; subsoil: clay, till and rock; land: 19.4% tillage, 66.8% bog waste and mountain pasture, 11.1% pasture, 1.4% plantation, 1.3% roads; 6 brooks and 6 springs; farms: 4 under 10 acres, 6 under 20 acres, 10 under 50 acres, 4 over 50 acres; manures: lime, 1 and a quarter miles from quarry, 1 and quarter miles from locality used; shells, nearest quarry 5 miles; communications: branch to the Dungiven and to the Newtownlimavady roads, good; markets: Londonderry, 7 miles.

27, Tamnymore, proprietor Acheson Lyle Esquire, tenure 3 lives and 31 years and some at will; 346 acres 1 rood 37 perches; winds: southerly, exposed to the same, sheltered from north easterly; ground levels: highest 521 feet, lowest 130 feet, average 430 feet; surface: mountainous and sloping; soil: depth from 6 inches to 1 foot 2 inches, loam; subsoil: clay, till and rock; land: 43.7% tillage, 19.3% bog waste and mountain pasture, 2.3% meadow, 28% pasture, 3.8% plantation, 2.9% roads; 2 rivers, 2 brooks and 2 springs; farms: 3 under 20 acres, 2 under 50 acres, 3 over 50 acres; manures: lime, 1 and a quarter miles from quarry, 7 and a half miles from locality used; communications: road from Derry to Dungiven and branch to Newtownlimavady, good; markets: Londonderry, 6 miles.

28, Tamnyreagh, proprietor William H. Ash, Esquire, tenure at will; 231 acres 1 rood 29 perches; winds: north westerly, exposed to the same, sheltered from south easterly; ground levels: highest 400 feet, lowest 180 feet, average 300 feet; surface: hilly and sloping; soil: depth from 4 inches to 1 foot, loam; subsoil: blue clay and till; land: 50.2% tillage, 12.5% bog waste and mountain pasture, 33.7% pasture, 3.5% roads; 2 brooks and 8 springs; farms: 3 under 10 acres, 3 under 20 acres, 5 under 50 acres; manures: lime, 1 mile from quarry; shells, nearest source 5 and three-quarter miles; communications: 3 branches to the Dungiven and to the Newtownlimavady roads, good; markets: Londonderry, 6 and a quarter miles.

29, Teenaght, proprietor Richard Hunter Esquire, tenure 21 years and 1 life; 333 acres 2 roods 33 perches; winds: northerly , exposed to the same, sheltered from south easterly; ground levels: highest 435 feet, lowest 280 feet, average 350 feet; surface: hilly, sloping and undulating; soil: depth from 4 inches to 1 foot 4 inches, gravelly clay; subsoil: blue clay, red gravel and rock; land: 49.7% tillage, 15.7% bog waste and mountain pasture, 31.8% pasture, 0.1% plantation, 2.7% roads; 1 river, 3 brooks and 5 springs; farms: 5 under 10 acres, 15 under 20 acres, 4 under 50 acres; manures: lime, half a mile from quarry, 3 and three-quarter miles from locality used; communications: road from Moneymore to the Derry and Dungiven road, good; markets: Londonderry, 11 miles, Dungiven 9 miles.

30, Toneduff, proprietor Skinners' Company, tenure [blank] lives and [blank] years and at will; 503 acres 3 roods 20 perches; winds: north easterly, exposed to the same, sheltered from southerly; ground levels: highest 500 feet, lowest 152 feet, average 350 feet; surface: hilly and mountainous; soil: depth from 7 inches to 1 foot 4 inches, gravelly clay and loam; subsoil: blue clay and rock; land: 31.8% tillage, 46.8% bog waste and mountain pasture, 17.4% pasture, 2% plantation, 2% roads; 1 river, 5 brooks, 1 lake and 8 springs; farms: 4 under 10 acres, 3 under 20 acres, 4 under 50 acres, 3 over 50 acres; manures: lime, 1 mile

Parish of Cumber

from quarry, three-quarters of a mile from locality used; communications: branch road to Strabane and Derry, and branch road to Dungiven, good; markets: Londonderry, 6 miles.

Cultivation, its Mode and Results

[Table contains the following headings: name, depth and kind of soil cost of manures and quantity used per acre, rotation of crops, analysis of crops, time of sowing and harvest, quantity of seed and produce, woods, stock].

Wheat, sown 1st November and 1st February, harvested 15th August and September; cost of seed 6s 1d per bushel, produce 5s 4d ha'penny per bushel.

Barley, sown 10th to 30th April, harvested 1st to 20th September; cost of seed 3s 7d 3 farthings per bushel, produce 2s 9d farthing per bushel.

Oats, sown February and May, harvested August and December; cost of seed 2s 11d farthing per bushel, produce 2s 4d ha'penny per bushel.

Rye, sown March and April, harvested September and October; cost of seed 3s 8d per bushel, produce 3s per bushel.

Potatoes, sown April and May, harvested October and December; cost of seed 1s 7d farthing per bushel, produce 8d farthing per bushel.

Flax, sown April and May, harvested August; cost of seed 11s 6d per bushel, produce 46s 6d per cwt.

Vetches, sown May, harvested November; cost of seed 8s 2d per bushel, produce 16s 9d per ton.

Turnips, seed 1s 3d per bushel, produce 18s 1d ha'penny per ton;

Hay, sown 1st April to 20th May, harvested 20th June to 1st August; clover seed 10d ha'penny per lb, grass seed 3s 4d per bushel, produce 40s per ton.

1, Ardground, soil: depth from 6 inches to 1 foot 2 inches, red clay; cost of manures per acre: compost 54s 6d, dung 24s 6d, lime 31s; 76 tons of compost used per acre, 34 tons of dung, 4.7 tons of lime; rotation of crops: 1st rotation, oats, potatoes, oats, flax, grass; 2nd rotation, oats, potatoes or turnips, oats, flax, hay, grass; renovating crops: potatoes 34.9, turnips 0.3, vetches 1.3; exhausting crops 110.8 acres; pasture 72.3 acres; meadow 2.6 acres; oats, 5.4 bushels seed per acre, 32 bushels produce; potatoes, 23 bushels seed per acre, 178 bushels produce; flax, 2.7 bushels seed per acre, 3.1 cwt produce; turnips, 2.3 lbs seed per acre, 15.5 tons produce; hay, 2.3 bushels grass seed, 1.6 tons produce; woods: one-quarter acre firs, planted in 1802 and 4 acres natural oak, hazel and birch, none cut; stock: 19 horses, 98 cattle, 13 sheep, 356 poultry, 6 beehives.

2, Ballygroll, soil: depth from 4 inches to 1 foot 2 inches, clay and loam; cost of manures per acre: compost 53s, dung 24s 6d, lime 31s 6d, shells 36s 3d; 66 tons of compost used per acre, 28 tons of dung, 3.7 tons of lime, 7 tons of shells; rotation of crops: 1st rotation, potatoes, oats, oats, grass, grass; 2nd rotation, potatoes, oats, flax, oats, grass, grass; 3rd rotation, potatoes, flax or oats or vetches, oats, grass, grass, grass; renovating crops: potatoes 19.7, vetches 0.3; exhausting crops 59.1; pasture 29.7; oats, 5.5 bushels seed, 28.5 bushels produce; potatoes, 23 bushels seed, 116 bushels produce; flax, 2.7 bushels seed, 2.7 cwt produce; vetches, 2.7 bushels seed; woods: none; stock: 10 horses, 1 ass, 43 cattle, 22 sheep, 2 hogs, 119 poultry.

3, Ballynamore, soil: depth from 4 inches to 1 foot 4 inches, clay, loam and bog; cost of manures per acre: compost 80s, dung 28s, lime 16s; 70 tons of compost used per acre, 35 tons of dung, 1.5 tons of lime; rotation of crops: 1st rotation, oats, potatoes, oats, flax, oats, grass, grass; 2nd rotation, potatoes, oats, flax or vetches, oats, grass, grass; 3rd rotation, oats, potatoes, oats, flax, oats, hay, grass, grass; renovating crops: potatoes 59.4, vetches 4.8; exhausting crops 133.3; pasture 91; meadow 2.6; oats, 4.7 bushels seed, 33 bushels produce; potatoes, 18.6 bushels seed, 186 bushels produce; flax, 2.7 bushels seed, 3.8 cwt produce; vetches, 3.1 bushels seed, 7.7 tons produce; hay, 7.8 lbs clover, 0.8 bushels grass seed, 1.6 tons produce; woods: some trees about the houses; stock: 23 horses, 78 cattle, 5 sheep, 11 hogs, 341 poultry.

4, Brackfield, soil: depth from 3 inches to 1 foot 4 inches, gravelly clay; cost of manures per acre: compost 60s 6d, dung 31s 6d, lime 37s 7d; 54 tons of compost used per acre, 39 tons of dung, 4.5 tons of lime; rotation of crops: 1st rotation, oats, potatoes, flax or oats, oats, grass, grass, grass; 2nd rotation, oats, potatoes, oats, flax, oats, grass, grass, grass; 3rd rotation, oats, potatoes or turnips, oats, flax, oats or vetches, grass, grass, grass; renovating crops: potatoes 31.9, turnips 0.3, vetches 1.3; exhausting crops 170.4; pasture 114.9; meadow 5.2; oats, 4.7 bushels seed, 36 bushels produce; potatoes, 23 bushels seed, 170 bushels produce; flax, 2.3 bushels seed, 3.5 cwt produce; vetches, 2.3 bushels seed, 4.7 tons produce; turnips, 1.9 lbs seed, 4.3 tons produce; hay, 1.2 tons produce; woods: 30 acres oak, birch and natural wood, none cut or sold; stock: 17 horses, 105 cattle, 20 sheep, 5 hogs, 156 poultry, 1 beehive.

5, Brockagh, soil: depth from 3 to 10 inches, loam; cost of manures per acre: compost 85s 3d, dung 28s, shells 14s 6d; 124 tons of compost used per acre, 41 tons of dung, 4.7 tons of shells; rotation of crops: 1st rotation, potatoes, oats, flax, oats, grass; 2nd rotation, oats, potatoes, oats, flax or vetches, oats, grass, grass, grass; renovating crops: potatoes 31.3, vetches 0.9; exhausting crops 69.5; pasture 53.6; meadow 2.6; oats, 4.7 bushels seed, 31 bushels produce; potatoes, 23 bushels seed, 140 bushels produce; flax, 2.7 bushels seed, 2.5 cwt produce; vetches, 3.1 bushels seed, 6.2 tons produce; hay, 1.6 tons produce; woods: 7 acres beech, fir, alder, planted in 1834, unfit for use; stock: 14 horses, 53 cattle, 45 sheep, 2 goats, 7 hogs, 243 poultry, 5 beehives.

6, Clonmakane, soil: depth from 4 inches to 1 foot, clay and loam; cost of manures per acre: compost 56s, dung 28s, shells 13s 9d; 74 tons of compost used per acre, 39 tons of dung, 4.7 tons of shells; rotation of crops: 1st rotation, oats, potatoes, flax, potatoes, oats, grass, grass, grass; 2nd rotation, oats, potatoes or turnips, oats or wheat, flax, oats, grass, grass, grass; renovating crops: potatoes 8.4, turnips 0.6; exhausting crops 35.2; pasture 11.6; wheat, 3.1 bushels seed, 19.4 bushels produce; oats, 5.2 bushels seed, 27.9 bushels produce; potatoes, 23.2 bushels seed, 154.8 bushels produce; flax, 2.6 bushels seed, 2.7 cwt produce; turnips, 1.9 lbs seed, 7.7 tons produce; woods: none; stock: 3 horses, 57 cattle, 6 sheep, 2 goats, 50 poultry.

7, Crossballycormick, soil: depth from 4 inches to 1 foot 3 inches, gravelly clay; cost of manures per acre: compost 77s 9d, dung 29s 9d, lime 17s; 109 tons of compost per acre, 43 tons of dung, 1.5 tons of lime; rotation of crops: 1st rotation, oats, flax, oats, potatoes or turnips, wheat, grass, grass; 2nd rotation, oats, flax, potatoes or turnips or vetches, barley or oats, grass, grass, grass; 3rd rotation, oats, potatoes or turnips, wheat, flax, oats, hay, grass, grass; renovating crops: potatoes 31.6, turnips 5.5, vetches 3.2; exhausting crops 115.1; pasture 99.4; meadow 7.7; wheat, 3 bushels seed, 30 bushels produce; barley, 3.2 bushels seed, 35.5 bushels produce; oats, 5.3 bushels seed, 34.1 bushels produce; potatoes, 21.7 bushels seed, 230 bushels produce; flax, 2.4 bushels seed, 3.5 cwt produce; vetches, 2.7 bushels seed, 10.8 tons produce; turnips, 2.3 lbs seed, 19.4 tons produce; hay, 7.8 lbs clover, 1.2 grass seed, 1.9 tons produce; woods: 8 and a half acres ash, alder, beech, fir, oak, planted since 1802, none cut; stock: 13 horses, 4 asses, 87 cattle, 4 sheep, 19 hogs, 217 poultry, 9 beehives.

8, Ervey, soil: depth from 6 inches to 1 foot 3 inches, clay and bog; cost of manures per acre: compost 44s 6d, lime 49s 7d, shells 50s; 62 tons of compost used per acre, 4.5 tons of lime, 7.7 tons of shells; rotation of crops: 1st rotation, oats, oats, potatoes, oats, grass, grass, grass; 2nd rotation, oats, flax or oats, potatoes, oats, grass, grass, grass; 3rd rotation, oats, potatoes or turnips, oats, flax or vetches, oats, grass, grass, grass; renovating crops: potatoes 20.6, vetches 0.9; exhausting crops 72.3; pasture 35.5; oats, 4.6 bushels seed, 36.2 bushels produce; potatoes, 24.8 bushels seed, 155 bushels produce; flax, 2.7 bushels seed, 1.9 cwt produce; vetches, 2.7 bushels seed, 6.2 tons produce; turnips, 1.9 lbs seed, 4.6 tons produce; woods: 57 acres ash, oak, fir, beech, planted since 1813, farming uses; stock: 15 horses, 67 cattle, 14 sheep, 3 hogs, 172 poultry.

9, Fawney, soil: depth from 3 inches to 1 foot 2 inches, red clay; cost of manures per acre: compost 46s, lime 39s, shells 41s; 62 tons of compost used per acre, 3.2 tons of lime, 7.7 tons of shells; rotation of crops: 1st rotation, potatoes, oats, flax or oats, grass, grass, grass; 2nd rotation, potatoes, flax or oats or wheat, oats, grass, grass, grass; 3rd rotation, oats, potatoes or turnips, oats or wheat, flax or vetches, oats, hay, grass, grass; renovating crops: potatoes 29.9; exhausting crops 111.7; pasture 70; meadow 3.2; wheat, 2.7 bushels seed, 32 bushels produce; oats, 4.6 bushels seed, 31 bushels produce; potatoes, 21.7 bushels seed, 194 bushels produce; flax, 2.7 bushels seed, 3.5 cwt produce; vetches, 3.1 bushels seed, 6.2 tons produce; hay, 7.8 lbs clover, 0.8 bushels grass seed, 1.6 tons produce; woods: none; stock: 20 horses, 1 ass, 46 cattle, 8 sheep, 1 goat, 1 hog, 160 poultry, 1 beehive.

10, Gortinreid, soil: depth from 4 inches to 1 foot 3 inches, loam; cost of manures per acre: compost 68s, dung 30s 6d, shells 10s; 95 tons of compost used per acre, 43 tons of dung, 3 tons of shells; rotation of crops: 1st rotation, oats, potatoes, oats or wheat, flax or oats, grass, grass; 2nd rotation, oats, flax or oats, potatoes or turnips, wheat, grass, grass; 3rd rotation, oats, potatoes or turnips, oats or wheat, flax or oats, grass, grass; renovating crops: potatoes 11.9, turnips 0.6; exhausting crops 45.5; pasture 53.6; wheat, 2.7 bushels seed, 27.2 bushels produce; oats, 5.2 bushels seed, 31 bushels produce; potatoes, 21.7 bushels seed, 193 bushels produce; flax, 2.3 bushels seed, 3.1 cwt produce; turnips, 2.3 lbs seed, 5.4 tons produce; woods: 13 acres alder, beech, firs, oak, 12 years planted, cut and sold; stock: 7 horses, 23 cattle, 2 sheep, 1 goat, 1 hog, 58 poultry, 1 beehive.

11, Gosheden, soil: depth from 4 inches to 1

Parish of Cumber

foot 3 inches, clay and loam; cost of manures per acre: dung 31s 6d, lime 19s 10d; 39 tons of dung used per acre, 2.3 tons of lime; rotation of crops: 1st rotation, oats, potatoes, oats, flax, potatoes, oats, grass, grass; 2nd rotation, potatoes, oats, flax, hay or oats, grass, grass, grass; 3rd rotation, oats, potatoes or turnips or vetches, oats, flax, potatoes, oats, grass, grass; renovating crops: potatoes 19, turnips 1.3, vetches 1.3; exhausting crops 80.4; pasture 54.8; meadow 3.9; oats, 4.7 bushels seed, 33.5 bushels produce; potatoes, 23 bushels seed, 201 bushels produce; flax, 2.7 bushels seed, 3.5 cwt produce; vetches, 3 bushels seed, 9.3 tons produce; turnips, 2.3 lbs seed, 15.5 tons produce; hay, 9.3 lbs clover, 2.3 bushels grass seed, 1.9 tons produce; woods: 27 acres natural wood, mostly birch, some cut and sold; stock: 10 horses, 56 cattle, 4 sheep, 5 goats, 110 poultry, 1 beehive.

12, Highmoor, soil: depth from 6 inches to 1 foot 3 inches, loam; cost of manures per acre: compost 73s, dung 29s, shells 20s; 97 tons of compost used per acre, 39 tons of dung, 4.7 tons of shells; rotation of crops: 1st rotation, potatoes, oats, flax or rye, oats, grass, grass; 2nd rotation, oats, potatoes, oats or rye, flax, oats, hay, grass, grass; renovating crops: potatoes 42.6, turnips 0.3 vetches 0.3; exhausting crops 62.6; pasture 82.6; meadow 7.7; oats, 4.7 bushels seed, 34 bushels produce; rye, 2.7 bushels seed, 38.7 bushels produce; potatoes, 18.6 bushels seed, 186 bushels produce; flax, 2.5 bushels seed, 3.1 cwt produce; hay, 7.8 lbs clover, 1.6 bushels grass seed, 1.6 tons produce; woods: half an acre alder, ash and fir, 25 years planted, none cut; stock: 7 horses, 42 cattle, 6 sheep, 1 hog, 153 poultry.

13, Kildoag, soil: depth from 4 inches to 1 foot 4 inches, gravelly clay and loam; cost of manures per acre: compost 64s 6d, dung 22s, lime 10s 6d; 81 tons of compost used per acre, 31 tons of dung, 1.2 tons of lime; rotation of crops: 1st rotation, oats, flax or potatoes, oats, oats, grass, grass, grass; 2nd rotation, oats, flax, potatoes, oats, oats, oats or vetches, grass, grass; 3rd rotation, oats, potatoes or vetches, barley or oats, oats or vetches, oats, grass, grass, grass; renovating crops: potatoes 36.7, vetches 1.3; exhausting crops 133.3; pasture 44.5; meadow 8.1; barley, 2.7 bushels seed, 35.5 bushels produce; oats, 4.6 bushels seed, 28 bushels produce; potatoes, 18.6 bushels seed, 194 bushels produce; flax, 2.3 bushels seed, 3 cwt produce; vetches, 2.7 bushels seed, 6.2 tons produce; hay, 1.6 tons produce; woods: 13 acres natural wood; stock: 32 horses, 89 cattle, 55 sheep, 3 goats, 4 hogs, 176 poultry.

14, Killaloo, soil: depth from 4 inches to 1 foot, loam; cost of manures per acre: compost 34s 6d, dung 29s, lime 45s; 58 tons of compost used per acre, 39 tons of dung, 4.7 tons of lime; rotation of crops: 1st rotation, oats, potatoes, oats, flax, grass, grass; 2nd rotation, oats, oats, potatoes or turnips, flax or wheat, grass, grass, grass; 3rd rotation, oats, potatoes or turnips, wheat, hay, grass, grass; renovating crops: potatoes 32.3, turnips 1.9, vetches 4; exhausting crops 78.4; pasture 62.6; meadow 32.3; wheat, 3.1 bushels seed, 27.2 bushels produce; oats, 5.4 bushels seed, 32 bushels produce; potatoes, 23 bushels seed, 136 bushels produce; flax, 2.7 bushels seed, 3.5 cwt produce; turnips, 1.9 lbs seed, 23.2 tons produce; hay, 7.8 lbs clover, 1.2 bushels grass seed, 1.6 tons produce; woods: 1 and a quarter acres ash, oak, larch, planted in 1817, none cut; and 8 acres hazel and birch, natural wood, none cut; stock: 12 horses, 38 cattle, 40 sheep, 4 hogs, 141 poultry, 4 beehives.

15, Killenan, soil: depth from 5 inches to 1 foot 6 inches, loam and boggy clay; cost of manures per acre: compost 53s 6d, lime 42s 6d, shells 61s; 69 tons of compost used per acre, 3.5 tons of lime, 9.3 tons of shells; rotation of crops: 1st rotation, oats, flax or oats, potatoes, oats, hay, grass, grass; 2nd rotation, oats, potatoes or vetches, oats or wheat, flax or vetches, grass, grass, grass; 3rd rotation, oats, flax or vetches, oats, potatoes or turnips, oats, grass, grass, grass; renovating crops: potatoes 39.3, turnips 1.6, vetches 2.8; exhausting crops 138.9; pasture 97.2; meadow 6.1; wheat, 2.7 bushels seed, 29 bushels produce; oats, 5.4 bushels seed, 35.7 bushels produce; potatoes, 21.7 bushels seed, 174 bushels produce; flax, 2.7 bushels seed, 3.4 cwt produce; vetches, 2.7 bushels seed, 7 tons produce; turnips, 1.9 lbs seed, 5.4 tons produce; hay, 6.2 lbs clover, 1.6 bushels grass seed, 1.6 tons produce; woods: none; stock: 20 horses, 44 cattle, 3 sheep, 5 goats, 3 hogs, 175 poultry, 2 beehives.

16, Lackagh, soil: depth from 1 inch to 1 foot 3 inches, clay and loam; cost of manures per acre: compost 43s 6d, dung 24s 6d, lime 7s 6d; 54 tons of compost used per acre, 31 tons of dung, 1.2 tons of lime; rotation of crops: 1st rotation, oats, flax, potatoes, oats, oats, grass, grass; 2nd rotation, oats, flax, oats, potatoes, oats, oats, grass, grass; renovating crops: potatoes 14.2; exhausting crops 90.5; pasture 31.3; meadow 9; oats, 4.7 bushels seed, 31 bushels produce; potatoes, 20 bushels seed, 227 bushels produce; flax, 2.3 bushels seed, 2.7 cwt produce; hay, 1.6 tons produce; woods: 30 acres hazel, oak, natural wood; stock: 16 horses, 60 cattle, 14 sheep, 118 poultry.

17, Legahory, soil: depth from 3 inches to 1 foot 2 inches, clay; cost of manures per acre: compost 50s, dung 33s 6d, lime 45s; 70 tons compost used per acre, 47 tons of dung, 5.8 tons of lime; rotation of crops: 1st rotation, potatoes, oats or wheat, flax, grass, grass; 2nd rotation, oats, potatoes or turnips, flax or wheat or vetches, hay, grass, grass, grass; renovating crops: potatoes 53.6, turnips 7.5, vetches 3.2; exhausting crops 140.4; pasture 94.3; meadow 51.6; wheat, 2.5 bushels seed, 29 bushels produce; oats, 4.7 bushels seed, 31.1 bushels produce; potatoes, 23 bushels seed, 197 bushels produce; flax, 2.7 bushels seed, 3.9 cwt produce; turnips, 1.9 lbs seed, 23.2 tons produce; hay, 1.6 bushels grass seed, 2.3 tons produce; woods: 39 acres firs, alder, ash, elm <elim>, beech and birch, planted since 1807, then used for paling; and 5 acres natural wood, hazel and birch, none cut; stock: 25 horses, 1 ass, 93 cattle, 64 sheep, 17 hogs, 216 poultry, 1 beehive.

18, Lettermire, soil: depth from 4 inches to 1 foot 3 inches, boggy clay and loam; cost of manures per acre; compost 44s, dung 31s 6d, lime 36s 6d; 55 tons of compost used per acre, 39 tons of dung, 4.7 tons of lime; rotation of crops: oats, potatoes, flax or oats, grass, grass; 2nd rotation, potatoes, oats, flax, oats, grass, grass; 3rd rotation, oats, potatoes, oats, flax or vetches, grass, grass, grass; renovating crops: potatoes 16.1, vetches 0.2; exhausting crops 55.2; pasture 28.1; meadow 6.1; oats, 4.7 bushels seed, 36 bushels produce; potatoes, 21.7 bushels seed, 155 bushels produce; flax, 2.7 bushels seed, 4.2 cwt produce; vetches, 2.3 bushels seed; hay, 1.6 tons produce; woods: none; stock: 10 horses, 32 cattle, 12 sheep, 1 hog, 102 poultry.

19, Lettershendony, soil: depth from 6 inches to 1 foot 4 inches, gravel and clay; cost of manures per acre: compost 61s, dung 25s, shells 36s; 81 tons of compost used per acre, 35 tons of dung, 6 tons of shells; rotation of crops: 1st rotation, oats, potatoes, flax or oats, grass, grass, grass; 2nd rotation, oats, flax, potatoes or vetches, oats, grass, grass, grass; 3rd rotation, oats, potatoes or turnips, oats, flax, hay, grass, grass; renovating crops: potatoes 21.3; exhausting crops 57.8; pasture 44.9; meadow 2.6; oats, 4.6 bushels seed, 37 bushels produce; potatoes, 21.7 bushels seed, 194 bushels produce; flax, 2.5 bushels seed, 3.5 cwt produce; vetches, 2.7 bushels seed, 4.7 tons produce; turnips, 2.3 lbs seed, 7.8 tons produce; hay, 3.1 bushels grass seed, 1.9 tons produce; woods: none; stock: 10 horses, 33 cattle, 5 sheep, 115 poultry.

20, Listress, soil: depth from 4 inches to 1 foot 3 inches, red clay; cost of manures per acre: compost 39s, dung 25s, lime 30s; 54 tons of compost used per acre, 34 tons of dung, 3 tons of lime; rotation of crops: 1st rotation, oats, flax or oats, potatoes, grass, grass, grass; 2nd rotation, potatoes, oats, flax or vetches, grass, grass; renovating crops: potatoes 19, vetches 1.3; exhausting crops 37.1; pasture 36.2; oats, 4.6 bushels seed, 31 bushels produce; potatoes, 23 bushels seed, 116 bushels produce; flax, 2.5 bushels seed, 2.3 cwt produce; vetches, 2.7 bushels seed; woods: 20 acres ash, oak and firs, partly natural, cut for farming uses; stock: 12 horses, 1 ass, 48 cattle, 10 sheep, 116 poultry.

21, Mullaboy, soil: depth from 4 inches to 1 foot, gravelly clay and loam; cost of manures per acre: compost 82s, dung 24s, shells 14s per acre; 103 tons of compost used per acre, 31 tons of dung, 3.9 tons of shells; rotation of crops: 1st rotation, oats, flax, oats, potatoes, oats, grass; 2nd rotation, oats, potatoes, oats, flax or vetches, grass, grass; renovating crops: potatoes 30.6, turnips 0.8; exhausting crops 64.6; pasture 23.2; meadow 3.2; oats, 4.8 bushels seed, 28.6 bushels produce; potatoes, 26 bushels seed, 155 bushels produce; flax, 2.5 bushels seed, 2.7 cwt produce; vetches, 2.3 bushels seed, 4.7 tons produce; hay, 1.6 tons produce; woods: none; stock: 22 horses, 63 cattle, 11 sheep, 2 goats, 4 hogs, 329 poultry.

22, Oghill, soil: depth from 8 inches to 1 foot 3 inches, loam; cost of manures per acre: compost 57s 9d, dung 28s, lime 16s 6d, shells 16s 5d; 81 tons compost used per acre, 39 tons of dung, 1 ton of lime, 3.1 tons of shells; rotation of crops: 1st rotation, potatoes, oats, flax, oats, grass, grass, grass; 2nd rotation, oats, potatoes, oats, flax or oats, oats, hay, grass, grass; 3rd rotation, oats, potatoes or turnips, flax or vetches, oats, grass, grass, grass; renovating crops: potatoes 25.2; exhausting crops 91; pasture 76.2; meadow 1.3; oats, 4.7 bushels seed, 28.7 bushels produce; potatoes, 18.6 bushels seed, 215 bushels produce; flax, 2.5 bushels seed, 3.5 cwt produce; vetches, 2.7 bushels seed, 9.7 tons produce; turnips, 1.9 lbs seed, 15.5 tons produce; hay, 6.2 lbs clover, 1.6 bushels grass seed, 1.4 tons produce; woods: none; stock: 15 horses, 34 cattle, 15 sheep, 1 goat, 5 hogs, 194 poultry.

23, Oughtagh, soil: depth from 3 inches to 1 foot 3 inches, red clay; cost of manures per acre: compost 42s, dung 26s 6d, lime 44s; 56 tons of compost used per acre, 35 tons of dung, 45 tons of lime; rotation of crops: 1st rotation, potatoes, oats, flax, oats, grass; renovating crops: potatoes 33.2; exhausting crops 52.6; pasture 65.4; meadow

Parish of Cumber

1.3; oats, 4.7 bushels seed, 31 bushels produce; potatoes, 28 bushels seed, 155 bushels produce; flax, 2.7 bushels seed, 3.5 cwt produce; hay, 1 ton produce; woods: 34 acres alder, ash, beech, firs, oak, planted since 1800, none cut; stock: 11 horses, 50 cattle, 20 sheep, 2 hogs, 183 poultry.

24, Slaghtmanus, soil: depth from 3 inches to 1 foot 3 inches, red clay and bog; cost of manures per acre: compost 43s 6d, lime 49s, shells 83s per acre; 58 tons of compost used per acre, 3.9 tons of lime, 10.8 tons of shells; rotation of crops: 1st rotation, potatoes, oats, oats, grass, grass; 2nd rotation, potatoes, oats, flax or oats, grass, grass, grass; 3rd rotation, oats, potatoes or vetches, oats, flax, grass, grass, grass; renovating crops: potatoes 35.8, vetches 0.2; exhausting crops 103.9; pasture 47.8; oats, 4.6 bushels seed, 18 bushels produce; potatoes, 23 bushels seed, 62 bushels produce; flax, 2.7 bushels seed, 1.9 cwt produce; vetches, 2.3 bushels seed; woods: none; stock: 39 horses, 1 ass, 147 cattle, 40 sheep, 196 poultry.

25, Strathall, soil: depth from 3 inches to 1 foot 4 inches, bog, clay and sand; cost of manures per acre: compost 61s, dung 39s, lime 24s; 81 tons of compost used per acre, 54 tons of dung, 2.9 tons of lime; [insert addition: bone dust, quantity four-fifths of a ton, cost 102s 6d per acre]; rotation of crops: 1st rotation, oats, potatoes, wheat, grass, grass; 2nd rotation, oats, potatoes or turnips, oats, hay or wheat, grass; renovating crops: potatoes 16.1, turnips 3.9, vetches 2.6; exhausting crops 27.1; pasture 27.1; meadow 38.7; wheat, 2.7 bushels seed, 34.8 bushels produce; oats, 4.6 bushels seed, 42.5 bushels produce; potatoes, 20 bushels seed, 262 bushels produce; turnips, 2.3 lbs seed, 23.2 tons produce; hay, 3.1 bushels grass seed, 2.3 tons produce; woods: 39 acres oak, ash, beech, fir and alder, planted since 1798, some cut, farming uses; stock: 6 horses, 69 cattle, 14 sheep, 18 goats, 9 hogs, 160 poultry, 10 beehives.

26, Tamnaherin, soil: depth from 5 inches to 1 foot 1 inch, clay and loam; cost of manures per acre: compost 49s, dung 32s 6d, lime 5s, shells 17s; 71 tons of compost used per acre, 47 tons of dung, 1.7 tons of lime, 6 tons of shells; rotation of crops: 1st rotation, oats, potatoes, oats, flax or vetches, grass; 2nd rotation, oats, potatoes, oats or vetches, flax or oats, grass, grass; 3rd rotation, flax or oats, potatoes, oats or wheat, oats or vetches, grass, grass; renovating crops: potatoes 40.2, turnips 0.8, vetches 2.3; exhausting crops 116; pasture 88.4; meadow 0.5; wheat, 2.7 bushels seed, 27.2 bushels produce; oats, 4.7 bushels seed, 25.7 bushels produce; potatoes, 23.2 bushels seed, 140 bushels produce; flax, 2.3 bushels seed, 3.1 cwt produce; vetches, 2.3 bushels seed, 6.9 tons produce; woods: 11 acres ash, alder, firs, oak, 4 to 20 years planted, none cut; stock: 20 horses, 82 cattle, 11 sheep, 2 goats, 3 hogs, 235 poultry, 2 beehives.

27, Tamnymore, soil: depth from 6 inches to 1 foot 2 inches, loam; cost of manures per acre: compost 60s 9d, dung 25s 9d, lime 19s; 93 tons of compost used per acre, 39 tons of dung, 1.5 tons of lime; rotation of crops: 1st rotation, oats, potatoes, barley or oats, flax or oats, grass, grass; 2nd rotation, oats, flax or oats, potatoes, oats, hay, grass, grass; 3rd rotation, oats, potatoes or turnips, flax or oats or wheat, oats or vetches, grass, grass; renovating crops: potatoes 31, turnips 0.3, vetches 0.6; exhausting crops 119.4; pasture 97.5; meadow 8.1; wheat, 3.1 bushels seed, 31 bushels produce; barley, 4.2 bushels seed, 33.3 bushels produce; oats, 4.6 bushels seed, 37.2 bushels produce; potatoes, 23.2 bushels seed, 232 bushels produce; flax, 2.7 bushels seed, 3.8 cwt produce; vetches, 2.7 bushels seed, 11.6 tons produce; turnips, 2 lbs seed, 15.6 tons produce; hay, 6.2 lbs clover, 0.8 bushels grass seed, 1.2 tons produce; woods: 13 acres ash, beech, birch, firs and oak, planted from 4 to 100 years, no use [?]; stock: 16 horses, 82 cattle, 10 sheep, 2 hogs, 165 poultry.

28, Tamnyreagh, soil: depth from 4 inches to 1 foot, loam; cost of manures per acre: compost 66s, dung 30s 6d, shells 9s 9d; 88 tons of compost used per acre, 43 tons of dung, 4.7 tons of shells; rotation of crops: 1st rotation, potatoes, flax or oats, oats, oats, grass, grass, grass; 2nd rotation, potatoes, oats, flax, oats, grass, grass, grass; 3rd rotation, potatoes, oats, flax, oats, grass, grass; renovating crops: potatoes 24.2, vetches 1.2; exhausting crops 91.4; pasture 78.8; oats, 5.2 bushels seed, 31 bushels produce; potatoes, 22 bushels seed, 209 bushels produce; flax, 2.7 bushels seed, 1.5 cwt produce; woods: none; stock: 15 horses, 33 cattle, 2 sheep, 3 goats, 1 hog, 134 poultry.

29, Teenaght, soil: depth from 4 inches to 1 foot 4 inches, gravelly clay; cost of manures per acre: compost 49s, dung 24s 9d, lime 43s 6d; 65 tons of compost used per acre, 33 tons of dung, 4.5 tons of lime; rotation of crops: 1st rotation, oats, flax or potatoes, oats, oats, grass, grass, grass; 2nd rotation, oats, potatoes, oats, flax, oats, grass, grass, grass; 3rd rotation, potatoes or turnips, oats, flax or oats, grass, grass, grass; renovating crops: potatoes 39, turnips 0.3, vetches 0.6; exhausting crops 126.5; pasture 105.9; oats, 4.6 bushels seed, 33 bushels produce; potatoes, 20 bushels seed, 201 bushels produce; flax, 2.3 bushels seed, 2.7 cwt produce; turnips, 2.3 lbs seed, 15.5 tons produce; woods: half an acre alder and firs, planted 30 years, none cut; stock: 26 horses, 81 cattle, 85 sheep, 3 goats, 18 hogs, 242 poultry.

30, Toneduff, soil: depth from 7 inches to 1 foot 4 inches, gravelly clay and loam; cost of manures per acre: compost 41s 6d, dung 35s 6d, lime 10s 6d; 56 tons of compost used per acre, 47 tons of dung, 1.7 tons of lime; rotation of crops: 1st rotation, oats, flax, potatoes, oats, grass, grass; 2nd rotation, potatoes, oats or vetches, flax, oats, grass, grass, grass; 3rd rotation, oats, flax or vetches, potatoes or turnips, oats, flax, grass, grass, grass; renovating crops: potatoes 51, turnips 0.6, vetches 3.2; exhausting crops 125.2; pasture 87.5; oats, 4.7 bushels seed, 25.7 bushels produce; potatoes, 24.8 bushels seed, 140 bushels produce; flax, 2.5 bushels seed, 2.3 cwt produce; vetches, 2.3 bushels seed, 6.2 tons produce; turnips, 2.3 lbs seed, 12.4 tons produce; woods: 10 acres natural wood, alder, ash, birch and hazel; stock: 18 horses, 73 cattle, 21 sheep, 4 hogs, 255 poultry, 2 beehives.

Application of Power

[Table contains the following headings: name of townland, labour subdivided into working farmers and subholders, family labour, agricultural servants, occasional labour, average days worked per acre, average days worked in arable; auxiliary power in farming, auxiliary power in quarrying, capacity of water mills].

1, Ardground, labour: 10 working farmers, 17 family males, 14 family females; 45 male and 9 female occasional labourers; total days worked: farmers and family 9,703, constant hired labour 4,695, occasional male labour 868, occasional female labour 110; average days worked per acre: 35 per townland, 46 arable; quarrying: 1 quarry, 3 men, 480 days labour per annum; object: building and roads, limestone quarry; 9 ploughs, 15 harrows, 1 roller, 11 cars, 14 carts, 19 horses, 37 spinning wheels.

2, Ballygroll, labour: 8 working farmers, 14 family males, 16 family females; 1 male farming servant; 22 male occasional labourers; total days worked: farmers and family 9,390, constant hired labour 1,878, occasional male labour 590; average days worked per acre: 35 per townland, 108 arable; 7 ploughs, 9 harrows, 7 cars, 7 carts, 10 horses, 31 spinning wheels.

3, Ballynamore, labour: 13 working farmers, 27 family males, 21 family females; 98 male and 28 female occasional labourers; total days worked: farmers and family 15,024, constant hired labour 3,443, occasional male labour 768, occasional female labour 198; average days worked per acre: 39 per townland, 73 arable; 10 ploughs, 20 harrows, 1 roller, 4 cars, 11 carts, 23 horses, 65 spinning wheels.

4, Brackfield, labour: 11 working farmers, 15 family males, 15 family females; 3 male farming servants; 14 male occasional labourers; total days worked: farmers and family 9,390, constant hired labour 5,321, occasional male labour 720, occasional female labour 72; average days worked per acre: 35 per townland, 63 arable; quarrying: 1 quarry, 4 men, 768 days labour per annum; object: building; 10 ploughs, 14 harrows, 1 roller, 1 corn-fan, 9 cars, 10 carts, 17 horses, 51 spinning wheels.

5, Brockagh, labour: 13 working farmers, 24 family males, 27 family females; 54 male occasional labourers; total days worked: farmers and family 15,963, constant hired labour 2,191, occasional male labour 378; average days worked per acre: 33 per townland, 123 arable; 8 ploughs, 10 harrows, 6 cars, 6 carts, 14 horses, 69 spinning wheels.

6, Clonmakane, labour: 3 working farmers, 4 family males, 5 family females; 24 male and 5 female occasional labourers; total days worked: farmers and family 2,817, constant hired labour 313, occasional male labour 364, occasional female labour 62; average days worked per acre: 9 per townland, 63 arable; 2 ploughs, 3 harrows, 1 roller, 1 car, 2 carts, 3 horses, 14 spinning wheels.

7, Crossballycormick, labour: 6 working farmers, 8 family males, 4 family females; 6 male and 2 female farming servants; 39 male and 30 female occasional labourers; total days worked: farmers and family 3,756, constant hired labour 6,886, occasional male labour 622, occasional female labour 347; average days worked per acre: 35 per townland, 43 arable; 6 ploughs, 10 harrows, 2 horse-hoes, 3 rollers, 2 corn-fans, 2 cars, 12 carts, 13 horses, 10 spinning wheels.

8, Ervey, labour: 9 working farmers, 10 family males, 14 family females; 3 male farming servants; 7 male occasional labourers; total days worked: farmers and family 7,512, constant hired labour 5,634, occasional male labour 318; average days worked per acre: 26 per townland, 73 arable; 7 ploughs, 13 harrows, 12 cars, 6 carts, 15 horses, 41 spinning wheels.

9, Fawney, labour: 16 working farmers, 27 family males, 27 family females; 1 male farming servant; 41 male and 18 female occasional labourers; total days worked: farmers and family 16,902, constant hired labour 1,878, occasional

Parish of Cumber

male labour 689, occasional female labour 88; average days worked per acre: 65 per townland, 94 arable; 10 ploughs, 15 harrows, 2 rollers, 1 corn-fan, 6 cars, 11 carts, 12 horses, 47 spinning wheels.

10, Gortinreid, labour: 5 working farmers, 8 family males, 10 family females; 23 male and 9 females occasional labourers; total days worked: farmers and family 5,634, constant hired labour 939, occasional male labour 252, occasional female labour 71; average days worked per acre: 50 per townland, 55 arable; 4 ploughs, 4 harrows, 1 car, 5 carts, 7 horses, 17 spinning wheels.

11, Gosheden, labour: 5 working farmers, 8 family males, 13 family females; 2 male farming servants; 17 occasional male labourers; total days worked: farmers and family 6,573, constant hired labour 2,817, occasional male labour 226; average days worked per acre: 17 per townland, 51 arable; 5 ploughs, 9 harrows, 1 car, 7 carts, 10 horses, 29 spinning wheels.

12, Highmoor, 6 working farmers; 9 family males, 7 family females; 1 male farming servant; 33 male and 3 female occasional labourers; total days worked: farmers and family 5,008, constant hired labour 939, occasional male labour 234, occasional female labour 18; average days worked per acre: 10 per townland, 36 arable; 5 ploughs, 8 harrows, 3 cars, 5 carts, 7 horses, 32 spinning wheels.

13, Killdoag, 18 working farmers; 24 family males, 22 family females; 1 male farming servant; 15 male and 9 female occasional labourers; total days worked: farmers and family 14,398, constant hired labour 3,443, occasional male labour 992, occasional female labour 332; average days worked per acre: 27 per townland, 80 arable; quarrying: 2 quarries, 3 men, 720 days labour per annum; object: [for] lime, not used, [the other] for building and flagging and slating; 14 ploughs, 26 harrows, 24 cars, 9 carts, 32 horses, 55 spinning wheels.

14, Killaloo, 5 working farmers, 7 family males, 7 family females; 4 male farming servants; 46 male and 10 female occasional labourers; total days worked: farmers and family 4,382, constant hired labour 5,008, occasional male labour 1,043, occasional female labour 300; average days worked per acre: 39 per townland, 52 arable; quarrying: 1 quarry, not in use; object: building; 7 ploughs, 9 harrows, 6 cars, 8 carts, 12 horses, 25 spinning wheels.

15, Killenan, 8 working farmers, 13 family males and 19 family females; 2 male farming servants; 48 male and 19 female occasional labourers; total days worked: farmers and family 10,016, constant hired labour 5,008, occasional male labour 670, occasional female labour 121; average days worked per acre: 44 per townland, 55 arable; quarrying: 1 quarry, not in use, [object] building and roads; 7 ploughs, 15 harrows, 1 horse-hoe, 2 rollers, 1 corn-fan, 1 car, 13 carts, 20 horses, 1 threshing machine, 43 spinning wheels.

16, Lackagh, 8 working farmers, 8 family males, 10 family females; 2 male and 2 female occasional labourers; total days worked: farmers and family 5,634, constant hired labour 3,130, occasional male labour 84, occasional female labour 24; average days worked per acre: 14 per townland, 61 arable; quarrying: 1 quarry, used occasionally; object: limestone; 7 ploughs, 14 harrows, 1 roller, 13 cars, 7 carts, 16 horses, 18 spinning wheels.

17, Legahory, 9 working farmers, 25 family males, 20 family females; 15 male farming servants; 67 male and 30 female occasional labourers; total days worked: farmers and family 14,085, constant hired labour 9,077, occasional male labour 1,419, occasional female labour 724; average days worked per acre: 44 per townland, 67 arable; 10 ploughs, 23 harrows, 1 horse-hoe, 4 rollers, 1 corn-fan, 5 cars, 15 carts, 25 horses, 49 spinning wheels.

18, Lettermire, 11 working farmers, 16 family males, 22 family females; 13 male and 1 female occasional labourers; total days worked: farmers and family 11,894, constant hired labour 1,252, occasional male labour 758, occasional female labour 10; average days worked per acre: 35 per townland, 131 arable; 9 ploughs, 11 harrows, 14 cars, 1 cart, 10 horses, 30 spinning wheels.

19, Lettershendony, 7 working farmers, 9 family males, 11 family females; 3 male farming servants; 20 male occasional labourers; total days worked: farmers and family 6,260, constant hired labour 1,565, occasional male labour 582; average days worked per acre: 28 per townland, 68 arable; 8 ploughs, 8 harrows, 2 rollers, 1 car, 10 carts, 10 horses, 29 spinning wheels.

20, Listress, 8 working farmers, 9 family males, 13 family females; 23 male and 2 female occasional labourers; total days worked: farmers and family 6,886, constant hired labour 1,565, occasional male labour 608, occasional female labour 4; average days worked per acre: 29 per townland, 80 arable; 9 ploughs, 10 harrows, 6 cars, 5 carts, 12 horse, 31 spinning wheels; grain water mill: 1 breast wheel, diameter of wheel 12 feet; 44,800 lbs of oats ground, [overall] maximum quantity 291,200 lbs; average time working 8 weeks, 1 attendant including miller; flax water mill: 1

undershot water wheel, diameter of wheel 10 feet; raw quantity 8,160 lbs, tow quantity 2,040 lbs; average time working 4 weeks, 4 male attendants.

21, Mullaboy, 17 working farmers, 26 family males, 22 family females; 1 male farming servant; 33 male occasional labourers; total days worked: farmers and family 15,024, constant hired labour 3,756, occasional male labour 347; average days worked per acre: 30 per townland, 157 arable; 16 ploughs, 23 harrows, 24 cars, 5 carts, 22 horses, 44 spinning wheels.

22, Oghill, 14 working farmers, 23 family males, 22 family females; 2 male farming servants; 83 male and 14 female occasional labourers; total days worked: farmers and family 14,085, constant hired labour 3,756, occasional male labour 635, occasional female labour 196; average days worked per acre: 69 per townland, 96 arable; 13 ploughs, 15 harrows, 1 roller, 1 car, 14 carts, 15 horses, 23 spinning wheels.

23, Oughtagh, 6 working farmers, 12 family males, 16 family females; 48 male and 16 female occasional labourers; total days worked: farmers and family 8,764, constant hired labour 1,878, occasional male labour 438, occasional female labour 96; average days worked per acre: 17 days per townland, 167 arable; 6 ploughs, 11 harrows, 5 cars, 5 carts, 11 horses, 24 spinning wheels.

24, Slaghtmanus, 27 working farmers, 58 family males, 50 family females; 1 male occasional labourer; total days worked: farmers and family 33,804, constant hired labour 313, occasional male labour 30; average days worked per acre: 76 per townland, 180 arable; quarrying: 1 quarry, not in use; object: building; 15 ploughs, 21 harrows, 33 cars, 10 carts, 39 horses, 78 spinning wheels.

25, Strathall, 10 male servants, 8 male and 9 female occasional labourers; total days worked: constant hired labour 4,382, occasional male labour 200, occasional female labour 820; average days worked per acre: 26 per townland, 37 arable; 2 ploughs, 4 harrows, 1 horse-hoe, 1 roller, 1 corn-fan, 4 carts, 6 horses, 18 spinning wheels.

26, Tamnaherin, 17 working farmers, 23 family males, 22 family females; 78 male and 33 female occasional labourers; total days worked: farmers and family 14,085, constant hired labour 3,130, occasional male labour 982, occasional female labour 430; average days worked per acre: 24 per townland, 73 arable; quarrying: 3 quarries: one, 10 men, 720 days labour per annum, object: lime; [other two] used occasionally, object building; 13 ploughs, 14 harrows, 2 corn-fans, 4 cars, 16 carts, 20 horses, 56 spinning wheels.

27, Tamnymore, 4 working farmers, 9 family males, 8 family females; 40 male and 32 female occasional labourers; total days worked: farmers and family 5,321, constant hired labour 3,756, occasional male labour 775, occasional female labour 337; average days worked per acre: 29 per townland, 38 arable; quarrying: 1 quarry, not in use; object: building; 5 ploughs, 11 harrows, 1 horse-hoe, 1 roller, 1 corn-fan, 4 cars, 8 carts, 16 horses, 40 spinning wheels.

28, Tamnyreagh; 11 working farmers, 21 family males and 18 family females; 57 male and 12 female occasional labourers; total days worked: farmers and family 12,207, constant hired labour 1,878, occasional male labour 886, occasional female labour 152; average days worked per acre: 65 per townland, 78 arable; 11 ploughs, 15 harrows, 1 roller, 1 car, 13 carts, 15 horses, 23 spinning wheels.

29, Teenaght, 24 working farmers, 40 family males, 48 family females; 1 male farming servant; 10 male occasional labourers; total days worked: farmers and family 27,544, constant hired labour 1,565, occasional male labour 220; average days worked per acre: 88 per townland, 107 arable; 21 ploughs, 21 harrows, 22 cars, 11 carts, 26 horses, 49 spinning wheels.

30, Toneduff, 13 working farmers, 25 family males, 22 family females; 51 male and 2 female occasional labourers; total days worked: farmers and family 14,711, constant hired labour 5,321, occasional male labour 714, occasional female labour 24; average days worked per acre: 41 per townland, 80 arable; 10 ploughs, 16 harrows, 1 corn-fan, 11 cars, 13 carts, 18 horses, 20 spinning wheels; grain water mill: 1 breast wheel, diameter of wheel 11 feet; 56,000 lbs of oats ground, [overall] maximum quantity 448,000 lbs; average time working 12 weeks, 2 attendants including miller.

[Insert footnote referring to quarries [?], townland nos 1, 4, 13, 14, 16, 24, 26, 27: "abandoned, being unprofitable"].

Manufactures and Manufacturing Processes

[Table contains the following headings: tanning, with amounts and value of hides; weaving, subdivided into woollen, linen and cotton work; bleaching, subdivided by power, materials and product].

1, Ardground, tanning: 16 pits, 4 men; materials: 400 cow hides, 200 calf hides, 40 horse hides, value 520 pounds; value of work 275 pounds, value of leather product 860 pounds; weaving of linen: 6 independent looms; materials: 2,120 yards

Parish of Cumber

of yarn, value 95 pounds; product: 2,492 yards, value 110 pounds; weaving of cotton: 2 dependent looms; materials: 605 yards of yarn, value 38 pounds; product: 5,368 yards, value 89 pounds.

2, Ballygroll, weaving of linen: 6 independent looms; materials: 1,420 yards of yarn, value 64 pounds; product: 2,522 yards, value 101 pounds.

3, Ballynamore, weaving of linen: 25 independent looms; materials: 11,177 yards of yarn, value 613 pounds; product: 21,511 yards, value 964 pounds.

4, Brackfield, weaving of linen: 1 independent loom; materials: 107 yards of yarn, value 10 pounds; product: 260 yards, value 14 pounds.

5, Brockagh, weaving of linen: 5 independent looms; materials: 1239 yards of yarn, value 67 pounds; product: 2,402 yards, value 106 pounds.

6, Clonmakane, weaving of linen: 1 independent loom; materials: 812 yards of yarn, value 15 pounds; product: 1,120 yards, value 26 pounds.

7, Crossballycormick, weaving of linen: 9 independent looms; materials: 25,088 yards of yarn, value 401 pounds; product: 27,976 yards, value 520 pounds.

8, Ervey, weaving of linen: 9 independent looms; materials: 2,795 yards of yarn, value 244 pounds; product: 6,812 yards, value 325 pounds.

9, Fawney, weaving of linen: 18 independent and 2 dependent looms; materials: 36,891 yards of yarn, value 685 pounds; product: 45,034 yards, value 922 pounds.

10, Gortinreid, weaving of linen: 1 independent loom; materials: 168 yards of yarn, value 14 pounds; product: 416 yards, value 22 pounds.

11, Gosheden, weaving of linen: 2 independent looms; materials: 299 yards of yarn, value 13 pounds; product: 500 yards, value 19 pounds.

12, Highmoor, weaving of linen: 7 independent looms; materials: 1,771 yards of yarn, value 147 pounds; product: 4,316 yards, value 225 pounds.

13, Kildoag, weaving of linen: 20 independent and 4 dependent looms; materials: 4,670 yards of yarn, value 283 pounds; product: 9,950 yards, value 466 pounds; weaving of cotton: 4 dependent looms; product: 1,100 yards of yarn, value 74 pounds; product: 5,208 yards, value 138 pounds.

14, Killaloo, weaving of linen: 2 independent and 2 dependent looms; materials: 1,143 yards of yarn, value 46 pounds; product: 1,965 yards, value 73 pounds.

15, Killenan, weaving of linen: 11 independent and 5 dependent looms; materials: 4,073 yards of yarn, value 348 pounds; product: 8,810 yards, value 417 pounds.

16, Lackagh, weaving of linen: 3 independent looms; materials: 512 yards of yarn, value 43 pounds; product: 1,248 yards, value 66 pounds; weaving of cotton: 2 dependent looms; materials: 280 yards of yarn, value 19 pounds; product: 1,736 yards, value 44 pounds; bleaching: 34 men, time of process 12 months, time employed 2 months; auxiliary power: 2 water wheels; materials: value 2,600 pounds; product: 338,000 yards bleached, value of process 4,225 pounds.

17, Legahory, weaving of linen: 6 independent and 1 dependent loom; materials: 1,372 yards of yarn, value 89 pounds; product: 2,872 yards, value 139 pounds.

18, Lettermire, weaving of linen: 8 independent and 1 dependent loom; materials: 1,591 yards of yarn, value 108 pounds; product: 3,414 yards, value 166 pounds.

19, Lettershendony, weaving of linen: 6 independent looms; materials: 2,483 yards of yarn, value 113 pounds; product: 4,826 yards, value 187 pounds.

20, Listress, weaving of linen: 5 independent looms; materials: 2,079 yards of yarn, value 92 pounds; product: 3,723 yards, value 141 pounds.

21, Mullaboy, weaving of linen: 21 independent looms; materials: 5,599 yards of yarn, value 360 pounds; product: 12,169 yards, value 553 pounds.

22, Oghill, weaving of linen: 11 independent looms; materials: 2,482 yards of yarn, value 212 pounds; product: 6,032 yards, value 322 pounds.

23, Oughtagh, weaving of linen: 1 independent loom; materials: 75 yards of yarn, value 5 pounds; product: 156 yards, value 7 pounds.

24, Slaghtmanus, weaving of wool: 1 dependent loom; material: 780 yards of yarn, value 59 pounds; product: 750 yards, value 69 pounds; weaving of linen: 11 independent looms; materials: 2,499 yards of yarn, value 113 pounds; product: 4,486 yards, value 174 pounds.

25, Strathall, [blank].

26, Tamnaherin, weaving of linen: 6 independent looms; materials: 713 yards of yarn, value 47 pounds; product: 1,596 yards, value 77 pounds.

27, Tamnymore, weaving of linen: 10 independent looms; materials: 2,823 yards of yarn, value 241 pounds; product: 6,740 yards, value 374 pounds.

28, Tamnyreagh, weaving of linen: 10 independent looms; materials: 2,493 yards of yarn, value 160 pounds; product: 5,564 yards, value 238 pounds.

29, Teenaght, weaving of wool: 1 dependent loom; materials: 1,080 yards of yarn, value 81 pounds; product: 1,620 yards, value 108 pounds; weaving of linen: 3 independent looms; materials: 2,184 yards of yarn, value 84 pounds; product: 3,554 yards, value 123 pounds.

30, Toneduff, [blank].

Trades and Professions

[Table contains the following headings: manufacturing subdivided by trades supplementary to internal and external production, and auxiliary to internal production; distribution subdivided by trades auxiliary to internal and external production; professions auxiliary to instruction and benevolence].

Manufacturing trades: Supplementary to internal production: 9 flax dressers, 7 masons, 15 shoemakers, 3 thatchers, total 34; supplementary to external production: 4 dressmakers, 16 smiths, 9 tailors, total 29; auxiliary to internal production: 13 carpenters, 4 coopers, 3 gardeners, total 20.

Trades of distribution: Auxiliary to internal production: 6 spirit dealers; auxiliary to external production: 4 grocers.

Professions: Auxiliary to instruction: 2 divines, 2 teachers, total 14; auxiliary to benevolence: 4 midwives.

Summary of Productive Agents

[Table of labour contains the following headings: farming, quarrying, mills, secondary manufactures, manufacturing trades, distribution trades, professions, servants, total].

Farming labour: farmers and family 1,044, servants in farming 309, cottiers 406, total 1,759; labour in quarrying 20; labour in mills: grain millers and attendants 3, flax millers and attendants 4, total 7; labour in secondary manufactures: tanning 4, bleaching 34; weaving, 2 woollen looms, 239 linen looms, 8 cotton looms, total 287.

Labour in manufacturing trades: supplementary to internal production 34, supplementary to external production 29, auxiliary to internal production 20, total 83; labour in trades of distribution: auxiliary to internal production 6, auxiliary to external production 4, total 10.

Professions: auxiliary to instruction 14, auxiliary to benevolence 4, total 18.

General total 2,184. [Signed] J.E. Portlock, 30th April 1838.

Distribution of Livestock and Utensils

[Table] Stock on a given area.

Horses: most on farms from 10 to 15 acres, least on farms above 50 acres.

Asses: most on farms from 2 to 3 acres, least on farms from 15 to 20 acres.

Cattle: most on farms from 2 to 3 acres, least on farms above 50 acres.

Sheep: most on farms above 50 acres, least on farms 1 acre and under.

Hogs: most on farms 1 acre and under, least on farms above 50 acres.

Poultry: most on farms 1 acre and under, least on farms above 50 acres.

Ploughs: most on farms from 10 to 15 acres, least on farms from 2 to 3 acres.

Harrows and breaks: most on farms from 10 to 15 acres, least on farms from 2 to 3 acres.

Carts and cars: most on farms from 10 to 15 acres, least on farms above 50 acres.

Table of Stock on Farms

Extract from table of averages (table 2).

[Table] Farms at will: pleasure horses 1 to 2,453 acres, agricultural horses 1 to 22.1 acres, transport horses 1 to 9,810.5 acres; asses 1 to 1,226 acres; cattle 1 to 6.9 acres; sheep 1 to 25.8 acres; hogs 1 to 12.2 acres; poultry 1 to 1.1 acres; ploughs 1 to 32 acres; harrows and breaks 1 to 28.7 acres; carts and cars 1 to 20.3 acres.

Farms let on lease: pleasure horses 1 to 1,435 acres, agricultural horses 1 to 22.9 acres, transport horses 1 to 1,674 acres; asses 1 to 1,507 acres; cattle 1 to 6.9 acres; sheep 1 to 33.8 acres; hogs 1 to 13.4 acres; poultry 1 to 1.3 acres; ploughs 1 to 36.6 acres; harrows and breaks 1 to 31.9 acres; carts and cars 1 to 21.9 acres.

Total farms: pleasure horses 1 to 2,049 acres; agricultural horses 1 to 22.3 acres; transport horses 1 to 4,177.5 acres; asses 1 to 1,293 acres; cattle 1 to 6.9 acres; sheep 1 to 27.6 acres; hogs 1 to 12.4 acres; poultry 1 to 1.1 acres; ploughs 1 to 33.1 acres; harrows and breaks 1 to 29.5 acres; carts and cars 1 to 20.7 acres.

Thus: there are more pleasure and transport horses on farms let on lease; and more agricultural horses, asses, sheep, hogs, poultry, ploughs, harrows, carts and cars on farms at will. The number of cattle is the same on both, viz. 1 to 6.9 acres. The comparative amount of the several kinds of stock, *on large and small farms* at will and on lease, is best shown by the general table of averages, (table 2).

Notes on Weaving and Tanning

[Notes refer to the following townlands: Ballyvannon, Gortinreid, Tamnyreagh, Ballygroll and Gosheden].

Parish of Cumber

It is conceived that the profit per yard to the weaver should bear a proportion to the value per lb of the yarn, as the latter must mainly depend on its texture; and [as] a larger expenditure of labour and superior degree of skill are required in the manufacturing of the finer linens, consequently a higher rate of renumeration would be effected. In a comparison of these points, it is found, with the exception of the following townlands, this rule greatly generally prevails: Brackfield, Ervey, Killennan, Brockagh. In the text observations, it is stated "although [remainder blank]."

How even this small profit is made out for the statements in the table, is not easy to conceive. The following are the details: value of hides 520 pounds, bark 275 pounds, labour of 4 men at 9s per week 1,872. It is feared that some misconception relating to the details of the tanning establishment must have led to very inaccurate information being obtained on the subject. Added to the value of the skin and bark, the cost of the labour, the total will exceed the value of the leather procured, taking the wages of the workmen at 1s 6d a day; but even at 1s, the profit would only be 10 pounds for investment of capital, rent of premises etc.

[In a different hand] It may be observed that 4 men appears an excessive number, for to carry the operations of tanning 640 skins throughout a year. It would be satisfactory to know the numbers of tons of bark and the rate per ton on which the quantities are based, to enable a comparison to be formed with the quantity used for a given quantity of hides and the rates paid in other places. The total value [of] bark here bears a most exhorbitant proportion to the number of skins tanned.

Rotation of Crops

There is much difficulty experienced in establishing a connection between the rotation of crops and the proportions of the different kinds of land. When rotations of one townland differ essentially, a very lengthy calculation would be necessary; but when the grass crops are equal in number, as in Altaghaney, a comparison is readily made. Thus in each of them, the 8-year rotation, there are 3 years' grass and 5 years' tillage. Therefore the grazing or pasture-land, according to Captain Portlock's definition of pasture-land, should be in the ratio to tilled land of 3 to 5. Refer to the land distribution and it will be found that the pasture-land is 55 over 1,000, and each to an equal extent would require an equal proportion of land for tillage and for pasture.

Productive Economy Tables for Upper Cumber by Captain J.E. Portlock, July 1838

PRODUCTIVE ECONOMY

Distribution of Land

[Table contains the following headings: name of townland, proprietor, chief tenure, acreage, aspect, ground levels, surface, soil, subsoil, proportions of land, supply of water, size of farms, manures: lime, bog and shells, distances estimated in miles from the quarry and other locality to the centre of the townland, communications, markets].

1, Alla Lower, proprietor Revd Francis Brownlow, tenure at will; 506 acres 3 roods 24 perches; winds: northerly, exposed to the same, sheltered from southerly; ground levels: highest 580 feet, lowest 250 feet, average 420 feet; surface: mountainous and sloping; soil: depth from 4 inches to 1 foot 1 inch, loam and bog; subsoil: till and blue clay; land: 19.3% tillage, 63.3% bog waste and mountain pasture, 11.8% meadow, 2.2% pasture, 1.2% mountain, 2.2% roads; 2 rivers, 3 brooks, 4 springs; farms: 2 under 10 acres, 4 under 20 acres, 1 under 50 acres, 4 over 50 acres; manures: lime, half a mile from quarry, half a mile from locality used; communications: branch to road from Cookstown to Derry, good; markets: Derry, 11 miles distant, Strabane 13 miles distant.

2, Alla Upper, proprietor Revd Francis Brownlow, tenure at will; 312 acres 1 rood 13 perches; winds: south easterly, exposed to the same, sheltered from north westerly; ground levels: highest 642 feet, lowest 500 feet, average 570 feet; surface: mountainous and sloping; soil: depth from 4 to 11 inches, loam, clay and bog; subsoil: blue clay and rock; land: 25.6% tillage, 57.2% bog waste and mountain pasture, 14.6% pasture, 0.7% meadow, 1.9% roads; 2 brooks, 5 springs; farms: 2 under 10 acres, 5 under 20 acres, 9 under 50 acres; communications: road from Strabane to Stewartstown, joining the Derry road, good; markets: Derry, 12 miles distant, Strabane 12 miles distant.

3, Altaghoney, proprietor Robert Ogilby Esquire, tenure at will; [?] 163 acres 3 roods 6 perches; winds: south easterly, exposed to the same, sheltered from north westerly; ground levels: highest 1,062 feet, lowest 380 feet, average 650 feet; surface: mountainous and sloping; soil: depth from 3 to 11 inches, red clay; subsoil: till, rock and clay; land: 18.7% tillage, 73.8% bog waste and mountain pasture, 5.5% pasture, 0.7% meadow, 1.3% roads; 2 rivers, 2 springs; farms: 2 under 10 acres, 6 under 20 acres, 6 under 50 acres; communications: branch to road from Derry to Dungiven, bad; markets: Derry, 14 and a quarter miles distant.

4, Ballyartan, proprietor Robert Ogilby Esquire, tenure at will and 31 years and 3 lives; 786 acres 1 rood 24 perches; winds: north easterly, exposed to the same, sheltered from south westerly; ground levels: highest 870 feet, lowest 194 feet, average 530 feet; surface: hilly, mountainous and sloping; soil: depth from 3 inches to 1 foot 4 inches, loam and bog; subsoil: red clay, blue clay; land: 22.7% tillage, 61% bog waste and mountain pasture, 11.4% pasture, 2.4% meadow, 0.3% plantation, 2.2% roads; 1 river, 5 brooks, 5 springs; farms: 1 under 10 acres, 8 under 20 acres, 2 under 50 acres, 4 over 50 acres; manures: lime, half a mile from quarry, half a mile from locality used; communications: road to Derry with branch to Strabane, good; markets: Derry, 9 and a quarter miles distant.

5, Ballycallaghan, proprietor Robert Ogilby Esquire, tenure at will; 301 acres 30 perches; winds: north easterly, exposed to the same, sheltered from south westerly; ground levels: highest 680 feet, lowest 304 feet, average 450 feet; surface: hilly, mountainous and sloping; soil: depth from 2 inches to 1 foot 3 inches, red clay and gravel; subsoil: till and rock; land: 34.3% tillage, 53.2% bog waste and mountain pasture, 15.8% pasture, 4.3% meadow, 0.4% plantation, 2% roads; 4 brooks, 6 springs; farms: 7 under 10 acres, 3 under 20 acres, 2 under 50 acres, 1 over 50 acres; manures: lime, 1 mile from quarry, 1 mile from locality used; communications: branch from Derry road to Strabane, good; markets: Derry, 10 and a quarter miles distant, Strabane 11 miles distant.

6, Ballyholly, proprietor Fishmongers' Company, tenure 21 years and at will; 681 acres 3 roods 13 perches; winds: north westerly, exposed to the same, sheltered from south easterly; ground levels: highest 820 feet, lowest 335 feet, average 660 feet; surface: hilly, mountainous and sloping; soil: depth from 4 inches to 1 foot 2 inches, loam: subsoil: blue clay and rock; land: 17.2% tillage, 70% bog waste and mountain pasture, 9.9% pasture, 0.6% meadow, 2.3% roads; 2 rivers, 3 brooks, 3 springs; farms: 3 under 20 acres, 4 under 50 acres, 10 over 50 acres; communications: road from Derry to Dungiven with branch to Newtownlimavady, indifferent; markets: Derry 13 miles distant, Dungiven, 7 and three-quarter miles distant, Newtownlimavady, 11 miles distant.

7, Ballymaclanigan, proprietor Fishmongers' Company, tenure 21 years and 1 life; 899 acres 13 perches; winds: northerly, exposed to the same, sheltered from southerly; ground levels: highest 970 feet, lowest 316 feet, average 640 feet; surface: hilly, mountainous and smooth; soil: depth from 3 inches to 1 foot 3 inches, loam and clay; subsoil: blue clay and rock; land: 24.9% tillage, 66.2% bog waste and mountain pasture, 7.2% pasture, 0.6% meadow, 1.1% roads; 1 river, 5 brooks, 5 springs; farms: 2 under 20 acres, 6 under 50 acres, 3 over 50 acres; manures: lime, 1 and a half miles from quarry, 1 and a half miles from locality used; communications: branch to road from Derry to Dungiven, good; markets: Derry, 11 and a quarter miles distant, Dungiven, 9 miles distant.

8, Ballyrory, proprietor John Beresford Esquire, tenure 21 years and 1 life; 426 acres 3 roods 14 perches; winds: north easterly, exposed to the same, sheltered from south westerly; ground levels: highest 854 feet, lowest 325 feet, average 590 feet; surface: hilly and mountainous; soil: depth from 4 to 11 inches, loam and clay; subsoil: till, clay and rock; land: 37.3% tillage, 45.5% bog waste and mountain pasture, 15.3% pasture, 1.9% roads; 1 river, 4 brooks, 3 springs; farms: 7 under 10 acres, 11 under 20 acres, 9 under 50 acres; manures: lime, half a mile from quarry, 1 and a half miles from locality used; communications: branch to Derry and Dungiven, also branch to Dungiven and Strabane road, good; markets: Derry 12 and a half miles distant, Dungiven, 10 and a quarter miles distant.

9, Barr Cregg, proprietor John Brown Esquire, tenure at will; 346 acres 2 roods 8 perches; winds: northerly, exposed to the same, sheltered from southerly; ground levels: highest 600 feet, lowest 372 feet, average 486 feet; surface: hilly and mountainous; soil: depth from 3 inches to 1 foot 3 inches, loam and clay; subsoil: till and red gravel; land: 5.2% tillage, 93.1% bog waste and mountain pasture, 1.7% pasture; 1 river, 3 brooks, 2 springs; farms: 3 over 50 acres; manures: lime, half a mile from quarry, 6 miles from locality used; no road; markets: Derry, 9 and a quarter miles distant.

10, Binn, proprietor John Brown Esquire, tenure at will; 581 acres 32 perches; winds: westerly, exposed to the same, sheltered from easterly; ground levels: highest 407 feet, lowest 248 feet, average 340 feet; surface: hilly; soil: depth from 5 inches to 1 foot, loam and clay; subsoil: till, rock and sand; land: 28.6% tillage, 51.1% bog waste and mountain pasture, 17.7% pasture, 1.4%

Parish of Cumber

plantation, 1.2% roads; 2 rivers, 2 brooks, 1 lake, 3 springs; farms: 2 under 10 acres, 11 under 20 acres, 7 under 50 acres, 1 over 50 acres; communications: road from Cookstown to Derry, good; markets: Derry, 11 miles distant.

11, Carnanbane, proprietor Robert Ogilby Esquire, tenure at will; 300 acres 3 roods; winds: south westerly, exposed to the same, sheltered from north easterly; ground levels: highest 856 feet, lowest 351 feet, average 660 feet; surface: hilly, mountainous and sloping; soil: depth from 4 inches to 1 foot, blue clay; subsoil: till and [?] blue rock; land: 26.3% tillage, 61.6% bog waste and mountain pasture, 8.7% pasture, 3.3% roads; 1 river, 4 brooks, 4 springs; farms: 17 under 10 acres, 6 under 20 acres; manures: lime, quarter of a mile from quarry, 1 and a half miles from locality used; communications: branch to road from Cookstown to Derry, good; markets: Derry, 12 and a half miles distant.

12, Carnanreagh, proprietor John Beresford Esquire, tenure 21 years and 1 life; 888 acres 3 roods 2 perches; winds: north westerly, exposed to the same, sheltered from south easterly; ground levels: highest 823 feet, lowest 370 feet, average 590 feet; surface: hilly, mountainous and sloping; soil: depth from 4 inches to 1 foot, clay and bog; subsoil: rock, till and blue clay; land: 24.7% tillage, 65.4% bog waste and mountain pasture, 8.1% pasture, 1.8% roads; 1 river, 3 brooks, 7 springs; farms: 5 under 10 acres, 30 under 20 acres, 7 under 50 acres; manures lime, 1 mile from quarry, 1 and a half miles from locality used; communications: road from Strabane to Dungiven, bad; markets: Derry, 13 and three-quarter miles distant.

13, Claudy, proprietor John H. Brown Esquire, tenure in perpetuity and at will; 1,154 acres 1 rood 26 perches; winds: northerly, exposed to the same, sheltered from southerly; ground levels: highest 938 feet, lowest 240 feet, average 600 feet; surface: hilly, mountainous and sloping; soil: depth from 3 inches to 1 foot 3 inches, loam and bog; subsoil: till, blue clay and rock; land: 18.9% tillage, 70.3% bog waste and mountain pasture, 6.4% pasture, 3.1% meadow, 0.3% plantation, 1% roads; 2 rivers, 7 brooks, 1 lake, 6 springs; farms: 5 under 10 acres, 10 under 20 acres, 12 under 50 acres, 2 over 50 acres; manures: lime, three-quarters of a mile from quarry, 1 and a half miles from locality used; communications: road from Derry to Dungiven and Strabane to Newtownlimavady, good; markets: Derry, 9 and a half miles distant, Dungiven, 10 miles distant.

14, Coolnacolpagh, proprietor Fishmongers' Company, tenure 21 years and at will; 664 acres 7 perches; winds: north westerly, exposed to the same, sheltered from south easterly; ground levels: highest 700 feet, lowest 327 feet, average 450 feet; surface: hilly, mountainous and sloping; soil: depth from 2 to 11 inches, loam and clay; subsoil: till, rock and blue clay; land: 31.6% tillage, 48.7% bog waste and mountain pasture, 18.5% pasture, 1.2% roads; 1 river, 3 brooks, 4 springs; farms: 1 under 20 acres, 7 under 50 acres, 4 over 50 acres; manures: lime, 1 and a half miles from quarry, 1 and a half miles from locality used; communications: branch to road from Dungiven to Derry, bad; markets: Derry, 12 and a half miles distant, Dungiven 8 and three-quarter miles distant.

15, Cregg, proprietor John H. Brown Esquire, tenure in perpetuity and at will; 681 acres 1 rood 12 perches; winds: south westerly, exposed to the same, sheltered from north easterly; ground levels: highest 800 feet, lowest 230 feet, average 450 feet; surface: mountainous, rough and sloping; soil: depth from 4 inches to 1 foot 2 inches, loam and bog; subsoil: till, rock and blue clay; land: 32.9% tillage, 40.5% bog waste and mountain pasture, 20.7% pasture, 2.6% meadow, 2.1% plantation, 1.2% roads; 1 river, 4 brooks, 5 springs; farms: 5 under 10 acres, 7 under 20 acres, 5 under 50 acres, 3 over 50 acres; manures: lime, 1 mile from quarry, 1 and a half miles from locality used; communications: road from Derry to Dungiven, good; markets: Derry, 8 and three-quarter miles distant, Dungiven, 10 and three-quarter miles distant.

16, Cumber, proprietor John H. Brown Esquire, tenure at will; 340 acres 3 roods 19 perches; winds: westerly, exposed to the same, sheltered from easterly; ground levels: highest 415 feet, lowest 230 feet, average 326 feet; surface: hilly and sloping; soil: depth from 5 inches to 1 foot 4 inches, loam, clay and bog; subsoil: till, blue clay and rock; land: 30.3% tillage, 23.2% bog waste and mountain pasture, 12.1% pasture, 12.7% meadow, 19.4% plantation, 2.3% roads; 2 rivers, 1 brook, 3 springs; farms: 2 under 10 acres, 4 under 20 acres, 2 under 50 acres, 1 over 50 acres; manures: lime, 1 mile from quarry, 1 mile from locality used; communications: branch to road from Derry to Dungiven and road to Newtownlimavady, good; markets: Derry, 10 and a quarter miles distant, Dungiven 10 and three-quarter miles distant.

17, Dunady, proprietor Robert Ogilby Esquire, tenure in perpetuity; 220 acres 30 perches; winds: easterly, exposed to the same, sheltered from westerly; ground levels: highest 1,050 feet, lowest 345 feet, average 697 feet; surface: mountainous and sloping; soil: depth from 3 inches to 1 foot, blue clay; subsoil: till and [?] blue rock; land: 22.7% tillage, 65.1% bog waste and mountain pasture, 9.5% pasture, 0.9% plantation, 1.8% roads; 1 river, 3 brooks, 2 springs; farms: 3 under 10 acres, 4 under 20 acres, 1 over 50 acres; manures: lime, 1 mile from quarry, 1 mile from locality used; communications: road from Strabane to Derry road at Claudy, bad; markets: Derry, 13 and a quarter miles distant.

18, Dungorkin, proprietor Fishmongers' Company, tenure 21 years; 308 acres 3 roods 20 perches; winds: southerly, exposed to the same, sheltered from northerly; ground levels: highest 500 feet, lowest 250 feet, average 380 feet; surface: hilly, mountainous and sloping; soil: depth from 4 inches to 1 foot 3 inches, loam and clay; subsoil: till, red clay and rock; land: 31.8% tillage, 53.4% bog waste and mountain pasture, 11% pasture, 0.8% meadow, 1.4% plantation, 1.6% roads; 1 river, 3 brooks, 1 lake, 3 springs; farms: 2 under 50 acres, 3 over 50 acres; manures: lime, 2 and a half miles from quarry, 2 and a half miles from locality used; communications: road through Fore glen from Derry to Dungiven, good; markets: Derry, 10 and a half miles distant, Dungiven, 7 and three-quarter miles distant.

19, Glenlough, proprietor Robert Ogilby Esquire, tenure at will; 664 acres 1 rood 12 perches; winds: northerly, exposed to the same, sheltered from southerly; ground levels: highest 860 feet, lowest 210 feet, average 540 feet; surface: hilly, mountainous and sloping; soil: depth from 4 inches to 1 foot 1 inch, loam and red clay; subsoil: till, red and blue clay; land: 14.7% tillage, 78.5% bog waste and mountain pasture, 5.1% pasture, 0.6% meadow, 1.1% roads; 6 brooks; farms: 2 under 50 acres, 4 over 50 acres; manures: lime, quarter of a mile from quarry, quarter of a mile from locality used; communications: road from Strabane going to Derry and Dungiven road, good; markets: Derry, 8 and a half miles distant.

20, Gortnaran, proprietor Robert Ogilby Esq., tenure at will; 268 acres 3 roods 36 perches; winds: westerly, exposed to the same, sheltered from easterly; ground levels: highest 430 feet, lowest 180 feet, average 355 feet; surface: sloping; soil: depth from 3 inches to 1 foot, gravelly clay and red clay; subsoil: blue clay and rock; land: 41.9% tillage, 32.9% bog waste and mountain pasture, 21.6% pasture, 0.3% meadow, 3.3% roads; 1 river, 1 brook, 3 springs; farms: 5 under 10 acres, 9 under 20 acres, 3 under 50 acres; manures: lime, half a mile from quarry, three-quarters of a mile from locality used; bog, half a mile distant; communications: road from Derry to Dungiven, indifferent; markets: Derry, 8 and three-quarter miles distant.

21, Gortilea, proprietor Fishmongers' Company, tenure 21 years and 1 life, perpetuity, and 21 years; 1,080 acres 1 rood 33 perches; winds: northerly, exposed to the same, sheltered from southerly; ground levels: highest 946 feet, lowest 320 feet, average 640 feet; surface: hilly, mountainous and smooth; soil: depth from 4 to 10 inches, loam and clay; subsoil: clay and rock; land: 17.7% tillage, 73% bog waste and mountain pasture, 8% pasture, 1.3% roads; 2 rivers, 6 brooks, 8 springs; farms: 2 under 10 acres, 7 under 20 acres, 8 under 50 acres, 4 over 50 acres; manures: lime, nearest natural locality half a mile distant, one 1 and a quarter miles distant used; communications: road from Newtownlimavady to the Derry and Dungiven road; markets: Derry, 12 miles distant, Dungiven, 8 and a quarter miles distant.

22, Gortnaskey, proprietor Robert Ogilby Esquire, tenure at will; 532 acres 37 perches; winds: northerly, exposed to the same, sheltered from southerly; ground levels: highest 802 feet, lowest 230 feet, average 520 feet; surface: hilly and sloping; soil: depth from 2 inches to 1 foot, red clay and gravel; subsoil: till and rock; land: 26.5% tillage, 54.7% bog waste and mountain pasture, 13.7% pasture, 3.2% meadow, 1.9% roads; 2 brooks, 4 springs; farms: 1 under 10 acres, 3 under 20 acres, 7 under 50 acres, 4 over 50 acres; manures: lime, nearest natural locality half a mile distant, same used; communications: road from Strabane to Derry and Dungiven road, good; markets: Derry, 9 and a half miles distant.

23, Gortscreagan, proprietor John Beresford Esquire, tenure 21 years and 1 life and at will; 316 acres 11 perches; winds: south easterly, exposed to the same, sheltered from north westerly; ground levels: highest 854 feet, lowest 339 feet, average 596 feet; surface: hilly and mountainous; soil: depth from 3 inches to 1 foot 2 inches, loam; subsoil: till and rock; land: 44.3% tillage, 24% bog waste and mountain pasture, 27.2% pasture, 1.3% plantation, 3.2% roads; 1 river, 4 brooks, 2 springs; farms: 15 under 10 acres, 12 under 20 acres, 2 under 50 acres; manures: lime, nearest natural locality 1 and a quarter miles distant, same used; communications: branch to Derry and Dungiven and branch to Dungiven and Strabane, good; markets: Derry, 13 and three-quarter miles distant, Dungiven, 10 and a quarter miles distant.

24, Kilcaltan, proprietor Robert Ogilby Es-

Parish of Cumber

quire, tenure at will; 310 acres 3 perches; winds: south westerly, exposed to the same, sheltered from north easterly; ground levels: highest 470 feet, lowest 170 feet, average 360 feet; surface: sloping; soil: depth from 5 inches to 1 foot 3 inches, loam and clay; subsoil: blue clay and rock; land: 21.3% tillage, 61.6% bog waste and mountain pasture, 9.4% pasture, 2.2% meadow, 4.2% plantation, 1.3% roads; 1 river, 2 brooks, 4 springs; farms: 4 under 10 acres, 3 under 20 acres, 2 under 50 acres, 1 over 50 acres; manures: lime, nearest natural locality half a mile distant, same used; communications: road from Derry to Dungiven and road to Strabane, indifferent; markets: Derry, 8 miles distant.

25, Kilculmagrandal, proprietor Fishmongers' Company, tenure 21 years; 481 acres 3 roods 28 perches; winds: northerly, exposed to the same, sheltered from southerly; ground levels: highest 500 feet, lowest 356 feet, average 300 feet; surface: hilly and mountainous; soil: depth from 5 inches to 1 foot 3 inches, loam and clay; subsoil: till, red clay and blue clay; land: 27% tillage, 55% bog waste and mountain pasture, 14.5% pasture, 2.3% roads; 1 river, 2 brooks, 2 lakes (Straid), 7 springs; farms: 8 under 50 acres, 2 over 50 acres; manures: lime, nearest natural locality 1 mile distant, one 4 miles distant used; communications: branch to Dungiven and Derry road, with branch to Newtownlimavady, good; markets: Derry 13 and a half miles distant, Dungiven, 8 miles distant, Newtownlimavady 12 and a half miles distant.

26, Kilgort, proprietor John Beresford Esquire, tenure 21 years and 1 life and at will; 1,029 acres 2 roods 16 perches; winds: northerly, exposed to the same, sheltered from southerly; ground levels: highest 1,198 feet, lowest 365 feet, average 786 feet; surface: hilly and mountainous; soil: depth from 2 inches to 1 foot, red sand, gravel and bog; subsoil: till and red clay; land: 25.7% tillage, 62.7% bog waste and mountain pasture, 9.2% pasture, 0.3% meadow, 1% mountain, 2.1% roads; 2 rivers, 6 brooks, 7 springs; farms: 31 under 10 acres, 9 under 20 acres, 4 under 50 acres, 1 over 50 acres; manures: lime, nearest natural locality half a mile distant, one 1 mile distant used; communications: road from Cookstown to Derry and branch to Strabane, good; markets: Derry, 13 and three-quarter miles distant, Dungiven, 10 and a half miles distant.

27, Killycor, proprietor Fishmongers' Company, tenure 21 years and 1 life; 579 acres 10 perches; winds: south easterly, exposed to the same, sheltered from north westerly; ground levels: highest 763 feet, lowest 265 feet, average 540 feet; surface: hilly and mountainous; soil: depth from 4 inches to 1 foot 2 inches, loam and clay; subsoil: till and rock; land: 45.3% tillage, 34% bog waste and mountain pasture, 16.1% pasture, 0.5% meadow, 0.2% plantation, 1.9% roads; 1 river, 4 brooks, 8 springs; farms: 1 under 10 acres, 6 under 20 acres, 10 under 50 acres, 2 over 50 acres; communications: road from Derry to Dungiven, with branch to Newtownlimavady, good; markets: Derry, 11 and a quarter miles distant, Dungiven, 8 miles distant.

28, Kinculbrack, proprietor Fishmongers' Company, tenure 21 years and 1 life; 554 acres 2 roods 35 perches; winds: westerly, exposed to the same, sheltered from easterly; ground levels: highest 710 feet, lowest 249 feet, average 480 feet; surface: hilly and mountainous; soil: depth from 6 inches to 1 foot 3 inches, loam and clay; subsoil: till, clay and rock; land: 43.3% tillage, 20.9% bog waste and mountain pasture, 30.3% pasture, 3.2% meadow, 2.3% roads; 2 rivers, 2 brooks, 7 springs; farms: 8 under 20 acres, 5 under 50 acres, 3 over 50 acres; manures: lime, nearest natural locality 1 mile distant, same used; communications: road from Derry to Dungiven, with branch to Newtownlimavady, good; markets: Derry, 10 and three-quarter miles distant, Dungiven, 8 and three-quarter miles distant.

29, Lear, proprietor John Beresford Esquire, tenure 21 years and 1 life; 2,010 acres 1 rood 38 perches; winds: north westerly, exposed to the same, sheltered from south easterly; ground levels: highest 1,612 feet, lowest 366 feet, average 990 feet; surface: hilly and mountainous; soil: depth from 4 inches to 1 foot, loam, gravelly clay and bog; subsoil: till, red clay and rock; land: 8.3% tillage, 81.2% bog waste and mountain pasture, 5.1% pasture, 0.9% meadow, 4% plantation, 0.5% roads; 2 rivers, 6 brooks, 3 springs; farms: 11 under 10 acres, 3 under 20 acres, 2 under 50 acres, 2 over 50 acres; manures: lime, nearest natural locality 1 mile distant, same used; communications: road from Cookstown to Derry and road to Dungiven, good; markets: Derry, 13 and three-quarter miles distant, Dungiven, 9 and a half miles distant.

30, Letterlougher, proprietor Fishmongers' Company, tenure 21 years; 297 acres 3 roods 14 perches; winds: northerly, exposed to the same, sheltered from southerly; ground levels: highest 507 feet, lowest 400 feet, average 450 feet; surface: hilly; soil: depth from 6 inches to 1 foot, loam and clay; subsoil: blue clay, red clay and rock; land: 37.8% tillage, 38.2% bog waste and mountain pasture, 21.6% pasture, 2.4% roads; 2

brooks, 3 springs; farms: 8 under 50 acres; manures: lime, nearest natural locality half a mile distant, one 1 mile distant used; communications: branch to road from Derry to Dungiven, bad; markets: Derry, 12 miles distant, Dungiven, 8 and three-quarter miles distant.

31, Lettermuck, proprietor Robert Ogilby Esquire, tenure 31 years and 3 lives and at will; 557 acres 3 roods 14 perches; winds: northerly, exposed to the same, sheltered from southerly; ground levels: highest 633 feet, lowest 232 feet, average 432 feet; surface: rough and sloping; soil: depth from 4 inches to 1 foot 1 inch, loam and bog; subsoil: blue clay and rock; land: 23.6% tillage, 61.6% bog waste and mountain pasture, 12.4% pasture, 0.5% plantation, 1.9% roads; 1 river, 3 brooks, 5 springs; farms: 5 under 10 acres, 1 under 20 acres, 7 under 50 acres, 1 over 50 acres; manures: lime, nearest natural locality 1 mile distant, same used; communications: branch to road from Derry to Dungiven, good; markets: Derry, 9 and a quarter miles distant, Dungiven, 6 miles distant.

32, Ling, proprietor Robert Ogilby Esquire, tenure at will; 507 acres 3 roods; winds: westerly, exposed to the same, sheltered from easterly; ground levels: highest 800 feet, lowest 285 feet, average 540 feet; surface: hilly and sloping; soil: depth from 4 inches to 1 foot 2 inches, blue clay; subsoil: blue clay, till, [?] red rock; land: 40% tillage, 36% bog waste and mountain pasture, 21.6% pasture, 2.4% roads; 1 river, 3 brooks, 3 springs; farms: 6 under 10 acres, 14 under 20 acres, 4 under 50 acres, 1 over 50 acres; manures: lime, nearest natural locality 1 mile distant, same used; communications: branch to road from Derry to Cookstown, good; markets: Derry, 13 and a quarter miles distant.

33, Lisbunny, proprietor Robert Ogilby Esquire, tenure at will; 840 acres 3 roods 14 perches; winds: northerly, exposed to the same, sheltered from southerly; ground levels: highest 1,000 feet, lowest 402 feet, average 600 feet; surface: mountainous and sloping; soil: depth from 3 inches to 1 foot 4 inches, loam and bog; subsoil: blue clay and rock; land: 21.2% tillage, 67.1% bog waste and mountain pasture, 9.8% pasture, 0.7% meadow, 1.2% roads; 5 brooks, 6 springs; farms: 10 under 10 acres, 9 under 20 acres, 11 under 50 acres; manures: lime, nearest natural locality half a mile distant, same used; communications: road from Strabane to Cookstown and Dungiven, indifferent; markets: Derry, 13 miles distant.

34, Mulderg, proprietor Fishmongers' Company, tenure at will and 21 years; 434 acres 3 roods 28 perches; winds: southerly, exposed to the same, sheltered from northerly; ground levels: highest 763 feet, lowest 323 feet, average 543 feet; surface: hilly and mountainous; soil: depth from 4 inches to 1 foot 3 inches, clay and loam; subsoil: blue clay and rock; land: 24.4% tillage, 63.2% bog waste and mountain pasture, 9.7% pasture, 0.7% meadow, 0.2% plantation, 1.8% roads; 1 river, 2 brooks, 7 springs; farms: 2 under 20 acres, 6 under 50 acres, 2 over 50 acres; manures: lime, nearest natural locality 1 and a half miles distant, same used; communications: road through Fore glen, Derry to Dungiven and branch to Newtownlimavady, good; markets: Derry, 12 and a quarter miles distant, Dungiven, 8 miles distant.

35, Raspberry Hill, proprietor Robert Ogilby Esquire, tenure at will; 167 acres 11 perches; winds: north westerly, exposed to the same, sheltered from south easterly; ground levels: highest 568 feet, lowest 275 feet, average 421 feet; surface: hilly, mountainous and rocky; soil: depth from 2 inches to 1 foot 2 inches, red clay and gravel; subsoil: rock; land: 31.2% tillage, 40.6% bog waste and mountain pasture, 22.2% pasture, 3% meadow, 3% roads; 1 river, 2 brooks, 2 springs; farms: 1 under 50 acres, 2 over 50 acres; manures: lime, nearest natural locality 1 and a quarter miles distant, one 2 miles distant used; communications: branch from Derry road to Strabane, good; markets: Derry, 10 and a half miles distant, Newtownlimavady 10 miles distant.

36, Sallowilly, proprietor Robert Ogilby Esquire, tenure at will; 412 acres 3 roods 17 perches; winds: easterly, exposed to the same, sheltered from westerly; ground levels: highest 1,062 feet, lowest 290 feet, average 670 feet; surface: mountainous and sloping; soil: depth from 4 inches to 1 foot, blue clay; subsoil: blue clay, rock and till; land: 36.4% tillage, 35.5% bog waste and mountain pasture, 24.7% pasture, 3.4% roads; 1 river, 4 brooks, 1 spring; farms: 3 under 10 acres, 17 under 20 acres, 2 under 50 acres; manures: lime, nearest natural locality 1 and a half miles distant, same used; communications: road from Strabane to Derry road at Claudy, bad; markets: Derry, 12 and a half miles distant.

37, Stranaganwilly [insert marginal note: county Donegal] [sic], proprietor Captain William Sinclair, tenure at will; 3,129 acres 1 rood 37 perches; winds: north westerly, exposed to the same, sheltered from south easterly; ground levels: highest 1,936 feet, lowest 419 feet, average 1,200 feet; surface: mountainous and sloping; soil: depth

Parish of Cumber

from 3 to 11 inches, blue clay and bog; subsoil: blue clay; land: 2.6% tillage, 95.2% bog waste and mountain pasture, 1.6% pasture, 0.1% meadow, 0.5% roads; 2 rivers, 8 brooks, 4 springs; farms: 38 under 10 acres, 8 under 20 acres; manures: lime, nearest natural locality 1 mile distant, same used; communications: road from Strabane to Cookstown and Derry road, bad; markets: Derry, 15 and a half miles distant, Newtownlimavady, 15 miles distant.

38, Tireighter, proprietor John Claudius Beresford Esquire, tenure 21 years and 1 life; 611 acres 1 rood 20 perches; winds: north easterly, exposed to the same, sheltered from south westerly; ground levels: highest 1,202 feet, lowest 400 feet, average 700 feet; surface: hilly, mountainous and smooth; soil: depth from 5 inches to 1 foot, loam and clay; subsoil: clay and rock; land: 47.6% tillage, 20.5% bog waste and mountain pasture, 28.9% pasture, 0.5% plantation, 2.5% roads; 2 rivers 3 brooks, 9 springs; farms: 11 under 10 acres, 18 under 20 acres, 12 under 50 acres; manures: lime, nearest natural locality half a mile distant, same used; communications: road from Cookstown to Derry and road to Dungiven, good; markets: Derry, 15 miles distant, Dungiven, 9 miles distant.

39, Tullintrain, proprietor Revd Francis Brownlow, tenure at will; 571 acres 3 roods 13 perches; winds: north westerly, exposed to the same, sheltered from south easterly; ground levels: highest 760 feet, lowest 270 feet, average 517 feet; surface: sloping; soil: depth from 6 inches to 1 foot, loam and clay; subsoil: till and blue clay; land: 43.9% tillage, 24.8% bog waste and mountain pasture, 28.5% pasture, 1.1% meadow, 1.7% roads; 1 river, 5 brooks, 4 small lakes, 5 brooks; farms: 6 under 10 acres, 14 under 20 acres, 10 under 50 acres; manures: lime, nearest natural locality half a mile distant, one 1 and three-quarter miles distant used; communications: branch to road from Dungiven to Derry, good; markets: Derry, 11 and three-quarter miles distant, Dungiven, 10 and a quarter miles distant.

Cultivation, its Mode and Results

[Table contains the following headings: name, depth and kind of soil cost of manures and quantity used per acre, rotation of crops analysis of crops, time of sowing and harvest, quantity of seed and produce, woods, stock].

Wheat, sown 15th December, harvested 1st September; cost of seed 7s 2d per bushel, produce 5s 10d per bushel.

Barley, sown 10th April, harvested 12th September; cost of seed 3s 7d per bushel, produce 2s 8d per bushel.

Oats, sown 15th March and 4th May, harvested 15th August and 30th October; cost of seed 2s 10d ha'penny per bushel, produce 2s ha'penny per bushel.

Potatoes, sown 20th April and 12th July, harvested 21st October and 12th December; cost of seed 1s 6d per bushel, produce 1s farthing per bushel.

Flax, sown 20th April and 20th May, harvested 12th and 30th August; cost of seed 11s per bushel, produce 47s 7d per cwt.

Hay, sown April and May, harvested June and August; cost of seed from 10d to 5s per bushel, produce 43s per ton.

Turnips, sown 12th May, harvested 1st November; cost of seed 1s 4d ha'penny per lb, produce 15s per ton.

Vetches, sown 1st April, harvested 1st August; cost of seed 9s per bushel, produce 12s 6d per ton.

Mangel wurzel, sown 1st May, harvested 30th October; cost of seed 2s per lb, produce 30s per ton.

1, Alla Lower: soil loam and bog; cost of manures: compost 43s 7d per acre, dung 26s 4d, lime 15s 7d; 46 tons of compost used per acre, 35 tons of dung, 2 and one-third tons of lime; rotation of crops: 1st rotation, oats, potatoes, oats, flax, oats, grass, grass, grass; 2nd rotation, oats, oats or vetches, potatoes or turnips or mangel wurzel, oats, grass, grass, grass, grass; 3rd rotation, oats, flax or vetches, oats, potatoes or turnips, wheat or oats, hay, grass, grass; crops: wheat, 3.1 bushels of seed per acre, 32.5 bushels produce; oats, 4.6 bushels seed per acre, 35.5 tons produce; potatoes, 20.5 bushels seed per acre, 116.1 bushels produce; flax, 2.7 bushels seed per acre, 3.5 cwt produce; hay, 1.9 bushels seed per acre, 1.5 tons produce; turnips, 2.1 lbs seed per acre, 23.2 tons produce; vetches, 2.7 bushels seed per acre, 4.6 tons produce; mangel wurzel, 3.1 bushels seed per acre, 15.5 tons produce; woods: 6 acres ash, oak, firs, alder and beech, planted 1802, farm uses; stock: 19 horses, 73 cattle, 8 sheep, 6 goats, 13 hogs, 177 poultry, 2 beehives.

2, Alla Upper: soil loam, clay and bog; cost of manures: compost 37s 7d per acre, dung 24s 10d, lime 13s 7d; 47 tons of compost used per acre, 31 tons of dung, 2 and one-third tons of lime; rotation of crops: 1st rotation, oats, flax or potatoes, oats, potatoes, oats, grass, grass, grass; 2nd rotation, oats, flax, potatoes, oats, oats, grass, grass, grass; 3rd rotation, oats, flax, oats, potatoes, oats, flax, oats, grass; crops: oats, 4.8 bushels seed, 31.7 bushels produce; potatoes, 20.1 bushels seed, 81.3 bushels produce; flax, 2.7 bushels seed, 3.7 bushels produce; woods: none; stock: 12 horses, 43 cattle, 3 sheep, 7 hogs, 148 poultry.

3, Altaghoney: soil red clay; cost of manures: compost 51s per acre, dung 20s 8d, lime 21s 8d; 58 tons of compost used per acre, 23 tons of dung, 3 and one-third tons of lime; rotation of crops: 1st rotation, oats, potatoes, oats, flax, oats, grass, grass, grass; 2nd rotation, potatoes, oats, flax, potatoes, oats, grass, grass, grass; 3rd rotation, potatoes, oats, flax, oats, turnips, grass, grass, grass; crops: oats, 5.2 bushels seed, 23.2 bushels produce; potatoes, 20.1 bushels seed, 81 bushels produce; flax, 2.5 bushels seed, 2.3 cwt produce; woods: none; stock: 42 horses, 153 cattle, 94 sheep, 1 goat, 6 hogs, 255 poultry. [Insert footnote: Quantity of seed and produce per acre of turnips in townland of Altaghoney could not be ascertained; see remarks and replies].

4, Ballyartan: soil loam and bog; cost of manures: compost 45s 9d per acre, dung 22s 6d, lime 23s 6d; 61 tons of compost used per acre, 30 tons of dung, 3 and a half tons of lime; rotation of crops: 1st rotation, oats, potatoes, oats, potatoes or turnips, oats, grass, grass, grass; 2nd rotation, oats, flax, oats, potatoes or turnips, oats, grass, grass, grass; 3rd rotation, oats, oats, flax or potatoes or turnips, oats, grass, grass, grass; crops: oats, 5.2 bushels seed, 36 tons produce; potatoes, 20.1 bushels seed, 193.5 bushels produce; flax, 2.7 bushels seed, 3.2 cwt produce; turnips, 1.9 lbs seed, 11.6 tons produce; woods: 2 and a half acres, firs, ash, beech and alders, planted 1813, none cut; stock: 26 asses, 113 cattle, 133 sheep, 19 hogs, 237 poultry, 5 beehives.

5, Ballycallaghan: soil red clay and gravel; cost of manures: compost 40s per acre, dung 20s 9d, lime 35s 4d; 50 tons of compost used per acre, 26 tons of dung, 4 and a half tons of lime; rotation of crops: 1st rotation, potatoes, oats, oats or flax, grass, grass, grass; 2nd rotation, oats, oats, flax or potatoes, oats, grass, grass; 3rd rotation, oats, oats, potatoes or turnips, grass, grass, grass, grass; crops: oats, 4.6 bushels seed, 32.4 bushels produce; potatoes, 26.4 bushels seed, 193.5 bushels produce; flax, 2.7 bushels seed, 3.5 cwt produce; turnips, 1.9 lbs seed, 23.2 tons produce; woods: 1 and one-third acres of ash, oak, alder and firs, planted in 1807, cut and sold; stock: 15 horses, 45 cattle, 7 sheep, 1 hog, 90 poultry.

6, Ballyholly: soil loam; cost of manures: compost 39s 2d per acre, dung 23s 4d, lime 18s 6d; 49 tons of compost used per acre, 30 tons of dung, 1 and a half tons of lime; rotation of crops: 1st rotation, oats, potatoes, oats, flax, oats, grass, grass; 2nd rotation, oats, potatoes, oats, flax, oats, grass, grass; 3rd rotation, oats, flax, oats, turnips or potatoes, oats, flax, grass, grass; crops: oats, 4.3 bushels seed, 20.3 bushels produce; potatoes, 19.1 bushels seed, 117 bushels produce; flax, 2.2 bushels seed, 2.6 cwt produce; turnips, 2 lbs seed, 5.3 tons produce; woods: none; stock: 17 asses, 103 cattle, 30 sheep, 4 hogs, 117 poultry.

7, Ballymaclanigan: soil loam and clay; cost of manures: compost 66s 9d per acre, dung 31s 6d, lime 13s 9d; 89 tons of compost used per acre, 42 tons of dung, 1 and one-fifth tons of lime; rotation of crops: 1st rotation, oats, flax or oats, oats, turnips or potatoes or vetches, oats, grass, grass; 2nd rotation, oats, potatoes or turnips, oats, oats or flax or vetches, grass, grass, grass; 3rd rotation, potatoes or turnips, oats, oats or flax or vetches, oats, grass, grass; crops: oats, 4 bushels seed, 27.8 bushels produce; potatoes, 19.1 bushels seed, 160.4 bushels produce; flax, 2.2 bushels seed, 2.9 cwt produce; turnips, 2 lbs seed, 16 tons produce; vetches, 2.4 bushels seed, 8.4 tons produce; woods: none; stock: 23 horses, 2 asses, 115 cattle, 28 sheep, 1 goat, 6 hogs, 261 poultry, 4 beehives.

8, Ballyrory: soil loam and clay; cost of manures: compost 61s 7d per acre, dung 25s 7d, lime 8s 6d; 77 tons of compost used per acre, 32 tons of dung, 1 ton of lime; rotation of crops: 1st rotation, oats, potatoes, oats, oats or flax, grass, grass, grass; 2nd rotation, oats, potatoes, oats, oats or flax, oats, grass, grass, grass; crops: oats, 4.5 bushels seed, 22 bushels produce; potatoes, 20 bushels seed, 147.1 bushels produce; flax, 2.3 bushels seed, 2.9 cwt produce; woods: none; stock: 21 horses, 77 cattle, 73 sheep, 1 goat, 196 poultry.

9, Barr Cregg: soil loam and clay; cost of manures: compost 43s per acre, dung 31s 2d, lime 16s 6d; 54 tons of compost used per acre, 39 tons of dung, 1 ton of lime; rotation of crops: 1st rotation, oats, potatoes, oats, oats, oats, grass, grass, grass; 2nd rotation, oats, flax or potatoes, oats, oats, oats, grass, grass, grass; crops: oats, 4.6 bushels seed, 25.6 bushels produce; potatoes, 21.7 bushels seed, 116.1 bushels produce; flax, 2.3 bushels seed, 2.3 cwt produce; woods: none; stock: 4 horses, 20 cattle, 20 sheep, 19 poultry.

10, Binn: soil loam and clay; cost of manures: compost 66s 8d per acre, dung 28s; 77 tons of compost used per acre, 36 tons of dung; rotation of crops; 1st rotation, potatoes, oats, flax, oats, grass, grass, grass; 2nd rotation, oats, potatoes or turnips, oats, oats or vetches, oats, grass, grass;

Parish of Cumber

crops: oats, 4.9 bushels seed, 21.2 bushels produce; potatoes, 20.5 bushels seed, 149.4 bushels produce; flax, 2.4 bushels seed, 3.2 cwt produce; turnips, 1.9 bushels seed, 7.7 tons produce; vetches, 2.3 bushels seed, 4.7 tons produce; woods: 8 and three-tenth acres natural oak and birches; 1 acre, 1809, firs and beech, none cut; stock: 20 horses, 1 ass, 59 cattle, 7 sheep, 3 goats, 8 hogs, 261 poultry, 6 beehives.

11, Carnanbane: soil blue clay; cost of manures: compost 42s per acre, dung 21s, lime 23s 5d; 58 tons of compost used per acre, 31 tons of dung, 2 and two-fifth tons of lime; rotation of crops: 1st rotation, oats, potatoes, oats, oats, oats, grass, grass, grass; 2nd rotation, oats, turnips [5 written above] oats, flax, oats, grass, grass, grass; 3rd rotation, potatoes, oats, flax, oats, oats, grass, grass, grass; crops: oats, 5.4 bushels seed, 29 bushels produce; potatoes, 20.5 bushels seed, 100.4 bushels produce; flax, 2.7 bushels seed, 3.3 cwt produce; woods: none; stock: 18 horses, 2 asses, 42 cattle, 57 sheep, 114 poultry.

12, Carnanreagh: soil clay and bog; cost of manures: compost 46s 6d per acre, dung 24s, lime 26s 3d; 57 tons of compost used per acre, 30 tons of dung, 2 and four-fifth tons of lime; rotation of crops: 1st rotation, oats, potatoes, oats, flax, oats, grass, grass, grass; 2nd rotation, oats, potatoes, oats, flax or vetches, oats, grass, grass, grass; 3rd rotation, potatoes, oats, oats, oats, grass, grass, grass; crops: oats, 5.4 bushels seed, 28.7 bushels produce; potatoes, 20.1 bushels seed, 77.4 bushels produce; flax, 2.3 bushels seed, 3.3 cwt produce; vetches, 1.9 bushels seed, 3.8 tons produce; woods: none; stock: 38 horses, 112 cattle, 147 sheep, 11 hogs, 206 poultry.

13, Claudy: soil loam and bog; cost of manures: compost 43s 6d per acre, dung 18s 6d, lime 25s 8d; 63 tons of compost used per acre, 27 tons of dung, 3 and two-fifth tons of lime; rotation of crops: 1st rotation, oats, flax, oats, potatoes, grass, grass; 2nd rotation, oats, potatoes or turnips, oats, flax, oats, grass, grass, grass; 3rd rotation, oats, potatoes, oats, vetches, grass, grass; crops: oats, 4.9 bushels seed, [?] 26 bushels produce; potatoes, 19.4 bushels seed, 159 bushels produce; flax, 2.7 bushels seed, 3.3 cwt produce; turnips, 1.7 lbs seed, 14.7 tons produce; vetches, 2.3 bushels seed, 3.8 tons produce; woods: 3 and a half acres fir, ash and sycamore, planted 1811, used by proprietor; stock: 31 horses, 115 cattle, 93 sheep, 2 goats, 13 hogs, 241 poultry, 1 beehive.

14, Coolnacolpagh: soil loam and clay; cost of manures: compost 59s 2d per acre, dung 26s 6d, lime 10s 4d; 74 tons of compost used per acre, 33 tons of dung, 1 and a half tons of lime; rotation of crops: 1st rotation, oats, flax, potatoes, oats, oats, grass, grass, grass; 2nd rotation, oats, flax, turnips or potatoes, oats, grass, grass; 3rd rotation, potatoes, oats or flax, oats, potatoes, oats, grass, grass; crops: oats, 3.9 bushels seed, 17.8 bushels produce; potatoes, 19.1 bushels seed, 129.4 bushels produce; flax, 2.2 bushels seed, 1.9 cwt produce; turnips, 2 lbs seed, 3.7 tons produce; woods none; stock: 16 horses, 1 ass, 78 cattle, 30 sheep, 3 hogs, 241 poultry, 2 beehives.

15, Cregg: soil loam and bog; cost of manures: compost 40s 3d per acre, dung 20s 6d, lime 30s 9d; 62 tons of lime used per acre, 32 tons of compost, 4 and one-third tons of lime; rotation of crops: 1st rotation, oats, potatoes, oats, oats, grass, grass, grass; 2nd rotation, oats, potatoes, oats, flax, oats, grass, grass, grass; 3rd rotation, oats, oats, potatoes or turnips, oats, flax, oats, grass, grass; crops: oats, 4.9 bushels seed, 33 bushels produce; potatoes, 20 bushels seed, 240 bushels produce; flax, 2.7 bushels seed, 3.5 cwt produce; turnips, 1.6 lbs seed, 23 tons produce; woods: 14 acres, forest trees, part ancient and part recent, used by proprietor; stock: 24 horses, 103 cattle, 16 sheep, 7 hogs, 293 poultry, 7 beehives.

16, Cumber: soil loam clay and bog; cost of manures: compost 41s 6d per acre, dung 20s, lime 25s 6d; 58 tons of compost used per acre, 29 tons of dung, 3 and seven-tenth tons of lime; rotation of crops: 1st rotation, oats, flax or potatoes, oats, oats, grass, grass, grass; 2nd rotation, potatoes, oats, oats, flax or potatoes, grass, grass, grass; 3rd rotation, oats, oats or flax, potatoes or turnips, oats, grass, grass, grass, grass; crops: oats, 5.4 bushels seed, 31.7 bushels produce; potatoes, 20 bushels seed, 232 bushels produce; flax, 2.6 bushels seed, 3.3 cwt produce; turnips, 1.9 lbs seed, 20 tons produce; woods: 6 and a half acres, forest trees, greater part ancient, 5 acres recent, used by proprietor; stock: 13 horses, 49 cattle, 3 sheep, 1 goat, 10 hogs, 121 poultry.

17, Dunady: soil blue clay; cost of manures; compost 43s per acre, dung 23s 4d, lime 23s 3d; 53 tons of compost used per acre, 28 tons of dung, 2 and four-fifth tons of lime; rotation of crops: 1st rotation, oats, flax or potatoes, oats, oats, grass, grass; 2nd rotation, oats, potatoes, oats or flax, oats, grass, grass, grass; 3rd rotation, oats, flax, potatoes or turnips, oats, vetches, grass, grass, grass; crops: oats, 5.4 bushels seed, 31 bushels produce; potatoes, 20.1 bushels seed, 86 bushels produce; flax, 2.7 bushels seed, 3.3 cwt produce; turnips, 2.7 lbs seed, 6.9 tons produce; vetches, 2.7 bushels seed, 4.2 tons produce; woods: 2 acres firs, beech, ash and alder, planted 1808 and 1827, none cut; stock: 9 horses, 20 cattle, 6 sheep, 43 poultry.

18, Dungorkin: soil loam and clay; cost of manures: compost 50s 3d per acre, dung 29s 10d, lime 8s 10d; 67 tons of compost used per acre, 31 tons of dung, 1 ton of lime; rotation of crops: 1st rotation, oats, potatoes, turnips, oats, flax, grass, grass; 2nd rotation, oats, potatoes, oats or flax, oats, grass, grass; 3rd rotation, oats, potatoes or turnips, oats, flax or vetches, oats, grass, grass, grass; crops: oats, 4.1 bushels seed, 23.4 bushels produce; potatoes, 19.1 bushels seed, 148 bushels produce; flax, 2.3 bushels seed, 3.2 cwt produce; turnips, 2.3 lbs seed, 6.8 tons produce; vetches, 2.3 bushels seed, 5.6 tons produce; woods: 4 and a half acres firs, oak and ash, planted 1825, none cut; stock: 9 horses, 41 cattle, 4 sheep, 3 hogs, 91 poultry.

19, Glenlough: soil loam and red clay; cost of manures: compost 46s 4d per acre, dung 23s 6d, lime 24s 11d; 58 tons of compost used per acre, 29 tons of dung, 3 and nine-tenth tons of lime; rotation of crops: 1st rotation, oats, flax or potatoes, oats, oats, grass, grass, grass; 2nd rotation, oats, flax, oats, potatoes, oats or vetches, grass, grass, grass; crops: oats, 5.6 bushels seed, 33.6 bushels produce; potatoes, 21.7 bushels seed, 154.8 bushels produce; flax, 2.7 bushels seed, 3.5 cwt produce; vetches, 2.3 bushels seed, 4.6 tons produce; woods: 28 acres, brushwood; stock: 14 horses, 47 cattle, 9 sheep, 2 hogs, 105 poultry, 1 beehive.

20, Gortnaran: soil gravelly clay and red clay; cost of manures: compost 103s 6d per acre, lime 13s 6d; 65 tons of compost used per acre, 1 and nine-sixteenth tons of lime; rotation of crops: 1st rotation, oats, potatoes, oats, flax, oats, grass, grass, grass; crops: oats, 5.1 bushels seed, 32.4 bushels produce; potatoes, 20.1 bushels seed, 135.5 bushels produce; flax, 2.7 bushels seed, 3.5 cwt produce; woods: 4 acres of brushwood, no use; stock: 11 horses, 57 cattle, 1 sheep, 4 hogs, 164 poultry.

21, Gortilea: soil loam and clay; cost of manures: compost 61s per acre, dung 28s 3d, lime 9s 1d; 74 tons of compost used per acre, 37 tons of dung, 1 and one-tenth tons of lime; rotation of crops: 1st rotation, oats, potatoes, oats, flax, oats, grass, grass, grass; 2nd rotation, oats, flax, potatoes, oats, oats or vetches, grass, grass; 3rd rotation, oats, oats, potatoes or turnips, oats, hay, grass, grass; crops: oats, 4.8 bushels seed, 26.6 bushels produce; potatoes, 17.9 bushels seed, 169.7 bushels produce; flax, 2.3 bushels seed, 2.9 cwt produce; hay, 4.6 bushels seed, 1.6 tons produce; turnips, 2.1 lbs seed, 8 tons produce; vetches, 2.4 bushels seed, 7.1 tons produce; woods: none; stock: 22 horses, 71 cattle, 13 sheep, 1 hog, 244 poultry.

22, Gortnaskey: soil red clay and gravel; cost of manures: compost 40s per acre, dung 20s 9d, lime 30s 4d; 50 tons of compost used per acre, 26 tons of dung, 4 and two-fifth tons of lime; rotation of crops: 1st rotation, potatoes, oats, oats or flax, grass, grass, grass; 2nd rotation, potatoes, oats, oats or flax, oats, grass, grass, grass; 3rd rotation, oats, potatoes, oats or flax, oats or flax, grass, grass, grass; crops: oats, 5.1 bushels seed, 28.5 bushels produce; potatoes, 21.7 bushels seed, 124 bushels produce; flax, 2.7 bushels seed, 3.5 cwt produce; woods: 9 acres brushwood; stock: 19 horses, 72 cattle, 33 sheep, 3 goats, 5 hogs, 253 poultry.

23, Gortscreagan: soil loam; cost of manures: compost 61s 7d per acre, dung 24s 9d, lime 9s 1d; 77 tons of compost used per acre, 31 tons of dung, 1 and one-tenth tons of lime; rotation of crops: 1st rotation, oats, potatoes, oats, flax, oats, grass, grass; 3rd rotation, oats, potatoes, oats or flax, oats, grass, grass; crops: oats, 4.7 bushels seed, 22.5 bushels produce; potatoes, 20.1 bushels seed, 162 bushels produce; flax, 2.4 bushels seed, 2.3 cwt produce; woods: 4 acres, firs, beech, oak and alder, planted 1812, farming purposes; stock: 24 horses, 57 cattle, 31 sheep, 213 poultry, 1 beehive.

24, Kilcaltan: soil loam and bog; cost of manures: compost 51s 9d per acre, dung 26s 6d, lime 17s 9d; 90 tons of compost used per acre, 35 tons of dung, 2 and seven-tenth tons of lime; rotation of crops: 1st rotation, oats, potatoes, oats or vetches, flax, grass, grass; 2nd rotation, oats, turnips or potatoes, oats, grass, grass, grass; 3rd rotation, potatoes, flax or barley, oats, grass, grass, grass; crops: barley, 2.3 bushels seed, 43.2 bushels produce; oats, 4.6 bushels seed, 35.7 bushels produce; potatoes, 23.2 bushels seed, 108.8 bushels produce; flax, 2.6 bushels seed, 3.7 cwt produce; turnips, 1.7 lbs seed, 19.4 tons produce; vetches, 2.5 bushels seed, 6.5 tons produce; woods: 8 acres forest trees, planted 1760 and 1838, farming uses; 5 acres of natural wood, none cut; stock: 10 horses, 42 cattle, 2 sheep, 186 poultry, 2 beehives.

25, Kilculmagrandal: soil loam and clay; cost of manures: compost 50s per acre, dung 26s 6d, lime 15s 5d; 62 tons of compost used per acre, 39 tons of dung, 1 and one-fifth tons of lime; rotation of crops: 1st rotation, oats, flax, turnips or potatoes, oats, oats, oats, grass, grass; 2nd rotation, oats, potatoes, oats, oats or flax, oats or vetches, grass, grass, grass; 3rd rotation, oats, oats, potatoes or turnips, oats or vetches, oats or hay, grass, grass; crops: oats, 4.1 bushels seed, 19.8 bushels produce; potatoes, 17.9 bushels seed, 114 bushels produce; flax, 2.1 bushels seed, 2.5 cwt produce; hay, 3.7 bushels seed, 1.4 tons produce; turnips, 1.9 lbs seed, 5.6 tons produce; vetches, 2.1 bushels seed, 5.3 tons produce; woods: none; stock: 12 horses, 64 cattle, 21 sheep, 7 hogs, 99 poultry, 2 beehives.

26, Kilgort; soil loam, [?] red gravel, bog; cost of manures: compost 46s 4d per acre, dung 21s, lime 7s 9d; 58 tons of compost used per acre, 28 tons of dung, 1 ton of lime; rotation of crops: 1st rotation, oats, potatoes, oats or flax, oats, grass, grass; 2nd rotation, potatoes, oats, oats or flax, oats, grass, grass, grass; 3rd rotation, oats, potatoes, oats, flax, oats or vetches, grass, grass, grass; crops: oats, 4.8 bushels seed, 20.8 bushels produce; potatoes, 19.4 bushels seed, 131.6 bushels produce; flax, 2.3 bushels seed, 2.5 cwt produce; vetches, 2.3 bushels seed, 6.2 tons produce; woods: 10 and three-quarter acres forest trees, planted from 1808 to 1838, cut and sold; stock: 40 horses, 12 cattle, 140 sheep, 2 hogs, 411 poultry.

27, Killycor: soil loam and clay; cost of manures: compost 72s 7d per acre, dung 28s 7d, lime 5s 8d; 102 tons of compost used per acre, 37 tons of dung, nine-tenths of a ton of lime; rotation of crops: 1st rotation, oats, flax, potatoes or turnips, oats, grass, grass, grass; 3rd rotation, oats, oats or vetches, potatoes or turnips, oats, hay, grass, grass; crops: oats, 4.3 bushels seed, 26.5 bushels produce; potatoes, 19.1 bushels seed, 138.8 bushels produce; flax, 2.3 bushels seed, 3.5 cwt produce; hay, 4 bushels seed, 2.3 tons produce; turnips 1.9 lbs seed, 13.8 tons produce; vetches, 2.5 bushels seed, 6.1 tons produce; woods: 1 and three-quarter acres of an orchard, apple and cherry, planted 1829, family use; stock: 20 horses, 101 cattle, 17 sheep, 11 hogs, 286 poultry.

28, Kinculbrack: soil loam and clay; cost of manures: compost 66s 9d per acre, dung 30s 1d, lime 7s 2d; 89 tons of compost used per acre, 39 tons of dung, 1 ton of lime; rotation of crops: 1st rotation, oats, oats or vetches, potatoes, oats or wheat, grass, grass, grass; 2nd rotation, oats, flax, turnips or potatoes, oats, flax or oats, grass, grass, grass; 3rd rotation, oats, turnips or potatoes, oats, vetches or flax or oats, grass, grass, grass; crops: wheat, 2.5 bushels seed, 24 bushels produce; oats, 4.6 bushels seed, 26.5 bushels produce; potatoes, 19.1 bushels seed, 169.7 produce; flax, 2.1 bushels seed, 2.7 cwt produce; turnips, 2.3 lbs seed, 11.1 tons produce; vetches, 2.5 bushels seed, 8.3 tons produce; woods: none; stock: 27 horses, 104 cattle, 30 sheep, 2 goats, 38 hogs, 239 poultry, 4 beehives.

29, Lear: soil loam, gravelly clay and bog; cost of manures: compost 41s 3d per acre, dung 17s, lime 14s 1d; 55 tons of compost used per acre, 23 tons of dung, 2 tons of lime; rotation of crops: 1st rotation, potatoes, oats, oats, grass, grass, grass; 3rd rotation, oats, potatoes, oats, oats or flax or turnips, oats, grass, grass, grass; crops: oats, 4.6 bushels seed, 21.7 bushels produce; potatoes, 23.2 bushels seed, 135.6 bushels produce; flax, 2.4 bushels seed, 2.9 cwt produce; turnips, 2.7 lbs seed, 3.9 tons produce; woods: 80 acres, forest trees, part ancient, part recent, cut and sold; stock: 24 horses, 102 cattle, 66 sheep, 5 hogs, 173 poultry.

30, Letterlougher: soil loam and clay; cost of manures: compost 42s per acre, dung 22s 1d, lime 7s 2d; 55 tons of compost used per acre, 31 tons of dung, 1 ton of lime; rotation of crops: 1st rotation, potatoes, oats, flax, oats, grass, grass; 2nd rotation, oats, oats or flax or vetches, potatoes or turnips, oats, hay, grass, grass; 3rd rotation, oats, flax, potatoes, oats, oats, grass, grass, grass; crops: oats, 4.3 bushels seed, 24.7 bushels produce; potatoes, 18.5 bushels seed, 154 bushels produce; flax 2.3 bushels seed, 2.3 cwt produce; hay, 1.2 bushels seed, 1.5 tons produce; turnips, 2.5 lbs seed, 8 tons produce; vetches, 2.3 bushels seed, 6.2 tons produce; woods: none; stock: 12 horses, 39 cattle, 20 sheep, 8 hogs, 138 poultry, 3 beehives.

31, Lettermuck: soil loam and bog; cost of manures: compost 45s 9d per acre, dung 27s 9d, lime 26s; 61 tons of compost used per acre, 37 tons of dung, 3 and a half tons of lime; rotation of crops: 1st rotation, oats, potatoes, oats or flax, oats, grass, grass, grass; 2nd rotation, oats, flax, oats, potatoes, oats, oats, grass, grass, grass; crops: oats, 4.7 bushels seed, 30.1 bushels produce; potatoes, 18.6 bushels seed, 133.1 bushels produce; flax, 2.7 bushels seed, 3.3 cwt produce; woods: 3 and one-fifth acres, firs, beech, ash and alder, planted 1802, none cut; half an acre orchard; stock: 17 horses, 57 cattle, 8 sheep, 2 goats, 192 poultry.

32, Ling: soil blue clay; cost of manures: compost 42s per acre, dung 25s, lime 24s 2d; 58 tons of compost used per acre, 31 tons of dung, 2 and a quarter tons of lime; rotation of crops: 1st rotation, oats, flax or potatoes, oats, oats, grass, grass, grass; 2nd rotation, oats, potatoes, oats, flax, grass, grass, grass; 3rd rotation, oats, vetches or potatoes or turnips, oats or flax, oats or vetches, grass, grass, grass; crops: oats, 5.2 bushels seed, 25.6 bushels produce; potatoes, 20.6 bushels seed,

95 bushels produce; flax, 2.7 bushels seed, 3.3 cwt produce; turnips, 2.3 lbs seed, 12.4 tons produce; vetches, 2.5 bushels seed, 4.7 tons produce; woods: none; stock: 27 horses, 69 cattle, 27 sheep, 1 goat, 7 hogs, 195 poultry.

33, Lisbunny: soil loam and bog; cost of manures: compost 52s 6d per acre, dung 28s 6d, lime 20s 7d ha'penny; 70 tons of compost used per acre, 38 tons of dung, 3 and one-tenth tons of lime; rotation of crops: 1st rotation, oats, flax, potatoes, oats, oats, grass, grass, grass; 2nd rotation, potatoes, oats, oats or flax, oats, grass, grass, grass; 3rd rotation, potatoes, oats, oats or flax, oats, grass, grass, grass; crops: oats, 4.9 bushels seed, 31 bushels produce; potatoes, 27.9 bushels seed, 108.8 bushels produce; flax, 2.7 bushels seed, 3.4 cwt produce; woods: none; stock: 30 horses, 101 cattle, 63 sheep, 9 goats, 10 hogs, 276 poultry.

34, Mulderg: soil clay and loam; cost of manures: compost 33s 9d per acre, dung 24s 9d, lime 9s 3d; 45 tons of lime used per acre, 33 tons of dung, 1 and two-fifth tons of lime; rotation of crops: 1st rotation, oats, potatoes, oats, flax, oats, grass, grass; 2nd rotation, oats, flax, potatoes, flax, oats, oats or grass, grass; 3rd rotation, oats, oats, potatoes or turnips, oats, vetches or oats, grass, grass, grass; crops: oats 4.5 bushels seed, 24 bushels produce; potatoes, 20.3 bushels seed, 154 bushels produce; flax, 2.3 bushels seed, 2.7 cwt produce; turnips, 2.3 lbs seed, 9.2 tons produce; vetches, 2.5 bushels seed, 7.7 tons produce; woods: four-fifths of a acre of alder and firs, planted 1827, none cut; stock: 9 horses, 47 cattle, 5 sheep, 4 hogs, 114 poultry.

35, Raspberry Hill: soil red clay and gravel; cost of manures: compost 39s per acre, dung 15s 6d, lime 31s 6d; 52 tons of compost used per acre, 26 tons of dung, 3 and a half tons of lime; rotation of crops: 1st rotation, oats, potatoes, oats, flax, grass, grass, grass; 2nd rotation, oats, potatoes, oats, flax, oats, grass, grass, grass; 3rd rotation, oats, potatoes, oats or flax, oats, grass, grass, grass; crops: oats, 5.1 bushels seed, 31 bushels produce; potatoes, 21.7 bushels seed, 116.1 bushels produce; flax, 2.7 bushels seed, 3.1 cwt produce; woods: none; stock: 25 horses, 15 cattle, 6 sheep, 170 poultry.

36, Sallowilly: soil blue clay; cost of manures: compost 43s 9d per acre, dung 22s, lime 18s 10d; 50 tons of compost used per acre, 25 tons of dung, 2 tons of lime; rotation of crops: 1st rotation, potatoes, oats, oats or flax, grass, grass; 2nd rotation, oats or potatoes, flax, oats, vetches, grass, grass, grass; 3rd rotation, potatoes, oats, oats or flax, grass, grass, grass; crops: oats, 5.4 bushels seed, 25.6 bushels produce; potatoes, 20.1 bushels seed, 77.4 bushels produce; flax, 2.7 bushels seed, 3 cwt produce; vetches, 2.7 bushels seed, 4.3 tons produce; woods: none; stock: 17 horses, 52 cattle, 18 sheep, 141 poultry.

37, Stranaganwilly: soil red clay and bog; cost of manures: compost 41s 7d per acre, dung 19s 2d, lime 29s 9d; 52 tons of compost used per acre, 24 tons of dung, 3 and nine-tenth tons of lime; rotation of crops: 1st rotation, potatoes, oats, oats, oats, grass, grass, grass; 2nd rotation, oats, potatoes, oats, oats, flax, oats, grass, grass; 3rd rotation, oats, potatoes, oats, oats, flax, grass, grass; crops: oats, 5.1 bushels seed, 27 bushels produce; potatoes, 20 bushels seed, 102 bushels produce; flax, 2.7 bushels seed, 2.9 cwt produce; woods: none; stock: 36 horses, 114 cattle, 127 sheep, 17 hogs, 262 poultry.

38, Tireighter: soil loam and clay; cost of manures: compost 45s per acre, dung 26s, lime 7s 6d; 43 tons of compost used per acre, 28 tons of dung, 1 and one-tenth tons of lime; rotation of crops: 1st rotation, oats, potatoes, oats, flax, oats, grass, grass; 3rd rotation, oats, potatoes, oats, flax, oats, grass, grass, grass; crops: oats, 4.4 bushels seed, 26 bushels produce; potatoes, 19.4 bushels seed, 116 bushels produce; flax, 2.4 bushels seed, 3.5 cwt produce; woods: 3 acres, firs, ash and oak, planted 1818, none cut; stock: 36 horses, 127 cattle, 89 sheep, 1 goat, 6 hogs, 419 poultry.

39, Tullintrain: soil loam and clay; cost of manures: compost 42s per acre, dung 21s, lime 22s; 56 tons of compost used per acre, 28 tons of dung, 2 and one-third tons of lime; rotation of crops: 1st rotation, oats, potatoes, oats, flax or oats, oats, grass, grass, grass; 2nd rotation, potatoes, oats, oats or flax, oats, grass, grass, grass; 3rd rotation, oats, flax, potatoes, oats, oats, grass, grass, grass; crops: oats, 4.6 bushels seed, 26.4 bushels produce; potatoes, 19.4 bushels seed, 193.5 produce; flax, 2.3 bushels seed, 3.2 cwt produce; woods: none; stock: 27 horses, 119 cattle, 31 sheep, 1 goat, 18 hogs, 332 poultry.

[Signed] J.E. Portlock, Captain Royal Engineers, 10th July 1838.

Application of Power

[Table contains the following headings: name of townland, labour subdivided into working farmers and subholders, family labour, agricultural servants, occasional labour, average days work per acre, average days worked in arable; auxiliary power in farming, auxiliary power in quarrying,

Parish of Cumber

capacity of water mills. Insert note referring to mills: "No flour mills, no flour manufactures"].

1, Alla Lower, labour: 9 working farmers and subholders; family aid to farmers 50 persons; 4 male and 1 female domestic servants; 14 male farming servants; 25 male and 8 female occasional labourers; total days work: farmers and family 15,650, constant hired labour 5,947, occasional hired labour 248, general total 21,845 days; average days worked per acre: 43 per townland, 125 tillage; utensils and vehicles: 9 ploughs, 13 harrows, 1 roller, 1 corn-fan, 11 cars, 8 carts, 19 horses, 36 spinning wheels.

2, Alla Upper, labour: 16 working farmers and subholders; family aid to farmers 51 persons; 2 female domestic servants; 19 male and 1 female occasional labourers; total days work: farmers and family 15,963, constant hired labour 626, occasional hired labour 630, general total 17,219; average days work per acre: 55 per townland, 136 tillage; 2 quarries, lime, occasionally used; utensils and vehicles: 11 ploughs, 11 harrows, 11 cars, 9 carts, 12 horses, 38 spinning wheels.

3, Altaghoney, labour: 43 working farmers and subholders; family aid to farmers 137 persons; 6 male and 4 female domestic servants; 32 male and 3 female occasional labourers; total days work: farmers and family 42,881, constant hired labour 3,130, occasional hired labour 674, general total 46,685; average days work per acre: 40 per townland, 163 tillage; 1 quarry, 6 men, 120 days labour per annum, object: lime, tombstones; utensils and vehicles: 30 ploughs, 36 harrows, 37 cars, 13 carts, 42 horses, 83 spinning wheels.

4, Ballyartan, labour: 15 working farmers and subholders; family aid to farmers 56 persons; 18 male and 6 female domestic servants; 4 male farming servants; 58 male occasional labourers; total days work: farmers and families 17,528, constant hired labour 8,764, occasional hired labour 1,180, general total 27,472; total days work per acre: 35 per townland, 90 tillage; 1 quarry, limestone, used occasionally; utensils and vehicles: 13 ploughs, 20 harrows, 1 horse hoe, 3 rollers, 1 corn-fan, 14 cars, 16 carts, 26 horses, 69 spinning wheels; grain mills: 1 undershot water mill, diameter of wheel 14 feet, width of buckets 2 feet; 448,000 lbs of oatmeal ground, maximum quantity 672,000 lbs, average time working 36 weeks, 3 attendants including miller; flax mills: 1 undershot water mill, diameter of wheel 14 feet, width of buckets 2 feet; raw quantity 48,000 lbs, tow quantity 12,000 lbs, average time working 13 weeks, 4 male attendants.

5, Ballycallaghan, labour: 12 working farmers and subholders; family aid to farmers 45 persons; 3 male and 1 female domestic servants; 7 male farming servants; 2 male and 6 female occasional labourers; total days work: farmers and family 14,085, constant hired labour 3,443, occasional hired labour 100, general total 17,628; average days work per acre: 58 per townland, 134 tillage; utensils and vehicles: 10 ploughs, 16 harrows, 1 roller, 21 cars, 3 carts, 15 horses, 33 spinning wheels.

6, Ballyholly, labour: 17 working farmers and subholders; family aid to farmers 50 persons; 8 male and 1 female domestic servant; 1 male farming servant; 34 male occasional labourers; total days work: farmers and family 15,650, constant hired labour 3,130, occasional hired labour 718, general total 19,498; average days work per acre: 20 per townland, 71 tillage; 2 quarries, 8 men, 576 days labour per annum, object: lime and building, not in use; utensils and vehicles: 14 ploughs, 15 harrows, 18 cars, 6 carts, 17 horses, 27 spinning wheels.

7, Ballycallaghan, labour: 8 working farmers and subholders; family aid to farmers 31 persons; 8 male and 6 female domestic servants; 3 male farming servants; 51 male and 26 female occasional labourers; total days work: farmers and family 9,703, constant hired labour 5,321, occasional hired labour 2,143, general total 17,167; average days work per acre: 19 per townland, 58 tillage; 1 quarry, not worked; utensils and vehicles: 10 ploughs, 23 harrows, 2 horse-hoes, 1 roller, 1 corn-fan, 14 cars, 14 carts, 23 horses, 31 spinning wheels.

8, Ballyrory, labour: 25 working farmers and subholders; family aid to farmers 65 persons; 1 male and 1 female domestic servant; 15 male and 4 female occasional labourers; total days work: farmers and family 20,345, constant hired labour 626, occasional hired labour 442, general total 21,413; average days work per acre: 15 per townland, 95 tillage; utensils and vehicles: 16 ploughs, 17 harrows, 19 cars, 9 carts, 21 horses, 44 spinning wheels.

9, Barr Cregg, labour: 3 working farmers and subholders; family aid to farmers 9 persons; 1 male occasional labourer; total days work: farmers and family 2,817, occasional hired labour 15, general total 2,832; average days work per acre: 8 per townland, 14 tillage; utensils and vehicles: 2 ploughs, 3 harrows, 1 horse-hoe, 3 cars, 4 horses, 4 spinning wheels.

10, Binn, labour: 20 working farmers and subholders; family aid to farmers 69 persons; 12 male and 4 female domestic servants; 3 male farming servants; 65 male and 19 female occasional labourers; total days work: farmers and family 21,597, constant hired labour 5,947, occasional hired labour 1,159, general total 28,703; average days work per acre: 49 per townland, 104 tillage; 1 quarry, 2 men, 96 days labour per annum, lime; utensils and vehicles: 17 ploughs, 20 harrows, 12 cars, 17 carts, 20 horses, 47 spinning wheels.

11, Carnanbane, labour: 21 working farmers and subholders; family aid to farmers 74 persons; 5 male and 1 female occasional labourer; total days work: farmers and family 23,162, occasional hired labour 354, general total 23,516; average days work per acre; 78 per townland, 222 tillage; 1 quarry, lime, not in present use; utensils and vehicles: 13 ploughs, 15 harrows, 20 cars, 2 carts, 18 horses, 38 spinning wheels.

12, Carnanreagh, labour: 39 working farmers and subholders; family aid to farmers 170 persons; 2 male and 1 female domestic servant; 18 male occasional labourers; total days work: farmers and family 53,210, constant hired labour 939, occasional hired labour 658, general total 54,807; average days work per acre: 61 per townland, 188 tillage; utensils and vehicles: 30 ploughs, 31 harrows, 38 cars, 9 carts, 38 horses, 94 spinning wheels.

13, Claudy, labour: 22 working farmers and subholders; family aid to farmers 100 persons; 11 male and 9 female domestic servants; 11 male farming servants; 50 male and 5 female occasional labourers; total days work: farmers and family 31,300, constant hired labour 9,703, occasional hired labour 1,434, general total 42,437; average days work per acre: 37 per townland, 163 tillage; 1 quarry, not in use; utensils and vehicles: 18 ploughs, 25 harrows, 23 cars, 18 carts, 31 horses, 78 spinning wheels.

14, Coolnacolpagh, labour: 10 working farmers and subholders; family aid to farmers, 46 persons; 5 male and 3 female domestic servants; 4 male farming servants; 40 male and 11 female occasional labourers; total days work: farmers and family 14,398, constant hired labour 3,756, occasional hired labour 1,315, general total 19,469; average days work per acre: 32 per townland, 64 tillage; utensils and vehicles: 13 ploughs, 16 harrows, 1 horse-hoe, 1 roller, 1 corn-fan, 9 cars, 12 carts, 16 horses, 32 spinning wheels; flax mills: 1 undershot water mill, diameter of water wheel 12 feet, width of buckets 1 and three-quarter feet; raw quantity 24,000 lbs, tow quantity 6,000 lbs, average time working 8 weeks, 2 male attendants.

15, Cregg, labour: 17 working farmers and subholders; family aid to farmers 63 persons; 12 male and 5 female domestic servants; 4 male farming servants; 59 male and 11 female occasional labourers; total days work: farmers and family 19,719, constant hired labour 6,573, occasional hired labour 1,061, general total 27,353; average days work per acre: 40 per townland, 69 tillage; utensils and vehicles: 15 ploughs, 23 harrows, 1 roller, 1 corn-fan, 8 cars, 15 carts, 24 horses, 34 spinning wheels; grain mills: 1 breast water mill, diameter of water wheel 15 feet, width of buckets 2 and a half feet; 224,000 lbs of oatmeal ground, maximum quantity 291,200 lbs, average time working 24 weeks, 2 attendants including miller; flax mills: 1 breast water mill, diameter of water wheel 14 feet, width of buckets 2 and 1 third feet; raw quantity 288,000 lbs, tow quantity 72,000 lbs, average time working 21 weeks, 4 male attendants.

16, Cumber, labour: 6 working farmers and subholders; family aid to farmers 26 persons; 2 male and 1 female domestic servant; 15 male farming servants; 5 male occasional labourers; total days work: farmers and family 8,138, constant hired labour 5,634, occasional hired labour 90, general total 13,862; average days work per acre: 40 per townland, 54 tillage; utensils and vehicles: 9 ploughs, 13 harrows, 1 horse-hoe, 1 roller, 1 corn-fan, 8 cars, 7 carts, 13 horses, 25 spinning wheels.

17, Dunady, labour: 8 working farmers and subholders; family aid to farmers 22 persons; 1 male and 1 female domestic servant; 1 male farming servant; 1 male occasional labourer; total days work: farmers and family 6,886, constant hired labour 939, occasional hired labour 156, general total 7,981; average days work per acre: 36 per townland, 109 tillage; utensils and vehicles: 5 ploughs, 7 harrows, 8 cars, 2 carts, 9 horses, 14 spinning wheels.

18, Dungorkin, labour: 5 working farmers and subholders; family aid to farmers 10 persons; 1 male and 1 female domestic servant; 2 male farming servants; 15 male and 11 female occasional labourers; total days work: farmers and family 3,130, constant hired labour 1,252, occasional hired labour 358, general total 4,740; average days work per acre: 15 per townland, 34 tillage; utensils and vehicles: 4 ploughs, 7 harrows, 1 car, 5 carts, 9 horses, 15 spinning wheels; flax mills: 1 undershot water mill, diameter of water wheel 13 feet, width of buckets 1 and five-sixth feet; raw quantity 57,600 lbs, tow quantity 14,400 lbs, average time working 19 weeks, 4 male attendants.

Parish of Cumber

19, Glenlough, labour: 6 working farmers and subholders; family aid to farmers 22 persons; 8 male and 4 female domestic servants; 17 male occasional labourers; total days work: farmers and family 6,886, constant hired labour 3,756, occasional hired labour 195, general total 10,837; average days work per acre: 16 per townland, 80 tillage; 1 quarry, 3 men, 132 days labour per annum, limestone; utensils and vehicles: 6 ploughs, 14 harrows, 9 cars, 5 carts, 14 horses, 29 spinning wheels.

20, Gortnaran, labour: 13 working farmers and subholders; family aid to farmers 59 persons; 3 male domestic servants; 6 male farming servants; 14 male occasional labourers; total days work: farmers and family 18,467, constant hired labour 2,817, occasional hired labour 448, general total 21,732; average days work per acre: 81 per townland, 126 tillage; utensils and vehicles: 7 ploughs, 9 harrows, 8 cars, 4 carts, 11 horses, 41 spinning wheels.

21, Gortilea, labour: 20 working farmers and subholders; family aid to farmers 72 persons; 4 male and 3 female domestic servants; 2 male farming servants; 41 male and 2 female occasional labourers; total days work: farmers and family 22,536, constant hired labour 2,817, occasional hired labour 692, general total 26,045; average days work per acre: 24 per townland, 95 tillage; utensils and vehicles: 19 ploughs, 22 harrows, 1 roller, 9 cars, 20 carts, 22 horses, 42 spinning wheels.

22, Gortnaskey, labour: 9 working farmers and subholders; family aid to farmers 55 persons; 2 male domestic servants; 1 male farming servant; 39 male and 13 female occasional labourers; total days work: farmers and family 17,215, constant hired labour 939, occasional hired labour 810, general total 18,964; average days work per acre: 36 per townland, 82 tillage; 1 quarry, not in present use, lime; utensils and vehicles: 13 ploughs, 13 harrows, 17 cars, 9 carts, 19 horses, 46 spinning wheels.

23, Gortscreagan, labour: 27 working farmers and subholders; family aid to farmers 94 persons; 2 male and 1 female domestic servant; 26 male occasional labourers; total days work: farmers and family 29,422, constant hired labour 939, occasional hired labour 176, general total 30,537; average days work per acre: 97 per townland, 132 tillage; utensils and vehicles: 24 ploughs, 24 harrows, 22 cars, 8 carts, 24 horses, 38 spinning wheels.

24, Kilcaltan, labour: 7 working farmers and subholders; family aid to farmers 27 persons; 2 male and 2 female domestic servants; 7 male farming servants; 20 male and 7 female occasional labourers; total days work: farmers and family 8,451, constant hired labour 3,443, occasional hired labour 753, general total 12,647; average days work per acre: 41 per townland, 110 tillage; utensils and vehicles: 5 ploughs, 7 harrows, 1 corn-fan, 4 cars, 6 carts, 10 horses, 22 spinning wheels.

25, Kilculmagrandal, labour: 6 working farmers and subholders; family aid to farmers 21 persons; 7 male and 5 female domestic servants; 1 male farming servant; 28 male and 10 female occasional labourers; total days work: farmers and family 6,573, constant hired labour 4,069, occasional hired labour 813, general total 11,455; average days work per acre: 24 per townland, 56 tillage; utensils and vehicles: 7 ploughs, 12 harrows, 1 roller, 1 corn-fan, 8 cars, 10 carts, 12 horses, 26 spinning wheels.

26, Kilgort, labour: 42 working farmers and subholders; family aid to farmers 134 persons; 1 female domestic servant; 21 male and 5 female occasional labourers; total days work: farmers and family 41,942, constant hired labour 313, occasional hired labour 312, general total 42,567; average days work per acre: 41 per townland, 117 tillage; utensils and vehicles: 27 ploughs, 34 harrows, 31 cars, 13 carts, 40 horses, 71 spinning wheels.

27, Killycor, labour: 15 working farmers and subholders; family aid to farmers 46 persons; 8 male and 4 female domestic servants; 3 male farming servants; 37 male and 15 female occasional labourers; total days work: farmers and family 14,398, constant hired labour 4,695, occasional hired labour 839, general total 19,932; average days work per acre: 34 per townland, 56 tillage; 2 quarries, [worked] occasionally, lime; utensils and vehicles: 16 ploughs, 25 harrows, 1 horse-hoe, 4 rollers, 15 cars, 14 carts, 26 horses, 61 spinning wheels; grain mills: 1 undershot water mill, diameter of water wheel 12 feet, width of buckets 2 feet; 134,400 lbs of oatmeal ground, maximum quantity 313,600 lbs; average time working 28 weeks, 3 attendants including miller; flax mills: 2 undershot water mills, diameter of water wheel 12 feet, width of buckets 2 feet and 1 and two-third feet; raw quantity 480,000 lbs, tow quantity 120,000 lbs, average time working 26 weeks, 9 male attendants.

28, Kinculbrack, labour: 14 working farmers and subholders; family aid to farmers 46 persons; 8 male and 5 female domestic servants; 31 male and 11 female occasional labourers; total days work: farmer and family 14,398, constant hired labour 4,069, occasional hired labour 644, general total 19,111; average days work per acre: 34 per townland, 45 tillage; 1 quarry, not worked; utensils and vehicles: 15 ploughs, 26 harrows, 4 rollers, 9 cars, 20 carts, 27 horses, 43 spinning wheels.

29, Lear, labour: 16 working farmers and subholders; family aid to farmers 64 persons; 5 male and 1 female domestic servant; 15 male farming servants; 33 male and 1 female occasional labourers; total days work: farmer and family 20,032, constant hired labour 6,573, occasional hired labour 1,000, general total 27,605; average days work per acre: 14 per townland, 75 tillage; 1 quarry, 4 men, 144 days labour per annum, lime; utensils and vehicles: 12 ploughs, 16 harrows, 1 roller, 1 corn-fan, 13 cars, 9 carts, 24 horses, 34 spinning wheels.

30, Letterlougher, labour: 8 working farmers and subholders; family aid to farmers 27 persons; 5 male and 3 female domestic servants; 3 male farming servants; 28 male and 7 female occasional labourers; total days work: farmers and family 8,451, constant hired labour 3,443, occasional hired labour 575, general total 12,469; average days work per acre; 43 per townland, 72 tillage; utensils and vehicles: 8 ploughs, 10 harrows, 1 roller, 1 corn-fan, 8 cars, 9 carts, 12 horses, 22 spinning wheels.

31, Lettermuck, labour: 14 working farmers and subholders; family aid to farmers 42 persons; 8 male and 4 female domestic servants; 30 male and 6 female occasional labourers; total days work: farmer and family 13,146, constant hired labour 3,756, occasional hired labour 417, general total 17,319; average days work per acre: 29 per townland, 80 tillage; utensils and vehicles: 10 ploughs, 12 harrows, 2 rollers, 11 cars, 8 carts, 17 horses, 43 spinning wheels.

32, Ling, labour: 25 working farmers and subholders; family aid to farmers 83 persons; 3 male and 2 female domestic servants; 18 male occasional labourers; total days work: farmer and family 25,979, constant hired labour 1,565, occasional hired labour 776, general total 28,320; average days work per acre: 55 per townland, 90 tillage; utensils and vehicles: 20 ploughs, 23 harrows, 28 cars, 8 carts, 27 horses, 40 spinning wheels; grain mills: 1 breast water mill, diameter of water wheel 14 feet, width of bucket 1 and one-sixth feet; 224,000 lbs of oatmeal ground, maximum quantity 448,000 lbs; average time working 20 weeks, 2 attendants including miller.

33, Lisbunny, labour: 26 working farmers and subholders; family aid to farmers 100 persons; 12 male and 5 female domestic servants; 31 male and 6 female occasional labourers; total days work: farmer and family 31,300, constant hired labour 5,321, occasional hired labour 1,416, general total 38,037; average days work per acre: 45 per townland, 104 tillage; 1 quarry, 2 men, 14 days labour per annum, lime; utensils and vehicles: 17 ploughs, 25 harrows, 1 roller, 34 cars, 8 carts, 30 horses, 66 spinning wheels.

34, Mulderg, labour: 10 working farmers and subholders; family aid to farmers 25 persons; 3 male and 2 female domestic servants; 1 male farming servant; 23 male and 2 female occasional labourers; total days work: farmer and family 7,825, constant hired labour 1,878, occasional hired labour 800, general total 10,503; average days work per acre: 24 per townland, 69 tillage; 4 quarries, 4 men, 288 days labour per annum, object: building; utensils and vehicles: 7 ploughs, 9 harrows, 1 horse-hoe, 7 cars, 5 carts, 9 horses, 14 spinning wheels.

35, Raspberry Hill, labour: 3 working farmers and subholders; family aid to farmers 11 persons; 2 male farming servants; 7 male and 2 female occasional labourers; total days work: farmer and family 3,443, constant hired labour 626, occasional hired labour 228, general total 4,297; average days work per acre: 26 per townland, 46 tillage; utensils and vehicles: 2 ploughs, 5 harrows, 2 cars, 2 carts, 5 horses, 11 spinning wheels; flax mills: 1 breast water mill, diameter of water wheel 12 feet, width of buckets 1 and a half feet; raw quantity 57,600 lbs, tow quantity 14,400 lbs, average time working 17 weeks, 2 male attendants.

36, Sallowilly, labour: 20 working farmers and subholders; family aid to farmers 63 persons; 2 male and 1 female domestic servants; 1 male farming servant; 21 male and 13 female occasional labourers; total days work: farmer and family 19,719, constant hired labour 1,252, occasional hired labour 1,028, general total 21,999; average days work per acre: 53 per townland, 87 tillage; utensils and vehicles: 15 ploughs, 18 harrows, 23 cars, 3 carts, 17 horses, 39 spinning wheels.

37, Stranaganwilly, labour: 43 working farmers and subholders; family aid to farmers 131 persons; 2 male and 2 female domestic servants; 15 male occasional labourers; total days work: farmer and family 41,003, constant hired labour 1,252, occasional hired labour 620, general total 42,875; average days work per acre: 14 per townland, 108 tillage; utensils and vehicles: 26 ploughs, 28 harrows, 33 cars, 7 carts, 36 horses, 69 spinning wheels; grain mills: 1 breast water mill, diameter of water wheel 12 feet, width of

Parish of Cumber

buckets 1 and one-third feet; 89,600 lbs of oatmeal ground, maximum quantity 268,800 lbs; average time working 36 weeks, 1 attendant including miller.

38, Tireighter, labour: 38 working farmers and subholders; family aid to farmers 165 persons; 8 male and 4 female domestic servants; 63 male and 2 female occasional labourers; total days work: farmers and family 51,645, constant hired labour 3,756, occasional hired labour 671, general total 56,072; average days work per acre: 92 per townland, 117 tillage; 1 quarry, 4 men, 48 days labour per annum, lime and building; utensils and vehicles: 36 ploughs, 36 harrows, 16 cars, 34 carts, 36 horses, 71 spinning wheels; grain mills: 1 breast water mill, diameter of water wheel 14 feet, width of buckets 3 and a half feet; 636,160 lbs of oatmeal ground, maximum quantity 1,111,040 lbs; average time working 24 weeks, 2 attendants including miller; flax mills: 1 breast water mill, diameter of water wheel 16 feet, width of buckets 2 and a half feet; raw quantity 38,400 lbs, tow quantity 9,600 lbs, average time working 13 weeks, 2 male attendants.

39, Tullintrain, labour: 27 working farmers and subholders; family aid to farmers 74 persons; 2 male and 3 female domestic servants; 3 male farming servants; 52 male and 14 female occasional labourers; total days work: farmer and family 23,162, constant hired labour 2,504, occasional hired labour 1,467, general total 27,133; average days work per acre: 47 per townland, 65 tillage; 1 quarry, lime; utensils and vehicles: 20 ploughs, 25 harrows, 21 cars, 16 carts, 27 horses, 58 spinning wheels.

Manufactures and Manufacturing Processes

[Table contains the following headings: primary manufactures subdivided into lime, tanning and paper; secondary manufactures subdivided into weaving and fulling].

1, Alla Lower, weaving of linen: 10 independent looms; materials: 4,269 lbs of yarn, value 125 pounds; product: 6,998 yards, value 217 pounds.

2, Alla Upper, weavng of linen: 8 independent looms; materials: 3,570 lbs of yarn, value 143 pounds; product: 6,404 yards, value 243 pounds.

3, Altaghoney, weaving of linen: 12 independent looms; materials: 4,391 lbs of yarn, value 94 pounds; product: 6,428 yards, value 150 pounds.

4, Ballyartan, weaving of linen: 3 independent and 3 dependent looms; materials: 1,228 lbs of yarn, value 116 pounds; product: 2,960 yards, value 168 pounds.

5, Ballycallaghan, weaving of linen: 1 independent loom; materials: 66 lbs of yarn, value 4 pounds 17s; product: 156 yards, value 7 pounds 9s.

6, Ballyholly, lime: 1 kiln, 3 men on average, 7 months employed, process 48 hours, 350 loads of turf, value 14 pounds; purpose: manure and building; 2,100 barrels, value 61 pounds.

7, Ballymaclanigan, weaving of linen: 2 independent looms; materials: 106 lbs of yarn, value 7 pounds; product: 260 yards, value 13 pounds.

8, Ballyrory, primary manufactures: none; weaving of linen: 9 independent looms; materials: 2,593 lbs of yarn, value 79 pounds; product: 4,122 yards, value 124 pounds.

9, Barr Cregg, weaving of linen: 1 independent loom; materials: 104 lbs of yarn, value 1 pound 14s; product: 150 yards, value 3 pounds.

10, Binn, weaving of linen: 9 independent looms; materials: 2,940 lbs of yarn, value 72 pounds; product: 4,196 yards, value 107 pounds.

11, Carnanbane, weaving of wool: materials, 33 lbs of yarn, value 2 pounds 4s; product, 36 yards, value 3 pounds 4s; weaving of linen: 1 independent and 3 dependent looms; materials: 671 lbs of yarn, value 14 pounds; product: 950 yards, value 23 pounds.

12, Carnanreagh, weaving of wool: 4 looms; materials: 1,261 lbs of yarn, value 87 pounds; product: 1,416 yards, value 124 pounds; weaving of linen: 2 independent and 1 dependent looms; materials: 2,433 lbs of yarn, value 50 pounds; product: 3,934 yards, value 94 pounds.

13, Claudy, weaving of linen: 13 independent looms; materials: 3,450 lbs of yarn, value 210 pounds; product: 7,216 yards, value 328 pounds.

14, Coolnacolpagh, weaving of linen: 2 independent looms; materials: 487 lbs of yarn, value 15 pounds; product: 728 yards, value 27 pounds.

15, Cregg, tanning: 17 pits, 3 men, 303 cow hides, 216 calf hides, 12 horse hides, total value 418 pounds, bark value 268 pounds, value of leather product 848 pounds; weaving of wool: 1 loom; materials: 128 lbs of yarn, value 10 pounds; product: 150 yards, value 12 pounds; weaving of linen: 3 independent and 1 dependent looms; materials: 824 lbs of yarn, value 70 pounds; product: 2,028 yards, value 110 pounds.

16, Cumber, weaving of linen: 2 independent looms; materials: 1,452 lbs of yarn, value 33 pounds; product: 1,936 yards, value 52 pounds.

17, Dunady, weaving of linen: 2 independent looms; materials: 262 lbs of yarn, value 5 pounds; product: 392 yards, value 8 pounds.

18, Dungorkin, weaving of linen: 2 independent looms; materials: 700 lbs of yarn, value 12 pounds; product: 980 yards, value 20 pounds.

19, Glenlough, weaving of linen: 7 independent looms; materials: 1,671 lbs of yarn, value 137 pounds; product: 4,004 yards, value 211 pounds; weaving of cotton: 4 looms, 4 men, 2 women and boys; materials: 1,512 lbs of yarn, value 113 pounds; product: 9,360 yards, value 222 pounds.

20, Gortnaran, weaving of linen: 4 independent looms; materials: 588 lbs of yarn, value 43 pounds; product: 1,404 yards, value 74 pounds.

21, Gortilea, weaving of linen: 6 independent looms; materials: 841 lbs of yarn, value 42 pounds; product: 1,928 yards, value 87 pounds.

22, Gortnaskey, weaving of linen: 8 independent looms; materials: 1,959 lbs of yarn, value 126 pounds; product: 4,128 yards, value 198 pounds.

23, Gortscreagan, weaving of linen: 4 independent looms; materials: 2,076 lbs of yarn, value 36 pounds; product: 2,816 yards, value 60 pounds.

24, Kilcaltan, weaving of linen: 3 independent looms; materials: 521 lbs of yarn, value 49 pounds; product: 1,300 yards, value 76 pounds.

25, Kilculmagrandal, weaving of linen: 5 independent looms; materials: 3,370 lbs of yarn, value 78 pounds; product: 4,396 yards, value 120 pounds.

26, Kilgort, weaving of linen: 2 independent looms; materials: 254 lbs of yarn, value 14 pounds; product: 516 yards, value 22 pounds.

27, Killycor, weaving of wool: 1 loom; materials: 310 lbs of yarn, value 21 pounds; product: 300 yards, value 24 pounds; weaving of linen: 2 independent looms; materials: 453 lbs of yarn, value 34 pounds; product: 1,092 yards, value 57 pounds.

28, Kinculbrack, weaving of linen: 2 independent looms; materials: 534 lbs of yarn, value 23 pounds; product: 1,024 yards, value 38 pounds.

29, Lear, [blank].

30, Letterlougher, weaving of linen: 4 independent looms; materials: 1,467 lbs of yarn, value 30 pounds; product: 1,722 yards, value 43 pounds.

31, Lettermuck, manufacture of paper: 1 water wheel, diameter 14 feet, width of buckets 4 feet, 1 rag engine, 2 vats, 2 presses, 52 hours employed, 10 days employed, 6 male and 1 female attendant; materials: 30 tons of rags and ropes, value 105 pounds; product: 910 reams of paper per annum, value 300 pounds; weaving of linen: 9 independent looms; materials: 3,077 lbs of yarn, value 155 pounds; product: 6,108 yards, value 266 pounds.

32, Ling, weaving of linen: 4 independent looms; materials: 851 lbs of yarn, value 16 pounds; product: 1,168 yards, value 26 pounds.

33, Lisbunny, weaving of cotton: 1 loom; materials: 432 lbs of yarn, value 32 pounds; product: 592 yards, value 56 pounds; weaving of linen: 4 independent looms; materials: 1,514 lbs of yarn, value 31 pounds; product: 2,045 yards, value 43 pounds.

34, Mulderg, weaving of linen: 2 independent looms; materials: 299 lbs of yarn, value 17 pounds; product: 728 yards, value 36 pounds.

35, Raspberry Hill, weaving of linen: 2 independent looms; materials: 77 lbs of yarn, value 3 pounds; product: 132 yards, value 4 pounds.

36, Sallowilly, weaving of linen: 6 independent looms; materials: 1,886 lbs of yarn, value 43 pounds; product: 2,802 yards, value 73 pounds.

37, Stranaganwilly, weaving of linen: 1 independent loom; materials: 324 lbs of yarn, value 7 pounds; product: 480 yards, value 10 pounds; fulling: 1 water wheel, diameter 12 feet, width of buckets 1 foot, 26 weeks employed, 366 days employed in process, 1 attendant; value of materials 29 pounds 15s; product: 2,380 yards dyed per annum, value of process 79 pounds 6s.

38, Tireighter, [blank].

39, Tullintrain, weaving of linen: 13 independent looms; materials: 4,062 lbs of yarn, value 152 pounds; product: 7,180 yards, value 256 pounds.

[Insert rough total: 170 independent looms, total product 96,813 yards].

[Signed] J.E. Portlock, Captain Royal Engineers, 10th July 1838.

Trades and Professions

[Table contains the following headings: manufacturing subdivided by trades supplementary to internal and external production, and auxiliary to internal production; distribution subdivided by trades auxiliary to internal and external production; professions auxiliary to instruction, benevolence and commerce. The numbers in each category living in Claudy are recorded].

Manufacturing trades, supplementary to internal production: 1 journeyman baker, total 1, in Claudy; 1 master basket maker, total 1; 12 master flax dressers, 1 journeyman, total 13, 2 in Claudy; 12 master masons, total 12; 24 master shoemakers, 1 journeyman, 1 apprentice, total 26, 4 in Claudy; 9 master stone cutters, total 9; 5 master thatchers, total 5, 1 in Claudy; total 63 masters, 3 journeymen, 1 apprentice, overall total 67, 8 in Claudy.

Manufacturing trades, supplementary to external production: 1 master bonnet maker, 2 journeymen, total 3, in Claudy; 9 master milliners, total 9, 2 in Claudy; 1 master glazier, total 1; 17

Parish of Cumber

master smiths, 2 journeymen, total 19, 1 in Claudy; 19 master tailors, total 19; total 47 masters, 4 journeymen, overall total 51, 6 in Claudy.

Manufacturing trades, auxiliary to internal production: 14 master carpenters and wheelwrights, 1 journeyman, 1 apprentice, total 16, 4 in Claudy; 2 master coopers, total 2; 2 master last makers, total 2; 1 master reed maker, total 1; 6 master gardeners, total 6; 7 master turners, total 7, 1 in Claudy; total 32 masters, 1 journeyman, 1 apprentice, overall total 34, 5 in Claudy.

Trades of distribution, auxiliary to internal production: 1 master butcher, total 1; 12 master spirit sellers, 1 journeyman, total 13, 5 in Claudy; 13 total masters, 1 journeyman, overall total 14, 5 in Claudy.

Trades of distribution, auxiliary to external production: 14 master grocers, total 14, 1 in Claudy; 8 master grocers and spiritsellers, 1 journeyman, 1 apprentice, total 10, 4 in Claudy; 1 master seller of ropes and rags, total 1, in Claudy; total 23 masters, 1 journeyman, 1 apprentice, overall total 25, 16 in Claudy.

Professions auxiliary to instruction: 6 master divines, total 6; 13 master teachers, total 13; 19 total masters.

Professions auxiliary to benevolence: 3 master surgeons, total 3; 6 master midwives, total 6; 9 total masters.

Professions auxiliary to commerce: 11 master excise officers, total 11; 2 master keepers of lodgings, total 2, in Claudy; total 13 masters; 1 land agent.

Summary of Productive Agents

[Table contains the following headings: number of persons in farming, quarrying, mills, secondary manufactures, manufacturing trades, trades of distribution, professions, servants, total].

Farming labour: farmers and family 2,435, servants 289, cottiers 333, total 3,057.

Labour in quarrying 33.

Labour auxiliary to trades 5.

Labour in mills: grain millers and attendants 13, flax millers and attendants 27, total 40.

Labour in primary manufactures 3.

Labour in secondary manufactures: tanning, 3 in tanning, 7 in paper, 1 in fulling, total 11; weaving, 17 in wool, 178 in linen, 4 men and women in cotton, total 189.

Labour in manufacturing trades: supplementary to internal production 66, to external production 51; auxiliary to internal production 33, 2 apprentices, total 152.

Labour in trades of distribution: auxiliary to internal production 14, to external production 24, 1 apprentice, total 39.

Professions: auxiliary to instruction 19, to benevolence 9, to commerce 13, to internal production 1, total 42.

Domestic servants: [?] 41.

General total 3,571, equivalent to machinery: 255.

[Signed] J.E. Portlock, Captain Royal Engineers, 12th July 1838.

www.ingramcontent.com/pod-product-compliance
Lightning Source LLC
Chambersburg PA
CBHW051212290426
44109CB00021B/2427